1/05

Photo courtesy of Jacques Lowe Visual Arts Projects, Inc.

TOM WOLFE

A Critical Companion

Brian Abel Ragen

CRITICAL COMPANIONS TO POPULAR CONTEMPORARY WRITERS
Kathleen Gregory Klein, Series Editor

Greenwood Press
Westport, Connecticut • London

Library of Congress Cataloging-in-Publication Data

Ragen, Brian Abel.
   Tom Wolfe : a critical companion / Brian Abel Ragen.
      p. cm.—(Critical companions to popular contemporary writers, ISSN 1082–4979)
   Includes bibliographical references and index.
   ISBN 0–313–31383–0 (alk. paper)
   1. Wolfe, Tom—Criticism and interpretation.   I. Title.   II. Series.
PS3573.O526 Z86   2002
818'.5409—dc21   2001050128

British Library Cataloguing in Publication Data is available.

Library of Congress Catalog Card Number: 2001050128
ISBN: 0–313–31383–0
ISSN: 1082–4979

First published in 2002

Greenwood Press, 88 Post Road West, Westport, CT 06881
An imprint of Greenwood Publishing Group, Inc.
www.greenwood.com

Printed in the United States of America

∞

The paper used in this book complies with the
Permanent Paper Standard issued by the National
Information Standards Organization (Z39.48–1984).

10 9 8 7 6 5 4 3 2 1

Copyright Acknowledgment

The author and publisher gratefully acknowledge the Jacques Lowe Visual Arts
Projects, Inc., for permission to use their photograph of Tom Wolfe.

To Sheryl L. Meyering

Contents

Series Foreword

The authors who appear in the series Critical Companions to Popular Contemporary Writers are all best-selling writers. They do not simply have one successful novel, but a string of them. Fans, critics, and specialist readers eagerly anticipate their next book. For some, high cash advances and breakthrough sales figures are automatic; movie deals often follow. Some writers become household names, recognized by almost everyone.

But, their novels are read one by one. Each reader chooses to start and, more importantly, to finish a book because of what she or he finds there. The real test of a novel is in the satisfaction its readers experience. This series acknowledges the extraordinary involvement of readers and writers in creating a best-seller.

The authors included in this series were chosen by an Advisory Board composed of high school English teachers and high school and public librarians. They ranked a list of best-selling writers according to their popularity among different groups of readers. For the first series, writers in the top-ranked group who had received no book-length, academic, literary analysis (or none in at least the past ten years) were chosen. Because of this selection method, Critical Companions to Popular Contemporary Writers meets a need that is being addressed nowhere else. The success of these volumes as reported by reviewers, librarians, and teachers led to an expansion of the series mandate to include some writers with wide critical attention—Toni Morrison, John Irving, and Maya Angelou, for example—to extend the usefulness of the series.

The volumes in the series are written by scholars with particular expertise in analyzing popular fiction. These specialists add an academic focus to the popular success that these writers already enjoy.

The series is designed to appeal to a wide range of readers. The general reading public will find explanations for the appeal of these well-known writers. Fans will find biographical and fictional questions answered. Students will find literary analysis, discussions of fictional genres, carefully organized introductions to new ways of reading the novels, and bibliographies for additional research. Whether browsing through the book for pleasure or using it for an assignment, readers will find that the most recent novels of the authors are included.

Each volume begins with a biographical chapter drawing on published information, autobiographies or memoirs, prior interviews, and, in some cases, interviews given especially for this series. A chapter on literary history and genres describes how the author's work fits into a larger literary context. The following chapters analyze the writer's most important, most popular, and most recent novels in detail. Each chapter focuses on one or more novels. This approach, suggested by the advisory board as the most useful to student research, allows for an in-depth analysis of the writer's fiction. Close and careful readings with numerous examples show readers exactly how the novels work. These chapters are organized around three central elements: plot development (how the story line moves forward), character development (what the reader knows of the important figures), and theme (the significant ideas of the novel). Chapters may also include sections on generic conventions (how the novel is similar to or different from others in its same category of science fiction, fantasy, thriller, etc.), narrative point of view (who tells the story and how), symbols and literary language, and historical or social context. Each chapter ends with an "alternative reading" of the novel. The volume concludes with a primary and secondary bibliography, including reviews.

The alternative readings are a unique feature of this series. By demonstrating a particular way of reading each novel, they provide a clear example of how a specific perspective can reveal important aspects of the book. In the alternative reading sections, one contemporary literary theory—way of reading, such as feminist criticism, Marxism, new historicism, deconstruction, or Jungian psychological critique—is defined in brief, easily comprehensible language. That definition is then applied to the novel to highlight specific features that might go unnoticed or be understood differently in a more general reading. Each volume defines two or three specific theories, making them part of the reader's understanding of how diverse meanings may be constructed from a single novel.

Taken collectively, the volumes in the Critical Companions to Popular Contemporary Writers series provide a wide-ranging investigation of the complexities of current best-selling fiction. By treating these novels seriously as both literary works and publishing successes, the series demonstrates the potential of popular literature in contemporary culture.

Kathleen Gregory Klein
Southern Connecticut State University

The Life of Tom Wolfe

I grow daily to honor facts more and more, and theory less and less.
—Thomas Carlyle

When *Harper's* published an issue celebrating its 150th anniversary in 1999, the cover was dominated by two men in white suits. On the left is Mark Twain; on the right, Tom Wolfe. While many would be quick to argue that the juxtaposition of Twain and Wolfe overstates Wolfe's importance in American literature, it is certainly true that Wolfe has followed Twain's example. He has both won for himself a reputation as a writer and created a public personality. Like Twain, he has used the white suit to mark himself as an outsider in the literary world of which he is also very much a part. In an era when most writers, even those most bound up with the artistic establishment, were seeking to appear bohemian and avant-garde, Wolfe took another stance. He presented himself as a courtly Southern gentleman and as a literary innovator. He made himself known as the champion of old forms of fiction and new forms of journalism. He has shown admiration for traditional values while criticizing entrenched establishments.

The decades after World War II have seen wave after wave of change—of changes that would have been unimaginable to earlier generations. The Civil Rights movement gained equal rights for black Americans. Great cities imploded and became impoverished shells of what they had been, while the suburbs became the sites of unparalleled wealth. The United States lost the war in Vietnam and put a man on the moon. Americans became richer than any people in human history and began dressing, even for important occasions, like laborers and beggars. The standards in several arts, especially music, came to be set by teenagers. The mainline Protestant churches that had shaped American society shrank almost to insignificance, while Americans became more interested in "spirituality" than ever before. Drug use, previously known only among a bohemian fringe, became briefly an important cultural force during the vogue of LSD and psychedelics and then returned as an intractable social problem in the crack epidemic of the 1980s. Men stopped wearing hats. Most of the stigmas against divorce and premarital sex disappeared, forms of sexual expression that would once have been barely discussed became commonplace, and AIDS killed thousands. Almost every institution that had been closed to women in 1960 was open to them by 1990. Stock car racing became a major sport.

DEFINING THE AGE

Wolfe's subject throughout his career has been this changing America. He has sought out the forces that were transforming the nation, for good or bad, where they were welling up most dramatically. That often took him to parts of the culture that the literary people pay little attention to, the worlds of car customizers and naval aviators and bond traders. Early in his career, he charted the emergence of the youth culture. For decades he examined the separation of high and popular culture. And throughout his career he has described the omnipresent influences of status and wealth. And he approached all these subjects, even those that might attract only derision, with enjoyment as well as dismay. Most important, he described all his subjects in language vivid enough to force people to remember what he reported. He has coined or popularized many of the phrases that have defined the age. "Good old boys" became the definition of a class after Wolfe wrote about Junior Johnson. The "Me-Decade" marked an era after Wolfe described the self-focus of much of that time's "spiritual" seeking. After Wolfe chronicled the space program, many heroes would be described as having "the right stuff," and almost every innovator would be said to be "pushing the envelope."

In the course of his career, Wolfe has created not only a distinctive literary voice, but also a distinctive public persona. The literary voice, which is more than just a distinctive style or a penchant for using punctuation in ways not taught in freshman English, will be discussed in the following chapters. While the literary voice appears in the pages of *Harper's* anniversary issue—a piece called "Rococo Marxists" could hardly be by anyone else—it was the public persona who appeared on its cover. The public persona also takes his place on the cover of *Time*, in TV and radio appearances, and in many printed interviews and profiles. (Interviewers cannot resist asking about his clothes; some even name his tailor.) This "Tom Wolfe" is easily recognized. He wears a white suit whose cut recalls the Edwardian era. His shoes are made so it appears that he is wearing spats. He carries an umbrella or a cane. He is soft-spoken and courtly, with a voice that still recalls the Virginia of his youth. He is more often wry than impassioned and seems much less interested in provoking people than is the voice in the books. This persona seems to serve several purposes for Wolfe. One may be, oddly enough, to protect his privacy, for Wolfe is quite reticent, especially for one so flamboyant, about his personal life. He has not, like other writers of his time (Norman Mailer, for example) made his private life part of his persona. Little of his work is autobiographical, and he keeps a zone of privacy despite his ostentation. For example, an interviewer who asks about Wolfe's love life before his marriage receives nothing more revealing than, "If you want me to describe my libidinous history, you've come to the wrong person!" (Cash). The persona keeps the focus off the private Wolfe and on itself, or, still better, his writing.

DRESSING TO BE NOTICED

The witty, soft-spoken, slightly self-mocking dandy image gives Wolfe a sort of "brand identity." The white suits, hats, and faux spats are a kind of logo or trademark for writing that manages to be at once elegant and aggressive. The outfits certainly attract attention, just as the prose style does. When the Victorian novelist Anthony Trollope discussed the prose style of his friend William Makepeace Thackeray, he compared it to clothing and wrote, "I hold that gentleman to be the best dressed whose dress no one observes" (200). Wolfe often expresses his admiration for Trollope and Thackeray, but he has never taken this piece of advice. Rather, he quotes Twain, "The last thing in the world I want is to be conspicuous, but I do want to be noticed" (Greig).

Wolfe's clothes serve another purpose. They are one of his research tools. They mark him as an outsider in the societies he visits, and he finds it is more useful for someone who wants to learn what is going on to frankly act as an outsider. He reports that "people really don't want you to try to fit in. They'd much rather fill you in. People like to have someone to tell their stories to" (Flippo 149). The coat and tie (usually not what he calls the full white rig) mark him as the outsider who will listen to your story rather than the interloper who may try to take your place in a status system.

The fastidious outfits also have a kind of political or cultural symbolism. They are, to use the term Wolfe suggests when something like "dandy" is applied to him, "counter-bohemian." Throughout the twentieth century, ever more elements of American society have adopted a bohemian stance—even those that are, unlike the traditional bohemian, part of the structures of power, rather than rebels against it. The tendency captured many writers as the century went on, and during and after the 1960s it conquered the world of academia and other parts of the cultural establishment. The jeans (often with designer labels) of the student and the predominantly black outfits of the artists at once proclaim a superiority to traditional status markers such as coats and ties and a desire to be fully part of an alternative status system. Wolfe always has an eye open for the affectation in such a stance and counters it with a forthright interest in style, status, and standards.

Finally, the white suit recalls a certain ideal of Southern manhood. The suits Wolfe wears are really more in the tradition of the English dandy than of the Southern gentleman in a linen suit and black string tie. Nevertheless, the white suit remains a badge of the South, thanks to cultural icons ranging from Mark Twain through Southern politicians for several generations down to the franchised icon of Kentucky Fried Chicken's Colonel Sanders. That Southern element in his persona is important to Wolfe, both because it separates him from the black-clad intellectuals of cultural centers of the Northeast and because it links him with the very parts of American culture that those writers are mostly likely to ignorantly despise.

Since graduating from college, Wolfe has not lived in the South for any length of time, and he is not considered a "Southern" writer in the way William Faulkner or Eudora Welty is. Nevertheless, Southern ways of one kind or another have influenced his life throughout his career— a career that has been centered on New York. His friends say that the essence of his personality is something he took from his youth in Richmond, a "Scotch-Irish sense of honor, of duty of family, about masculinity" (Applebome). Wolfe's interest in stock cars, test pilots, even real estate developers shows a continuing exploration of various types of Southern manhood. Besides marking him as "counter-bohemian" English dandy, the white suits show Wolfe's continuing allegiance to the South of good old boys and men in full.

A GENTEEL UPBRINGING

Thomas Kennerly Wolfe, Jr. was born in Richmond, Virginia, in 1931. (Even though all his books have been published under the name "Tom Wolfe," he is still sometimes confused with Thomas Wolfe [1900–1938], the North Carolina novelist, though probably never by anyone who has read both of them.) Unlike many writers, Wolfe recalls his childhood as happy. While he would chronicle the flowering of youth culture in the 1950s and 1960s, he himself did not take part in adolescent rebellion and seems pleased to have missed the opportunity. "I was lucky, I guess," he told one interviewer, "in my family in that they had a very firm idea of role: Father, Mother, Child. Nothing was ever allowed to bog down into those morass-like personal hangups" (Dundy 15).

The father in the family, Thomas Kennerly Wolfe, Sr., was evidently a man of several talents. He was a scholar with a Ph.D. from Cornell University who taught agronomy, the science of farming, at the Virginia Polytechnic Institution. He also had two farms of his own (Dundy 14). In addition, the elder Wolfe was involved in the business side of farming, serving as a director of a farmer's cooperative, which became a Fortune 500 Company (Applebome). While these varied activities allowed him to provide his family a lifestyle that is often described as genteel, his other pursuits were probably a more important model for his son, for he was also a journalist and author: he edited a journal called *The Southern Planter* and published books with titles such as *Production of Field Crops*. Wolfe, in fact, recalls him primarily as a working writer and reports once looking in a library card catalog and finding more entries under his father's name than under his own (McKeen 4). Wolfe seems to have inherited from his father an interest in style, especially in clothing. He makes it clear, however, that his father's insistence on custommade clothes was completely unpretentious and certainly nothing like Wolfe's own flamboyance.

The mother in the family, Helen Hughes Wolfe, fostered Wolfe's interests in literature and arts of all kinds. (Before his focus turned to sports, the young Wolfe's activities included tap dancing and ballet.) She taught him to sketch and to appreciate color, and also read to him frequently (McKeen 4). If Wolfe missed anything important in his childhood, it was that the family included only one other child, a sister five years his junior. He reports telling a Sunday school teacher at the age of five that he had eight siblings, and that the fantasy of having a brother still persisted (Dundy 17). Wolfe began writing early on. He began a biography of Napoleon at age nine (Fishwick 1) and both wrote and illustrated a picture version of a life of Mozart (Gorner 200). In both instances, he was describing unlikely figures—a child prodigy, a notoriously short provincial military officer—who through force of genius dazzled the world.

Wolfe was raised as a Presbyterian but was sent to an Episcopalian school in Richmond—St. Christopher's. There he seems to have been a model student, the antithesis of the disaffected, bohemian rebel that would soon be idolized by the youth culture. Rather, he was involved in everything. He was student council president and worked on the school's newspaper, serving as its editor in his senior year. He developed his talents in drawing and was an avid athlete. His column for the school newspaper, "The Bullpen," brought all those interests together. He both wrote and illustrated it, and as the title suggests, often devoted his attention to sports. He was graduated in 1947, and turned down an offer from Princeton to enroll at Washington and Lee University in Lexington, Virginia.

Washington and Lee was then, like many American colleges, all male. It was also the repository of several traditions that would be important, at least peripherally, in Wolfe's work. Its heritage is that of the old South: Robert E. Lee served as its president in the years after the Civil War. And Wolfe, whose grandfather was a Confederate infantryman, would always play, among other roles, that of the Southern gentleman. It was also one of the first liberal arts colleges to take journalism seriously. Its first journalism instructors were hired by General Lee himself, so the idea of training working writers as well as scholars was an old one by the time Wolfe enrolled.

A WRITER'S EDUCATION

At college Wolfe majored in English and took the fiction seminar offered by George Foster, but he also pursued his interests in literature and writing outside the classroom. He helped found the still influential literary magazine *Shenandoah*, published stories in it, and served on its editorial board. He worked on the college newspaper and was for a time its sports editor. He was already becoming interested in thinkers who joined fields that academia, journalism, and the literary world keep separate. Marshall Fishwick, who had been trained in American Studies at Yale, taught a course in that hybrid field at Washington and Lee. Unlike purely literary scholars, experts in American Studies and the fields that would later be called American culture and popular culture do not limit their analyses to high art. Rather, they look at everything a culture creates, both high and low, almost as an anthropologist studies all the artifacts of a primitive culture, from the most sacred images to the everyday drinking bowls. Fishwick's course ranged far beyond American literature to introduce students to American art and architecture. Fishwick also saw to it that his students looked at the creations of culture that intellectual elites often ignore, including country music and the crafts that allow one to rebuild a farmhouse or lay bricks (Thompson in Scura 220). This attention to the whole range of culture would become the hallmark of Wolfe's work, and he himself is now one of the heroes of the popular culture movement. One of its flagship organs, *The Journal of American Culture*, devoted a special issue to his work in 1991, with an introduction by his old teacher, Marshall Fishwick.

Wolfe's undergraduate thesis, *A Zoo Full of Zebras: Anti-Intellectualism in America*, shows Wolfe already acting as the cultural critic and also gives hints of his future style: "We wonder, all of us at some moment in our lives, if we have not managed to translate the dun bulk of material into our most spirited thoughts, deadening them, novocaining our self-expression and ultimately our conscience" (qtd in Fishwick 1). The years at Washington and Lee allowed Wolfe to experiment in styles outside his academic work as well. For a time he affected black shirts and white ties in imitation of the "tough guy" characters he saw in a Richard Widmark play (McKeen 5). He graduated *cum laude* in 1951.

Throughout his school and college years, Wolfe had been quite athletic. He became skilled as a baseball pitcher, played semipro ball during college, and even earned a tryout with the New York Giants in 1952. He was cut after three days, a misfortune he attributes to his never having developed a good fastball. Sports clearly remained important to him, however. In what might be called a pre-Title IX comment, he has said, "This country is made up of half failed athletes and half women. That's what America is" (Gorner 99). One of his continuing subjects has been that part of America made up of men trying to master some skill and win some prize—and failing as often as succeeding. While he has written less directly about sports than many of his contemporaries in literary journalism, he has often written about those who bring the values of sport—skill, daring, and willingness to risk defeat in the pursuit of glory—into other areas of life, including business, space exploration, and war.

After the baseball tryout, Wolfe returned to the academic world. Following Marshall Fishwick's example, he enrolled in the Ph.D. program in American Studies at Yale University in New Haven, Connecticut, in 1952. During his years at Yale, Wolfe studied with many of the great names of the movement in literary studies called the New Criticism, including Cleanth Books. That movement, which championed the method of analysis known as "close reading," often seemed to suggest that nothing outside the text, even the biography of the author or cultural milieu in which he or she was writing, had any relevance to a literary interpretation. As a student of American Studies, however, Wolfe was exposed to thinkers who did not believe that a literary work, or anything else, for that matter, could be studied in isolation. Wolfe would in later years often come into conflict with those writers who, like the New Critics and their successors in literary studies, thought that the text was essentially self-referential and independent of the world—a "verbal icon." Rather, he would argue that a literary work had to reflect the world to be of lasting interest, and he learned ways of understanding the world beyond the literary in his work in American Studies.

RELIGION A CONTINUING THEME

Many of these ideas were taken from sociology, and Wolfe would continue to invoke the great names in that field, such as Thorstein Veblen and Max Weber. In studying Weber (1864–1920), Wolfe found a model for dealing with what would be one of the continuing themes of his work—religion. In works such as *The Protestant Ethic and the Spirit of Capitalism*, Weber showed how religious ideas, attitudes, and feelings influence culture, often in unexpected ways. His work does not address the truth of a religion's doctrines but the ways in which a religion influences its adherents' behavior and satisfies their needs. Wolfe would find himself exploring religious movements for most of his career. He would see in the drug culture of the 1960s a new religious movement, and he would use the same terminology to describe the various self-help groups that sought transcendence through self-absorption in the 1970s. His large novel of the 1990s, *A Man in Full*, would reach its climax with a religious conversion—a conversion to classical Stoicism, of all things. Wolfe charts the religious impulse throughout his discussion of American culture without entering into questions of truth. He describes his own religious position genteelly as "lapsed Presbyterian" but when asked if he is an atheist, he frankly answers, "Well, yes [. . .]. Getting right down to it" (Cash).

While Wolfe finally earned his Ph.D. and was offered a job teaching history at a Midwestern university (Dundy 16), graduate school seems to be the one period of his life he looks back on without enthusiasm. His books contain several references to how stifling life in the library carrel is. Though in the late 1990s Wolfe announced that the subject of his next big novel might be academia, he had said earlier that, like others who had suffered through it, he had never been able to turn graduate school into a novel: "Such a novel would be a study of frustration, but a form of frustration so exquisite, so ineffable, nobody could describe it" (*New Journalism* 4). Many of his later works, especially those dealing with art and architecture, suggest that one of the things he disliked about graduate school was its tendency to encourage a slavish devotion to theory rather than a forthrightly critical look at the world. No deference to his alma mater prevents him from calling the inhuman, undecorated blocklike buildings of the International School the "Yale Box."

All the same, Wolfe's training served him in good stead when he left the academic world. "American Studies" blended several academic disciplines. His dissertation, *The League of American Writers: Communist Activity Among American Writers, 1929–1942*, was essentially historical but on a literary subject. Reading it, one sees what has been the most baleful influence of graduate education on many who have suffered through it: it deadens all sense of style. Wolfe's dissertation is, for the most part, in the same stilted, passive language as so many dissertations. But if the style gave little hint of the Tom Wolfe that was to come, the subject did. Wolfe treats the world of American writers, not as a group of artistic geniuses waiting for inspiration but as a social group like any other, one that can be treated as a "manipulable mass" (*League* 31) and influenced for various ends—in this instance political ones. Wolfe's research for the book included not only poring over tomes in a library carrel but also interviews with many of the grand old men of the "Lost Generation" of American writers, such as Malcolm Cowley, Archibald MacLeish, and James T. Farrell. He had also already developed an eye for what would later be the subject of one of his most famous books: the intersection of leftist politics and social climbing. He describes how the Communist-backed League of American Writers used "cause parties" with famous literati as a way of spreading its influence (*League* 249–250). The same intersection of fashionable parties and far left politics became the subject of *Radical Chic*.

For Wolfe, the frustration of graduate school went beyond the intellectual. It was also a matter of style and image. "It was the one time in life I was really stuck," he recalls. "I couldn't stand out because everybody was eccentric in graduate school. They had everything from genuine dirty-neck bohemians to true British fops" (qtd. in McKeen 6). Wolfe for a time tried the "dirty-neck bohemian" pose himself. After finishing his course work at Yale, he spent a few months in New Haven trying to live out the Jack London fantasy of immersing himself in the life of the laborer, working as a furniture mover and truck loader. He said afterward that he learned nothing from the experience, but he may have drawn on it when he created a thoroughly sympathetic portrait of a man trapped in a life of loading and unloading shelves in Conrad Hensley of *A Man in Full*.

THE FIRST NEWSPAPER JOB

There was also, for Wolfe, a bohemian allure to the next profession he entered, newspaper writing. The craft at that time still had a proletarian edge to it; journalism had not yet acquired the high-minded aura of nobility that would envelop it in the 1970s, when "investigative reporters" like Bob Woodward and Carl Bernstein were seen as the saviors of the Republic during the Watergate scandal. In the introduction to *The New Journalism*, Wolfe sketches the fantasy that attracted him: "Chicago, 1928, that was the general idea . . . Drunken reporters out on the ledge of the *News* peeing into the Chicago River at dawn [. . .] Nights down at the detective bureau—it was always nighttime in my daydreams of the newspaper life. Reporters didn't work during the day. I wanted the whole movie, nothing left out" (3). In reality, his first newspaper job was not in Chicago, but in Springfield, Massachusetts, at the *Springfield Union*, where he worked from 1956 to 1959 and doubtless discovered that journalism is not an entirely nocturnal profession. He also learned more important things. In later years he would hark back to the basic rules of journalism he learned while working on the paper (Buckley 87). He also discovered that "a city could be made up of more than one ethnic group that was politically powerful, that had its own way of life and its own restaurants" (Dundy 16), a realization that would later shape both his novels. While at the *Union*, Wolfe completed his dissertation, closing the academic chapter of his life as the journalistic one opened.

In 1959 Wolfe moved on to the *Washington Post*. He was for a time a foreign correspondent, filing reports from Cuba for which he received the Newspaper Guild's award for foreign reporting in 1961. That same year, the Guild also bestowed on him its award for humor, for he was also writing less orthodox journalistic pieces, some of them accompanied by his own drawings. A good example is his series, "The Dispensable Guide," which he wrote and illustrated in 1959 as a comic commentary on President Eisenhower's world tour. His commentary was not political; rather, he made sardonic observations on the cultures through which the president would be passing. (Wolfe at one time ascribed his getting the job on the *Post* to his very lack of interest in politics. The city editor was "amazed that Wolfe preferred cityside to Capitol Hill, the beat every reporter wanted" [Flippo 132]). But throughout his career, Wolfe has known that good stories are at least as often to be found on the fringes of culture as in the centers of power.

ENTERING FEATURE WRITING'S "GOLDEN AGE"

In 1962 Wolfe left the *Post* for the *New York Herald-Tribune*. The *Tribune* was, in the eyes of many, the most literary and certainly the most experimental of New York City's newspapers. Wolfe both did general reporting, as he had done on the *Union* and the *Post*, and wrote "feature articles," many of them for the paper's Sunday supplement magazine, *New York* (1962–1966). The "feature," as Wolfe describes it, was "anything that fell outside the category of hard news" (*New Journalism* 5). While reporters who stuck to hard news were constrained by the fairly narrow conventions of journalism at that time and could inject little that was stylistically flamboyant or "personal" in any way into their work, the conventions were looser for feature writers, especially when their stories appeared in the supplements, which were not considered serious journalism. The hard news, or "scoop," reporters competed with their peers mainly by finding some piece of information about a political or criminal situation and reporting it first. The feature writers competed by finding new subjects and writing about them in an engaging style. Wolfe describes his years on the *Herald-Tribune* as a sort of golden age of feature writing, when many of the writers who would later create the New Journalism were all working on New York papers. Wolfe and his colleagues at the *Herald-Tribune* were fortunate to have editors who welcomed the breaking of conventions. The most important of these was Clay Felker, editor of the Sunday magazine, who had come to the paper from *Esquire* and brought with him that magazine's tradition of welcoming innovative writing. Wolfe was writing on the subjects that would be the substance of his later work, but had yet to develop the voice that would make his work distinctive.

In 1963, during a four-month strike at the *Herald-Tribune*, Wolfe began writing the pieces for *Esquire*. While working on a piece on custom cars, he had the crisis of writer's block and stylistic breakthrough he describes in the introduction to his first book (see chapter 3). When the resulting article appeared in *Esquire* in 1964 as "There Goes (Varoom! Varoom!) That Kandy-Kolored Tangerine-Flake Streamline Baby," Wolfe became famous. Some readers loved it, others hated it, and many were confused by it. But it made an impression. And it set Wolfe free to explore a new, flamboyant literary style, utterly unlike conventional newspaper prose. He now felt free to use the widest range of vocabulary—from the scientific to the slangy—to manipulate point of view as a fiction writer would and use the odd punctuation and onomatopoeia that would make his style so recognizable. The flamboyance also evoked many, many parodies, including one by Lillian Ross in the *New Yorker*. Wolfe had already adopted the white suit as his personal emblem. He reports that he bought a white suit, planning to wear it, as Southern gentlemen did, during the summer, but found it too heavy for summer wear and so saved it for winter. When he appeared in the suit in the months when absolutely no other man was in white, he found the sensation, even the annoyance, it caused gratifying and made it his trademark.

In 1965, Wolfe published his first book, *The Kandy-Kolored Tangerine-Flake Streamline Baby*, which collected many of his pieces from the *Herald-Tribune*, *Esquire*, and other magazines. It also included a number of drawings. (That same year there was a one-man show of Wolfe's drawings at the Maynard Walker Gallery in New York.) Almost all the pieces deal, in one way or another, with the issue of status. The response to the book was largely positive, though some reviewers had no stomach for either his experiments in style or his insistence that popular culture, especially teenage culture, was the engine driving American society. In any case, by this point Wolfe had become what he would remain for the rest of the century, not just a writer but a literary celebrity.

TAKING ON THE *NEW YORKER*

Also in 1965, Wolfe ignited a controversy that would echo through much of the rest of his career. With the encouragement of Clay Felker, he wrote two articles to mark the fortieth anniversary of the *New Yorker* magazine. The magazine was very much a literary institution. It had, indeed, published some of the greatest writers of the century, and its editors had helped create a distinctive and classic prose style. It had also, however, taken on the airs of an institution beyond all criticism, refusing, as it would for many years to come, even to print letters to the editor. It sent the message that its word was final. The *New Yorker*'s editor, William Shawn, was treated as an oracular figure, beyond the criticism and analysis to which most writers and editors are subjected. Like Shawn himself, most of the *New Yorker*'s staffers refused to talk with Wolfe, but not because, as Wolfe would later assert, a memo directed them to remain silent. He was able, nevertheless, to attend one of the magazine's parties and get a lot of information secondhand. When the first of the articles, "Tiny Mummies! The True Story of the Ruler of 43rd Street's Land of the Walking Dead!" appeared in the *Herald-Tribune* Sunday supplement, it brought down a hail of criticism on Wolfe—and on any authors associated with him and his style of writing.

It is not hard to see why the response to the articles was so strong. Their style was outrageous. Wolfe and Felker had decided that the *New Yorker*'s prose was beyond parody—the dullness they saw in it could not be exaggerated—so they decided to describe the staid magazine in a style as distant from its own as possible, what Wolfe later called "a kind of screaming tabloid style" (McLeod 80). And rather than treating Mr. Shawn respectfully—or, as was the tradition, not discussing the editor of the *New Yorker* at all—it presented him in the worst possible light. The very first word of piece—*Omertà!*—presents him as a Mafia boss, *Omertà* being the mob's code of silence. But worse would come. Shawn is presented not as a creative editor but as the mere "museum curator, the mummifier, the preserver-in-amber, the smiling embalmer" of the *New Yorker* created by founding editor Harold Ross. Wolfe dwells upon Shawn's personal eccentricities, including his soft voice and his fear of crowds—and then ascribes them to a rumored cause. In keeping with the "true crime" style, the rumor he repeats is that Shawn was the intended victim in the Leopold and Loeb case, the notorious 1924 murder in which two wealthy Chicago boys tried to commit the "perfect murder." Their victim, Bobbie Franks, was indeed one of William Shawn's school classmates. Although Wolfe invokes the records in the Cook

County Criminal Court, no one else has been able to find evidence that Leopold and Loeb had their eyes on the young Shawn, much less that the trauma of a close brush with kidnappers explained Shawn's later eccentricities. Wolfe does not quite assert that the story is true, however; he uses it to capture the atmosphere of the *New Yorker* in an un-*New Yorker* style. The article also contains what seemed like allusions to the long-term affair between Shawn and *New Yorker* writer Lillian Ross, at least to those who knew about the affair already.

The pieces are wonderful to read. And they do, in their hyperbolic way, seem to capture a good deal of the unusual atmosphere of *The New Yorker* in Shawn's day. Decades later, books by those who consider themselves Shawn's fiercest partisans, such as Ved Mehta, Lillian Ross, and Renata Adler, would describe that same hermetic atmosphere, where, by endless query and revision, Shawn would lead some writers to produce the sort of prose he was after, drive others into self-conscious silence, and make many dependent on him—seeking both his professional and his fatherly approval. They would also confirm many of Shawn's eccentricities. It is, all the same, true that the pieces are unfair and often inaccurate. Denied direct access to the offices of the magazine he was writing about, Wolfe relied on second- and thirdhand information, and much of it was wrong. Still worse, many facts that he could have verified turned out to be wrong as well.

The response to "Tiny Mummies!" was as extreme as Wolfe's style. Shawn, having seen a copy of article before its publication, wrote a long letter to John Hay Whitney, owner of the *Herald-Tribune*. He called the piece "false and libelous" and asked—"[f]or your sake, and for mine, and, in the long run, even for the sake of Wolfe and his editor Clay Felker (God help me for caring about them)"—that Whitney "stop the distribution of the article" (Yagoda 338–339). Whitney and Felker stood behind Wolfe, and both "Tiny Mummies!" and its successor, "Lost in the Whichy Thicket," which deals with the *New Yorker*'s style as much as its personalities, appeared on schedule. Shawn's letter was also leaked to *Time* and *Newsweek*, which ran articles noting the irony of one of the mainstays of American journalism "asking a rival periodical to censor itself" (Yagoda 339).

No response to Wolfe's articles ever appeared in the *New Yorker* itself, nor did it take any legal action for libel, but writers associated with the magazine were quick to attack both Wolfe's accuracy and his fairness. The *New Yorker* has always been famous for its fact checking, and Shawn allowed two of his writers, Renata Adler and Gerald Joncas to go over Wolfe's pieces. Adler even flew to Chicago to see what there was in the records of the Cook County Criminal Court that linked Leopold and Loeb to William Shawn. The two *New Yorker* writers found many, many errors—and contested the idea that Shawn had been the kidnapper's intended victim (perhaps not noticing that Wolfe did not exactly assert that he was). After the *Herald-Tribune* declined to print their letter, they submitted it to the magisterial *Columbia Journalism Review*, which published it under a covering article that put the blame on Felker, asking, more than once, "Where was the editor?" (Lewin 32).

The *Herald-Tribune* did, however, publish a good many responses to Wolfe, and others appeared elsewhere. Writers including Joseph Alsop, Walter Lippmann, Murray Kempton, Muriel Spark, Ved Mehta, and even J.D. Salinger, who was already a recluse, came to Shawn's defense. E.B. White's letter was especially devastating, both because it came from a *New Yorker* writer renowned for his humanity and because it acknowledged Wolfe's powers and popularity:

> The virtuosity of the writer makes it all the more contemptible, and to me, as I read it, the spectacle was of a man being dragged for no apparent reason at the end of a rope by a rider on horseback—a rider, incidentally, sitting very high in the saddle these days and very sure of his mount. (531)

Wolfe took a lesson from this experience, but it was not to avoid antagonizing the great and good in the future. Rather, it was that literary quarrels are not, in fact, that serious:

> All these eminent people descended upon me, and I felt the sky was falling in.
> Then a few days later I woke up, and nothing had happened. It dawned on me that it's very difficult to get hurt in a literary fight. In a strange way, all the shouting and shooting and the explosions were part of the literary excitement. I took so much abuse at that time that I think it made me fireproof. So now if I am attacked in a review—and it happens quite often—I can't say that I like it, but I know that no matter what it says, the sky really isn't going to fall. (McLeod 183–184)

Wolfe was now, at age thirty-four, established as a literary enfant terrible. As the years went by, he felt free to puncture the self-importance of many cultural institutions almost as well entrenched as the *New Yorker*.

All the same, the *New Yorker* articles are like nothing else Wolfe has published. In them he clearly violated rules he himself says are impor-

tant. He got facts wrong—facts he could have got right. As the years
went by, Wolfe did little to defend the pieces in print, and he decided
to leave them out of his next collection, evidently out of deference to
Shawn's feelings. Shawn spoke with Roger Straus, Wolfe's editor at Farrar Straus Giroux, and told him that he hoped the pieces would not
appear in the forthcoming *Pump House Gang*. When Straus contacted
Wolfe, he replied, "Oh, well, you know, he feels so badly about it, and
I didn't mean to make him feel so badly. That wasn't the point of it. I
just thought it was an interesting article. We'll leave it out" (Yagoda 341).
Wolfe reprinted them only after Shawn's death, and, more important,
after Shawn's privacy had been thoroughly destroyed by his own intimates and defenders, including Lillian Ross and Renata Adler.

"BASTARD" JOURNALISM?

While the *New Yorker* remained silent, other magazines would publish
large-scale attacks on Wolfe—attacks by eminent writers. Dwight Mac-
Donald in the *New York Review of Books*, for example, did not limit his
criticism to Wolfe, much less to his *New Yorker* articles. Rather, he attacked the movement in journalism of which (much to the displeasure
of some of his peers) Wolfe was now the chief representative. MacDonald
called it "parajournalism," and described it as "a bastard form, having
it both ways, exploiting the factual authority of journalism and the at-
mospheric license of fiction. Entertainment rather than information is the
aim of its producers, and the hope of its consumers" (MacDonald, 1967).
He went on to brand several other writers, including Jimmy Breslin and
Gay Talese, with the title of parajournalist. In the face of such attacks,
Wolfe wisely chose not to defend the specifics of the *New Yorker* articles,
which he said were not even examples of the New Journalism, because
they "used neither the reporting techniques nor the literary techniques"
that characterized the "new genre" (*New Journalism* 24). Rather, he chose
to respond to the attacks made on the whole form of "New Journalism."
Those responses would grow into one of his most influential books.

The *Herald-Tribune* would not much longer be Wolfe's home base, not
because of the *New Yorker* controversy, but because, like many of the
greatest American newspapers, it simply found that it could not remain
in business as people more and more turned from print to television for
their news. In 1966 and 1967 Wolfe worked as a magazine writer for the
New York World Journal Tribune, a continuation of the *Herald-Tribune* and
other failing papers. All that finally survived from the *Herald-Tribune* was

New York magazine, which carried on the traditions of the *Herald-Tribune's* Sunday supplement after the newspaper itself folded, with Clay Felker continuing as editor. Wolfe served as a contributing editor to *New York* from 1968 to 1976. He later found new outlets for his work, including *Harper's*, and, most important, *Rolling Stone*.

New York City seemed to be the locus of cultural change in the early 1960s, but during the second half of the decade, the west coast and old England were the places where things seemed to be happening, and Wolfe went to where his subjects were. His next two books, *The Electric Kool-Aid Acid Test* and *The Pump House Gang* were published on the same day in July of 1968. The latter collects a number of pieces, mostly set in California and London. Their subjects include some of the cultural gurus of the 1960s, notably communications theorist Marshall McLuhan, and such representatives of the sexual revolution as the first silicone-enhanced stripper and Hugh Hefner, the founder *Playboy*, whom Wolfe describes as "the King of the Status Drop-Outs" enthroned in his bedroom in Chicago's "Playboy Mansion." The title story describes a California youth culture utterly separate from the adult world around it. Many of these pieces are first-rate, and they reveal that Wolfe did a lot of reporting in unusual places, but the book was overshadowed by *The Electric Kool-Aid Acid Test*, which made Wolfe the leading practitioner of the "nonfiction novel"—and the leading expert on the hippie movement and drug culture that fascinated part of the nation and perplexed or appalled the rest.

LETTERS LEAD TO KESEY

Wolfe's interest in the drug culture began in 1966, when novelist Larry McMurtry, author of *The Last Picture Show* and, later, *Lonesome Dove*, showed him two letters he had received from fellow novelist Ken Kesey. Kesey, facing charges of marijuana possession in California, had fled to Mexico. Wolfe found the letters engaging—and hardly what one would expect of a drug-crazed fugitive. (Another novelist, Robert Stone, was also attracted to the Kesey saga. He first obstructed Wolfe's research and then gave up his own project and turned his notes over to Wolfe.) Imagining an article on the fugitive writer in exile, Wolfe prepared to go to Mexico to search for Kesey, but before he could set out on his trip, Kesey had returned to California and been arrested. Wolfe actually first met him in the San Mateo County jail. Wolfe spent about a month with Kesey—who was quickly released on bail—and the band of disciples he had gathered about himself, the Merry Pranksters. Wolfe originally planned a single article, but it expanded into a three-part piece in the *World Journal Tribune*'s version of *New York*. Wolfe was not finished with the subject even then. He realized that the story was about something larger than one writer's legal troubles or even the growing drug sub-culture. What fascinated him about Kesey and his following was that they seemed to be as much a religious movement as a band of outlaws. Their use of drugs—especially the psychedelics, such as LSD—was not simple pleasure seeking. It was part of the movement of "self-actualization" and personal discovery that was the 1960s version of a spiritual awakening.

Wolfe proposed a book-length version of the story to Henry Robbins, his editor at Farrar Straus Giroux, and received a contract. He expanded his research widely, interviewing many of the participants in the Prank-sters' activities. He amassed a vast amount of material. But, as with "The Kandy-Kolored Streamline Baby," he found it difficult to get his research down on paper. (Considering how prolific he has been, it is surprising how often Wolfe has had to deal with serious bouts of writer's block.) Things changed when Wolfe faced a new sort of pressure. His father had become very ill, and Wolfe left New York to help his mother back in Richmond. He could only write between visits to the hospital. Together with his freedom from the distractions of New York, the very limits on his time unblocked Wolfe. "Since I had maybe a couple of hours in the morning, and an hour in the afternoon, and maybe an hour at night to work, I was *religious* about it. I never missed those hours. I would sit down and start writing" (Thompson in Scura 212). He also was encour-aged by both his deadline with Farrar Straus Giroux and the fear that the drug culture would either drop off the cultural map or be chronicled by another writer before his book was finished. As the project continued (and his father recovered), he set deadlines and page quotas for himself, so that he was again writing rapidly, as he had when he made his sty-listic breakthrough in the custom car piece. But before he wrote, he pre-pared, both by creating a traditional outline and by a more unusual technique that helped him write from the subjective perspective of his real-life characters. "I'd review my notes for a certain chapter, then I would close my eyes and try to imagine myself, as a Method actor would, into the scene . . . going crazy, for example . . . how it feels and what it's going to sound like if you translate it into words" (Thompson in Scura 213).

During his research, Wolfe maintained his role of journalist. He was an observer, not a participant. In groups that wore the various badges of the counter-culture—love beads, pants made from American flags, face paint—he wore the emblems of respectable journalism, a coat and tie and shiny black shoes. Most important, he did not accept Kesey's invitations to try LSD himself. (He noticed that other writers stopped being writers once they crossed that line.) In the course of writing the book, however, he decided that he needed to experience the drug once into order to convey what was one of the central experiences of his subject. He traveled to Buffalo, where he had a friend with access to the drug, and took 125 milligrams. At first he thought he was having a heart attack. The rest of his "trip" was strangely appropriate for someone who has been both fascinated with the details of style and the varieties of American culture. "As I began to calm down, I had the feeling that I had entered into the sheen of this nubbly twist carpet—a really *wretched* carpet, made of Acrilan—and somehow this represented the people of America, in their democratic glory. It was cheap and yet it had a certain glossy excitement to it [. . .]. At the time, it seemed like a phenomenal insight, a breakthrough" (Thompson in Scura 213). Wolfe does not consider that his vision meant "a goddamn thing," but perhaps it allowed him to so vividly describe people who did think that LSD opened what Aldous Huxley called "the doors of perception."

Most reviewers admired *The Electric Kool-Aid Acid Test*, though some were again baffled by its style. More important, the book found readers. Admirers of the new journalism read it, but so did the young people creating the youth culture it chronicled. It became one of the books that everyone of a certain age had to read, along with Tolkien, Herman Hesse, and Heinlein's *Stranger in the Strange Land*. Wolfe became a regular on the college lecture circuit—where he may have tired of being asked what Ken Kesey was up to now. The identification of Wolfe with the counter-culture was in many ways ironic, since his experimental style often conveyed a more conservative worldview. (And, while fair to the Pranksters, Wolfe's version of their quest is hardly an uncritical celebration: it ends, after all, with one of them chanting, "We Blew It!") As the years went by and the 1960s faded into memory, the book never went out of print, for it became one of the best introductions to a moment in American culture beyond recapture.

AT ODDS WITH NEW YORK

In the following years, Wolfe's focus shifted back to New York and the world of the arts that he had been chronicling off and on from his first book onward. His relationship with it, however, became increasingly confrontational. In part, he fell out with the artistic establishment because of his rhetorical stance as a social critic: no power structure likes to see its assumptions questioned by outsiders or its received ideas satirized. A power structure that thinks of itself as leftist and bohemian likes it all the less, since the very news that it *is* a power structure undermines its self-identity, and that was often the first message that Wolfe brought. While Wolfe dressed like a member of old society, he brought the bohemian world the awful news that the Society they so enjoyed railing against had disappeared. Still worse, they had taken its place. There was, undoubtedly, enough truth to Wolfe's accusation to make its sting all the sharper. A small group of critics and dealers—and the patrons who followed their lead—did control the "art world," which in fact had little to do with the vast amount of art Americans actually consumed. Almost all poets and many fiction writers had retreated to the university "creative writing program" and were writing more for each other than for a larger audience. The leaders of style in architecture were paying more attention to imported theories than to the wishes of those who would live or work in their buildings. The fashionable work in all these areas was widely disliked by most people, but the power centers, for all their leftist politics, felt at least as free to despise the vulgar masses as any aristocratic elite had. And as Wolfe noticed when he first arrived in New York, there indeed are many who "totally accept what is the current intellectual fashion and then pat themselves on the back for being nonconformists" (Gross 122). Nevertheless, his pointing out these ironies made many, to say the least, uncomfortable.

Wolfe also departed from the conventional stance of the literary and artistic world in that he thought many good things were happening in America. He genuinely liked some products of popular culture. More important, he recognized that in many ways the dream of the old Utopian socialists had been fulfilled. The working classes were now, in fact, flush with cash and able to create their own culture. From *The Pump House Gang* on, he pointed out that despite whatever other problems they faced, Americans were enjoying unrivaled prosperity. The opportunities for self-actualization that that wealth made possible for the masses of Americans was creating, in fact, a "Happiness Explosion" (*The Pump House Gang* 14). Since the assumption of the literary establishment was that things were bad in America, Wolfe's positive view put him out of step with his contemporaries.

The assumption that America was in desperate straits was never stronger than in the late 1960s. The Vietnam War was dragging on. Cities had erupted in race riots. Colleges had become hotbeds of protest—often unable even to offer classes. Along with serious political activism directed toward solving real problems, there was a great deal of political posturing, absurd talk of "revolution," and facile repetition of political pieties. Wolfe had a keen eye for the pomposity and hypocrisy of the fashionable left and made it the subject of his next book, *Radical Chic & Mau-Mauing the Flak-Catchers* (1970). The first half, originally published in *New York*, describes a famous party, one which Wolfe, frankly, crashed. (Even though he had not received an invitation, he called and RSVP'd.) The contrast between composer and conductor Leonard Bernstein and his society friends and the revolutionary Black Panthers they were entertaining gave Wolfe a rich field for his satirical eye—and for his exploration of status details. The irony of people trying to ensure their place in the society status hierarchy by embracing the revolutionary provided Wolfe with the perfect subject—and his relentless and open note taking ensured that he could not be attacked for the accuracy of his facts. He was, on the other hand, attacked for several other things, including writing about a party at which he was a guest and not being serious enough about the real issues of race relations. But many critics admired the book, and it was a lasting success.

Wolfe's willingness to mock liberal pieties in *Radical Chic*, which he himself compared to "laughter in church" (Gross 121), led parts of the literary establishment to begin to shun or marginalize him. But Wolfe was not unhappy to be out of the mainstream. Rather, he relished his position, questioning the reigning dogmas in several of the arts, starting with literature itself. In 1973 he published *The New Journalism*, which is as much about the deficiencies of modern fiction as it is about new paths in journalism. The book begins with a theoretical introduction by Wolfe, which collects a number of the essays Wolfe had prepared in the wake of the *New Yorker* brouhaha defending the New Journalism as a form, though not the offending pieces themselves. This introduction is a touchstone for most later discussions of how fictional techniques could be brought into nonfiction. It so thoroughly defined the form that many of Wolfe's peers took some umbrage at his appropriating the role of leader of a new literary movement. Wolfe, however, disclaimed that role, and in the second half of the book, which he edited with E.W. Johnson, he presents the New Journalism as the communal creation of many writers. It excerpts many of the finest examples of the new literary form. The collection as a whole remains the best introduction to the way literary journalism was transformed during the 1960s.

In the 1970s, Wolfe shifted his magazine home to two very different publications. One was the venerable *Harper's*. The other was *Rolling Stone*, the often outrageous rock and roll magazine that had published some of the most important pieces by Hunter S. Thompson, another pioneer in new journalism. *Rolling Stone* was the creation of the innovative editor Jann Wenner, who was one of Wolfe's greatest fans. He once amended a writer's reference to Wolfe to read, "the *great* Tom Wolfe" (McKeen 13.) His magazine gave Wolfe a subject that would occupy him for the next decade—and later made possible his transformation from journalist to novelist.

The subject was the space program. When in 1972 Wenner signed Wolfe to cover the launch of Apollo 17, the last American mission to the moon, the assignment itself made news—as would several of Wolfe's later contracts. The plan was to simply report what happened around the launch. Two years earlier another pioneer in the "nonfiction novel," Norman Mailer, had tried to capture the atmosphere of the first moon launch in *Of a Fire on the Moon*. When Wolfe wrote about that book in *The New Journalism*, he suggested it failed because Mailer's "autobiographical technique never succeeds in taking the reader inside the capsule, much less inside the points of view or central nervous systems of the astronauts themselves" (188). As Wolfe became more and more interested in the astronauts—and he went to the Apollo 17 launch in part because it was "going to be a regular reunion for all the astronauts who'd gone before" (McKeen 92)—he clearly set out to avoid that pitfall. What was meant to be a single article grew into the four-part series entitled "Post-Orbital Remorse," published in 1973. The title referred to the depression into which some astronauts fell after returning to Earth, but Wolfe's interest had already shifted away from their post-flight problems to the quality that allowed them to sit calmly atop a thirty-six-story pile of explosives that was about be to lit beneath them, a quality he was already calling "the right stuff." And rather than reporting, like Mailer, in the voice of the "literary gentleman in the grandstand," he wrote in what he called the "Astronauts' Collective Unspoken" (McKeen 92). With these articles, Wolfe began his research in the space program from its beginning, a project he would continue to work on for almost seven years.

RATTLING A "CLOSED" ART WORLD

But before turning his full attention back to the astronauts, he would begin grappling with the world of art. In 1975 he published *The Painted*

Word, which was first excerpted in *Harper's*. As the title suggests, Wolfe's central claim is that most modern art is not the purely visual experience that a majority of artists and critics, especially since the rise of abstract art, claim it is. Rather, it is often the illustration of a theory—even of the written manifesto of a school. Wolfe began his exploration of this idea by quoting Hilton Kramer, the art critic for the *New York Times*: "Realism does not lack its partisans, but it does rather conspicuously lack a persuasive theory. And [. . .] to lack a persuasive theory is to lack something crucial" (9). Wolfe was disturbed, doubtless, by the idea that realism lacked a persuasive theory; he had been working on one for literary realism for some time. Still more troubling for him, however, was the idea that what was most important—crucial—to art was theory. In several areas of criticism, especially literary studies, it was becoming fashionable to say that theory was "prior" to artwork (or text) itself—a view diametrically opposed to all traditional conceptions of the role of critic. Here Wolfe was identifying something still more disturbing. Even the most influential critics have only limited influence in the literary world, because even the least popular books have a mass audience. Almost anyone can afford one book, after all. The art world, in contrast, is a small and virtually closed society, comprised of a few wealthy collectors, a limited number of dealers, and a few influential critics. Wolfe went on to suggest that this small market is, in fact, manipulated by the critics and dealers for their own ends. He also suggests that the "popularity" of some movements, such as abstract impressionism, was almost entirely the creation of this closed art world. The book is a lively essay and illustrated with Wolfe's own drawings, which could hardly contrast more sharply with the art works he reproduces. (There had been another one-man show of his drawings at the Tunnel Gallery in New York the year before.)

The reaction to the book from the art world was negative, as might have been expected. Wolfe was treated by many reviewers as a philistine intruder into a world beyond his understanding. Others saw political implications in his attack on the art world: the *New Republic* called him a fascist and even compared him to the brain-washed soldier sent to destroy America in the film *The Manchurian Candidate*. And, in an odd trend that Wolfe considered an illustration of how inbred the art world was, there were a number of what he called "X-rated insults." One artist compared him to "A six-year-old at a pornographic movie; he can follow the action of the bodies but he can't comprehend the *nuances*." *Time* magazine art critic Robert Hughes used the same image—with the boy now eleven (Flippo 154). The *New York Times Book Review* used it once more, with a eunuch taking the place of the small boy (McKeen 86). And, in another pornographic image, the *Partisan Review* compared the author of *The Painted Word* to the star of the notorious pornographic film *Deep Throat*. To Wolfe, the similarity in the very language of abuse proved that the art world was a tiny community where people talked only to each other and could not help picking up each other's phrases. In any case, the intemperance of the responses to the book showed that Wolfe had hit a nerve.

IMPORTANT ESSAYS PUBLISHED

Wolfe collected several pieces from magazines, as well as some new ones, in *Mauve Gloves & Madmen, Clutter & Vine* in 1976, and the book includes some of his most important essays. Wolfe's only piece dealing directly with the Vietnam War, "Jousting with SAM and Charlie" can be seen as the root of *The Right Stuff*. (A "SAM" is a surface-to-air missile; "Charlie" was the nickname American soldiers gave to their enemies in the Vietnam War.) In describing the ethos of the fighter pilots sailing from the aircraft carrier *Coral Sea* to bomb North Vietnamese targets in or near Hanoi, he encapsulates the qualities that he would elsewhere call "the right stuff" and here can only call "it." Wolfe clearly admired the military ethos, and he later lamented that "[s]erious writers stopped looking at the military around 1919—in any sympathetic way or even empathetic way" (Flippo 135). They began presenting soldiers only as victims and never as warriors. Here Wolfe goes back to older traditions—invoked in the chivalric imagery of his title—of celebrating skill, daring, bravery, and prowess. Wolfe's interest in the astronauts was doubtless based on his true admiration for their virtues. But it also allowed him to describe the military ethos in the one context where even the most pacifist reader could admire it. In this essay, he risks the antiwar reader's revulsion by showing the fighting military—specifically, the officer corps—as a source of the qualities he values.

Mauve Gloves also includes "The Me-Decade and the Third Great Awakening," which had appeared in *Esquire* earlier that year. In it Wolfe both gave a lasting name to the 1970s and returned to his interest in religion. In an argument similar to that presented in *The Electric Kool-Aid Acid Test*, Wolfe suggests that some of the things that seem strangest and newest in American culture are, in fact, part of the old American pattern of seeking self-fulfillment through ecstatic religious experience. The first Great Awakening in the eighteenth century had seen a wave of emotional revivals throughout the colonies and given impetus both to the expansion of Methodism and New Light Presbyterianism. The Second Great Awakening from 1825 to 1850 led to the "atmosphere of Christian asceticism" that made it possible to "build communities in the face of great hardship" and led to the strengthening of traditional denominations and to the creation of uniquely American groups, such as the Mormons. Both movements had been characterized not so much by new doctrines as by new feelings. Eighteenth-century writers, such as Jonathan Edwards, describe the sweetness of religious sentiments that whole communities felt as the revival swept over them, and Wolfe describes the still more wild ecstasy of "hoedown camp-meeting revivalism [. . .] in which people barked, bayed, fell down in fits and swoons, rolled on the ground, talked in tongues, and even added a touch of orgy" (162). Wolfe saw a third, equally important, large-scale revival in the spiritual seeking of the 1970s, which included both the movement of evangelical Christianity into the mainstream with the election of Jimmy Carter as president and, perhaps more important, the rise of many other groups offering ecstasy or understanding—many of them "therapeutic" rather than religious in their terminology. Where this "Great Awakening" differed from its predecessors was that its focus was primarily on self, not on some transcendence beyond the ego. In many of these varied movements of the 1970s, such as EST and various sorts of "encounter groups"—and, more tellingly, one might add, in all the versions of twelve-step self-help programs that have become so important in American culture since then—the focus is on the self, on telling one's own story. The recitation of one's weaknesses and failures may seem humiliating on the surface, but the appeal is clear: "It is summed up in the notion: 'Let's talk about *Me.*' No matter whether you managed to renovate your personality through encounter sessions or not, you had finally focused your attention and your energies on the most fascinating subject on earth: *Me*" (146–147).

Since American culture has in the last decades gone a long way toward replacing "religion," which has to do with commitment to a body of doctrine and a community outside one's self, with "spirituality," which is often a self-created path to self-fulfillment, Wolfe was clearly on to something. He suggests another development that made possible the focus on the individual ego as well as many other changes in the culture— the loss of "man's age-old belief in serial immortality." That quality, the idea that one's fulfillment is less important than one's place in a "great biological stream," is what motivates "[t]he husband and wife who sacrifice their own ambitions and their material assets in order to provide a 'better future' for their children [and] the soldier who risks his life, or perhaps consciously sacrifices it, in battle" (165). In Wolfe's next big project, he would show men—men with large egos—who exemplified just that quality.

FINISHES *THE RIGHT STUFF*

In 1977, Wolfe got down to finishing the project on the astronauts he had begun five years before. Once again, the phrase "writer's block" shows up in descriptions of his work (Blue 104). Wolfe's problems with this project were also personal; he was "affected deeply" by the death of Thomas Kennerly Wolfe, Sr. But some saw the book, as he finally shaped it, with its early focus on Southerner Chuck Yeager, as a tribute not just to "the spirit of the rural south" but to his father (Thompson in Scura 214–215). Wolfe had been researching the story, which he imagined covering the "whole space program up to Skylab," for years. He wrote quickly for six months. When he had covered the Mercury program and the roots of the Astronauts' ethos in that of the test pilots of the 1940s and 1950s, he found that he had "got up to 450 pages and [. . .] said that's it, I think I've got a book" (Blue 104). He held on to the manuscript for a year, however, polishing it. (While rapidly getting everything down on paper had worked for Wolfe's books on the wild world of custom cars and the Merry Pranksters, several later books, including *Radical Chic*, went through several drafts.) When it was published in 1979 as *The Right Stuff*, it sold better than any of Wolfe's previous books and won both the American Book Award and the National Book Critics Circle Award.

The Right Stuff showed Wolfe drawing all his talents together. The book was clearly the result of a great deal of careful reporting. (Even Alan Shepard, who had declined to cooperate with the project and appears in it as a hero with a number of flaws, admitted that the "storyline was OK," while claiming that the "personalities [. . .] were off the mark" [qtd. in McKeen 94].) It is carefully structured, with a gripping narrative. Full of memorable phrases, whether Wolfe's or the astronauts' own, it made "the right stuff" and "pushing the envelope" part of the language. Besides being a storyteller, Wolfe showed he was still a sociologist, here one analyzing a subject that others would be embarrassed to talk about: heroism. To understand how the astronauts were able so coolly to risk their lives, Wolfe argued, you had to understand the culture they lived in, for "physical bravery only happens in a social context. There has to be a sphere of people, a fraternity which sets standards and whose approval is all-important to you—and there has to be no honorable alternative to bravery [. . .]. Otherwise you're just not going to have brave people" (Blue 104).

The critical response to *The Right Stuff* was overwhelmingly positive. Almost every important reviewer was lavish in praising the book. Some, however, objected to the portrait of Mercury astronaut John Glenn, who by then was a U.S. senator, which surprised Wolfe. Wolfe thought his presentation of him, the straight arrow in the Mercury Seven, showed him as "an exceptional and rather courageous figure" (Flippo 138). Glenn himself praised *The Right Stuff* in his memoirs—though he had fewer kind things to say about the movie that would be made from it. One major negative reaction to *The Right Stuff*—and to other recent examples of New Journalism, such as Norman Mailer's *The Executioner's Song*—showed the dust had not settled from the "Tiny Mummies!" flap. Writing in the *Yale Review*, John Hersey, whom Wolfe had labeled "boring" in his *New Yorker* article, called *The Right Stuff* "a vivid book, a tainted book" and fell into the pattern, set by Dwight MacDonald, of suggesting that the New Journalism is not a matter of applying fictional techniques to nonfiction, but of actually making things up: "The tricks of fiction he uses dissolve now and then into its very essence: fabrication" (5). Wolfe responded, as he had in *The New Journalism*, that "it's extremely important to be accurate, because a lot of the voltage of narrative nonfiction is that the reader is able to believe" (Gilder 162). He also noted that Hersey's own *Hiroshima* lacked footnotes and presented exactly the same problem in distinguishing fact and fiction that his own work did, assuming such a problem existed.

The year before the publication of *The Right Stuff*—at forty-seven, an age when many men of his generation were shedding a first wife for a younger "trophy wife"—Wolfe married for the first, and only, time. He seemed to have no regrets about his long bachelorhood. When asked if he was annoyed that in America men who dress flamboyantly are often assumed to be homosexual, he replied, "Sensitivity to homosexuality is very much a New York phenomenon. It never came up back home in Virginia. There always was the tradition of the honorable dandy and the honorable bachelor. I've always felt that people should be highly respected, if not actually rewarded, for long bachelorhoods" (Levine 170). If anything, his delaying marriage seems to be a sign of his seriousness about the step. His wife, Sheila Berger, was then art director at *Harper's*; she had met Wolfe while working at *Esquire*. A daughter, Alexandra Kennerly was born in 1980, and a son, Thomas, in 1985. While Wolfe reveals little of his personal life, his friends report him as delighting in his family. The writer Gay Talese once even described him as having "found glamour in family life" (Thompson in Scura 216). Other friends also report his having very clear and traditional private views on marriage and fidelity. His public writings show that he is very much a dissenter from general acceptance of divorce that has grown so rapidly in the last few decades. In both his novels, extramarital affairs lead to disaster, and an issue that comes up repeatedly in his work is the plight of the first wife abandoned for the trophy wife.

That issue appears several times in Wolfe's next book, *In Our Time* (1980). While the title harks back to Hemingway's first book of spare, chiseled, short stories, Wolfe's book is something else entirely. Published in coffee-table size, it is primarily a collection of drawings, and it collected almost all the drawings he had published to date. The centerpiece of the book is a series of pictures with brief prose commentaries that had appeared as a monthly series in *Harper's* from 1978 to 1980. In one, "The Birds and the Bees," a father explains the facts of life, as they were at the end of the "Me-Decade," to his son:

> No, no, son, that's not how it works. When you're forty-five or fifty, you'll get a new wife, a young one, a girl in her twenties.
> What happens to the old one?
> Well, she opens up a needlepoint shop and sells yarn to her friends and joins a discussion group. (34)

In both text and pictures, Wolfe satirized many of the fads of the time—from jogging to disco. Despite its original size, the book is a slight one, but much of it remains amusing.

ATTACKS MODERN ARCHITECTURE

Undaunted by the hostile response to *The Painted Word*, Wolfe produced a critique of another artistic establishment in 1981. *From Bauhaus to Our House* attacked the conventions of modern architecture. Wolfe especially deplored the abandonment of American traditions, such as that of Louis Sullivan, who had no hesitation to decorate even skyscrapers in a manner that would please the eye, by architects eager to embrace Europeans dogmas. Wolfe disliked most of all the International Style, derivative of Mies van der Roche, Le Corbusier, and Walter Gropius, a style that tended to produce undecorated boxes—sometimes all glass, sometimes windowless—instead of buildings that could be understood and admired by those who had to live and work in them. He clearly had two objections to modern architecture. One was essentially aesthetic. International School buildings, if not invariably ugly, were uniformly dull. The flat walls with horizontal windows and little, if any, molding or decoration, and the flat roofs, mandatory even in snowy climates, provide little for the eye to rest on. The second was to the same slavish adherence to theory that he had attacked in the art world—and that he had, and would again, attack in literature. Architects were simply following a prescribed theory—one based on a political philosophy at once dubious in itself and inapplicable to America. (Why model all buildings, from schools to corporate headquarters, on the uniform "worker's flats" designed for masses of proletarians in a land where the workers were all rich enough to buy their own suburban ranch houses?) The domination of the architectural profession by academics—like the domination of fiction writing by creative writing programs—was driving it to produce buildings that almost no one actually liked.

Similar arguments were being made by other critics—including even the Prince of Wales—and by many ordinary people. Architects themselves were tiring of the dogmas they had followed for so long. The growing "post-modern" movement forsook the undecorated box and returned to decoration of many kinds—though often with a jaded irony that mocked tradition even while returning to it. All the same, the response to Wolfe's foray into the domain of artistic experts was once again greeted with hostility. While many readers relished his attack on styles they found inhuman and compared him to the boy in the Hans Christian Andersen tale who points out that the emperor has no clothes, professional critics savaged him. *Time* critic Robert Hughes, for example, devoted several pages to denouncing him. Such extreme responses only contributed to the popularity of Wolfe's critique.

WINS HONORARY DEGREES, OTHER AWARDS

Despite any controversy, Wolfe was getting his share of honors, including an honorary doctorate from the Minneapolis College of Art in 1971 and the Frank Luther Mott Award for Research in Journalism in 1973. His home state seemed especially delighted to honor him. He was made an honorary doctor of humane letters by Washington and Lee in 1974, became Virginia Laureate for Literature in 1977, and was awarded another honorary doctorate by Virginia Commonwealth University in

1983. In 1984, he received another honorary degree from Long Island University's Southampton College, near which he has a summer home. In 1988, he received the Harold D. Vursell Memorial Award for distinguished service in the field of journalism from the American Institute of Arts and Letters and in 1986, the Benjamin Pierce Cheney Medal from Eastern Washington University and the Washington Irving Medal for literary excellence from the Nicholas Society. All these honors came before Wolfe turned from bringing nonfiction techniques into journalism to writing fiction itself. He was an established man of letters before he took the risk of trying to become a novelist. Wolfe's next book was more proof of the status he had acquired. *The Purple Decades: A Reader* (1982) contained no new material. Rather, it collected many of Wolfe's best pieces, including excerpts from the full-length books. The publication of a "reader" asserted that Wolfe had reached the level of a sort of "classic" author, and most reviewers were perfectly willing to accord him that status. Brought together in one volume, Wolfe's twenty years of nonfiction proved to be a truly impressive achievement. He now began trying to replicate that achievement in a new field of writing.

Wolfe had for many years considered writing a novel, and the sort of novel he wanted to write was clear. His models were the broad, panoramic nineteenth century novels that seemed to capture a whole society, novels like William Makepeace Thackeray's *Vanity Fair*. His subject was also clear: New York. Thackeray, in Wolfe's view, had tried "in one book to present the picture of ambition and status strife as he saw it in the London of his time. [...] And *nobody* has tried to do this for New York in our own time, despite the fact that New York has certainly been one of the most bizarre world capitals that has ever been" (Bellamy 43–44). The book Wolfe was imagining was in many ways out of step with fashion. The models he invoked were not the heroes of Modernism, like Joyce and Proust, but rather their predecessors—English writers Dickens and Trollope and French writers Balzac and Zola. He had, of course, little good to say about the contemporary novelists who were experimenting in "magical realism" and other forms of fiction that turned away from research-based realism. His novel, as much as his nonfiction, would be based on reporting: "I think the only future for the novel is reporting," he declared, "which means there's not going to be *much* difference between the best novels and the best nonfiction" (Bellamy 42).

Other projects, such as the monthly contributions to *Harper's*, kept Wolfe from getting down to work on his New York book for years, but in 1981 he gave them up in order to give it his full attention. The writing did not come easily. Wolfe did a great deal of research, much of it on the criminal justice system, since that is one area where different classes and races are sometimes forced to interact with each other. For a time he was a regular at the Manhattan Criminal Court, observing cases in a court presided over by his friend Burt Roberts, and even "sitting next to him on the bench during a calendar session" (Taylor 260). The actual writing, however, did not get very far, though Wolfe drafted a good deal, including four chapters on the art world, that would never see print. He continued his research in the even rougher courts of the Bronx. His friend, Attorney Edward Hayes, had worked as an assistant district attorney in the Bronx homicide squad, and he was able to provide Wolfe with access to still more parts of the world he wanted to put on his social canvas. "It was directly through Eddie, for example, that I was able to go down to the detention pen" (Thompson in Scura 260).

The new venue for his research led Wolfe to change the planned setting of his novel to the Bronx, and he completed an outline. But after working on the project for three years, he still had not really begun to write it. "I finally decided," he says, "I've got to get this book out; I can't afford to be blocked. It's so stupid to be blocked" (261). He arranged to overcome his block by once again imitating the Victorian novelists he so admired. Many of them had written their books for immediate serialization. One part of the novel would appear in a magazine or as a pamphlet before the next was even written. The expectation of the publisher—and the reader—for the next part to appear on time gave the writer the most inflexible of deadlines. No one had written and published a novel this way for decades, but Wolfe took what he had—"a 100-page outline and individual chapter summaries"—to Jann Wenner and proposed that *Rolling Stone* do what Thackeray's *Cornhill* and Dickens's *Household Words* had done a century before: publish a novel in parts as it was written. Wenner agreed, offering Wolfe "around $200,000" for his work.

The arrangement was a success. Wolfe's block disappeared, thanks to the deadlines. A new installment of *The Bonfire of the Vanities* appeared in each biweekly issue of *Rolling Stone* from July 1984 to August 1985. All the same, the method did not come as naturally to Wolfe as it had to Dickens or Trollope. They were able to make whatever adjustments in structure they had to on the fly, and the final versions of their novels that later appeared in hard covers hardly differed from those that had appeared in parts. Wolfe, on the other hand, found that his work was not flowing so smoothly. Fiction differed from journalism in two important ways. First, it is not ephemeral ("One of the great things about journalism is, it's thrown away," he said). Second, the structure is not largely provided by the facts but must be entirely created by the writer. "I don't think many people were as aware as I was of how many times the thing was going offtrack in terms of structure. I was making mistakes. And I was acutely aware of it" (Taylor 261). On top of those purely literary concerns, there was the problem of fiction being outpaced by the news. Wolfe dropped a strand of the plot involving violence on the subway when media attention devoted to "subway vigilante" Bernhard Goetz threatened to make it seem he was just repeating the events in the newspapers. In the end, Wolfe did not feel that the serialization—his "very public first draft"—was a great success: "I had the distinct impression the population was not thronging the docks waiting for the next issue, the way they did with Dickens" (Taylor 262).

After his novel finished its run in *Rolling Stone*, Wolfe set out to revise it. He did the job thoroughly. Hardly a page in the book exactly matches the corresponding passage in the magazine. Most important, Wolfe decided to change even the occupation of his central character, Sherman McCoy. In the first version, he is a writer, and even before the serialization ended, Wolfe began to consider changing that. Not only was the character "boring," but "You never saw him sitting down at the typewriter. I can't stand novels or movies in which people have an occupation and you never see them at it" (Taylor 262). By making McCoy a bond trader, Wolfe tapped into a part of American culture—Wall Street—that characterized the 1980s every bit as much as the drug culture characterized the 1960s. The change also required more reporting. He spent a day at a bond-trading desk at Salomon Brothers, "even listening in on the telephone conversations of traders" (Taylor 263). In the book version of the novel, McCoy's work is every bit as important as his legal woes—and you do see him at the business of making money.

The revisions and further research took almost two years, and *The Bonfire of the Vanities* finally appeared between hard covers in 1987. It was on the best-seller lists for weeks. And despite Wolfe's attacks on the literary establishment and especially the dominant trends in the literary novel, it was largely a critical success as well. Praise was not universal, however. When John Leonard of *Newsday* heard that Wolfe had almost won the National Book Critics Circle Award, he was appalled: "That the bailiffs almost gave their bauble to Tom Wolfe's catalogue of shoes—electric-blue lizard pumps! Snow-white Reeboks! Bench-made half-brogued English New & Lingwoods!—is scary" (McKeen 125). But most readers thought Wolfe's use of status details here, as in his earliest work, made his description of a society marked by class divisions all the more vivid. Others were troubled that few of the characters were sympathetic—forgetting that, as books like *Vanity Fair*, which Thackeray sub-titled *A Novel Without a Hero*, prove, fiction often works best when readers feel some distance from the characters. Still others thought Wolfe's female characters weak—a point he accepted (Taylor 263). Finally, some objected to Wolfe's depictions of African Americans as stereotypical. In response, Wolfe invoked his research and argued that many literary people are unwilling to address issues like race frankly: "There's a convention that says you can bring these topics up so long as the tension is resolved in the end. [. . .] Well, the tension isn't resolved in New York in real life—or it hasn't been yet." (Taylor 264). Whatever the objections of some, most readers thought that Wolfe had come close to his goal of writing the great New York novel.

In a sign of the popularity of *The Bonfire of the Vanities*, the movie rights to it sold for $750,000. The resulting film, released in 1990, became one of Hollywood's most celebrated catastrophes, despite Brian De Palma as director and stars including Tom Hanks, Melanie Griffith, and Morgan Freeman. Journalist Julie Salamon had been allowed to cover the whole production, and her book, *The Devil's Candy*: The Bonfire of the Vanities *Goes to the Movies*, describes the debacle. Salamon reports that Wolfe was unwilling to criticize the filmmakers. "I think it's bad manners in the Southern sense to be sharp and critical of it [. . .]. I did cash the check." (xii). Part of the problem was that the producers tried to avoid addressing the racial issues Wolfe raised. While Wolfe shows a Jewish judge trying to get a black crowd to share his belief in color-blind justice and going unheeded, the moviemakers put a similar speech into the mouth of a black judge—eliminating the very tension that was Wolfe's subject. There were, however, other problems with the film, which Salamon discusses at length. While she describes Wolfe as cringing over the movie, he seems not very upset by it: "The great thing about selling a book to the movies is that nobody blames the author" (408). Wolfe's earlier experience with film had hardly been better. The screen version of *The Right Stuff*, released in 1983 and directed by Philip Kaufman, while not a complete flop, was not a great success, either. It turned Wolfe's celebration of heroism into mostly low comedy. John Glenn even blamed it, in part, for derailing his presidential ambitions. He wrote that the "book was good, but what Hollywood did to it could have been titled *Laurel and Hardy Go to Space*. Somehow the movie's lukewarm reception had a chilling effect on the campaign" (349). Wolfe's own comments on the movie were more mild: "What was on the screen was not my book. It was something else. It was something else pretty good" (Salamon 23). Thus far, the only thoroughly successful film version of one of Wolfe's works

is *The Last American Hero*, the 1973 version of Wolfe's account of Junior
Johnson directed by Lamont Johnson and starring Jeff Bridges. That film
was strong enough to lead Pauline Kael to insist on publishing a good
review of it in the *New Yorker*, despite William Shawn's disinclination to
print something positive about anything connected with Wolfe (Yagoda
354–355). NBC is producing a multipart TV movie version of *A Man in
Full*. That form may be a better match for the broad scope of Wolfe's
fiction. As he told Salamon, "From my standpoint it's too bad that movies don't run nine or ten hours" (xiii)

LAUDED AS AUTHOR AND JOURNALIST

After the publication of *The Bonfire of the Vanities*, Wolfe received several further honors, as well as general recognition that he was both a
major novelist and a preeminent journalist. He was awarded the John
Dos Passos Prize for literature from Longwood College in 1987, and the
Wilbur Lucius Cross Medal from Yale, which is described as the "most
prestigious honor available" to a Yale graduate alumnus (Fishwick 5) in
1990. Wolfe was, nevertheless, still offending the cultural establishment.
In 1989 *Harper's* published "Stalking the Billion-Footed Beast: A Literary
Manifesto for the New Social Novel." In it Wolfe once again made many
of the points he had been making for years, arguing that realism—realism based on research—was the true source of the novel's power and
that the fashionable works that turned away from it were an artistic dead
end. He also described the writing of his own novel and made it the
model for what the novel should be. (That is not an unusual trap for
novelists writing theory to fall into. Many decades before Somerset
Maugham noted that in *Aspects of the Novel*, E.M. Forster described exactly the sort of novel E.M. Forster wrote.) The piece predictably attracted the ire of many other novelists. *Harper's*, in fact, encouraged
controversy. It invited a number of prominent writers to respond, and a
good number did. While Wolfe's points were largely supported by Walker Percy, most of those who responded disagreed to a greater or lesser
extent. Some, among them Allison Lurie, were moderate in tone and
made cogent points. (Lurie pointed out, quite correctly, that the literary
tradition Wolfe describes is almost entirely masculine.) Other resorted to
name-calling. Mary Gordon, proving that ethnic slurs can still be used
against one group, the Southern white, referred to him as "the thinking
man's redneck." And many made interesting points about how far realism had in fact been displaced by fabulation in American fiction. None

of this, of course, changed Wolfe's view that the large social novel was the real mainstay of fiction. It did show him in his old position of being both at the center of American literature and marginalized from it. His alienation from the literary establishment was also by now clearly political. Though Wolfe has never been one for taking political stands, neither has he been willing to follow the fashionable leftist line that most in the literary world and academia take. During the 1980s and 1990s he was willing to associate with such conservative writers as William F. Buckley, Jr., and George Will. He was entertained at the White House during the Reagan administration. Though Wolfe could never be called what was then known as a "movement" conservative, he was not afraid to be associated with them. Such connections said to the literary establishment that Wolfe was still an outsider and allowed some academic historians of American literature to dismiss him as simply a "neo-conservative gadfly," which is what *The Columbia Literary History of the United States* called him in 1988, a judgment that is clearly more political than literary (Molesworth 1036).

All the same, after *The Bonfire of the Vanities*, the expectations for Wolfe's next novel were high. In 1989 Wolfe signed a contract and received a $7.5 million advance (Cash). That advance, in effect a loan against the earnings the book would finally bring, put great pressure on Wolfe, as did his desire to top his previous achievement. Once again, he had to struggle with writer's block and the problem of early drafts simply not working. Looking back, he recalled several mistakes he had made as he embarked on the project. "I was 57 [. . .] and I thought the eight or nine years I'd spent on *Bonfire* had taught me what *not* to do the second time. So, I proceeded to make every blunder a beginning writer could stumble into. [. . .] I always recommend to people who ask me for helpful hints on writing that they start with an outline. Naturally, I didn't take my own advice and do an outline until I was years into the project" (Gray 89). A larger problem was setting. Part of the novel was always to be set in the quail plantations of south Georgia, but the rest of the book was again to take place in New York—and Wolfe realized after a time that he was repeating himself. By 1995, when he had amassed nearly 1,000 pages of manuscript, Wolfe "muse[d] wistfully" to Jonathan Galassi, his editor at Farrar Straus Giroux, that he wished he had set the novel in Atlanta. Galassi asked, "Then why don't you?" "The way he said it," Wolfe recalls, "gave me the confidence to jettison literally hundreds of pages" (Scott). The new setting gave Wolfe's novel the focus it lacked. The research he did in Atlanta and elsewhere gave the novel the realistic power that Wolfe talked about in his literary manifestos. The writing continued to be hard going, however, and Wolfe took on a number of smaller projects on subjects ranging from the creators of the microchip to sociobiology to neuroscience. ("If I were a college student today," he wrote, "I don't think I could resist going into neuroscience" [*Hooking Up* 107]).

In the middle of the project, Wolfe faced a major nonliterary crisis. He had, as he says, "few minor vices," and had taken good care of himself over the years. He even admitted to having been something of a "body snob" when he compared his own fitness with the paunches of other men his age (Rehm). He was avid for exercise, such as playing squash with his son. Exercise, however, was not helping Wolfe to get his mind off his troubles with the book. "One of the supposed benefits of exercise is that you don't think of your problems: not true. As I did aerobics or bicycled, I thought of nothing but my book, and how to finish it. I paid the price" (Grieg). During a workout in August of 1996, he suffered chest pains that turned out to be a heart attack. He had to undergo quintuple bypass surgery. Wolfe's recovery left him at first feeling "euphoric. I was so happy to be alive that I started writing constantly, though mostly on things not related to the novel" (Gray 94). But by January of 1997, he succumbed to the depression that often follows heart surgery. "I had never been depressed before," he said, "and I couldn't understand what was happening to me. I looked at the novel and thought it was a failure" (Gray 94). Wolfe was reluctant to seek help—therapy had attracted his scorn more than once—but he did at last contact a friend he had made through his neuroscience research, Dr. Paul McHugh, psychiatrist in chief at the Johns Hopkins hospital in Baltimore. McHugh offered to treat him himself, and Wolfe was back to normal in a few months. He would, however, now be able to describe the depression Charlie Croker, the central character the new novel, would fall into. He already knew firsthand the mounting pressure Croker feels closing in all around him.

Wolfe had by this point abandoned parts of his manuscript he decided could not be fit into the novel as it was developing. He cut what would have been a plot dealing with television news but did not abandon it entirely. Part of it became an independent novella, "Ambush at Fort Bragg," which appeared in *Rolling Stone* in 1996. With the heart attack and depression behind him and the focus of the novel now clear, Wolfe pressed on and completed the book.

A Man in Full was published in the fall of 1998. *Rolling Stone* earlier paid $600,000 to serialize it. It was a large book, and its appearance was an important event. There were prominent stories on Wolfe and his work in the major news magazines. The novel was nominated for a National

Book Award even before its publication. It was a best-seller for weeks, and many of the reviews were glowing. Wolfe seemed to have captured another important moment in the culture, for Atlanta was now, indeed, one of the places where American culture was being formed, just as New York and San Francisco had been in earlier decades. Wolfe had clearly tried to stretch himself. He wrote about the very areas reviewers had suggested he slighted in *The Bonfire of the Vanities*, such as the experience of women and minorities. Here important strands of the plot were told from the points of view of a woman and of a black man. He had also set out to counter the criticism that none of his characters was sympathetic by endeavoring to create, in Conrad Hensley, a portrait of a genuinely good man.

Nevertheless, response to the novel was by no means entirely positive. Some of the most negative reviews were from Wolfe's fellow novelists, including John Updike, Norman Mailer, and John Irving. Even their reviews were not entirely bad: Updike and Mailer both had good things to say about *A Man in Full*; it simply did not rise from the realm of entertainment into the world of true literary art. Wolfe had been addressing the charge that the realistic novel was "mere entertainment" for years and launched once again into its defense. The quarrel itself made for stories in *Newsweek* and the *New York Times*, but in many ways it seemed like a last echo of quarrels from the past. *The New York Review of Books*, which published Mailer's review, had been dismissing Wolfe since Dwight McDonald's time, and the *New Yorker*, Updike's literary home, had been on the outs with Wolfe since 1965. Some of the arguments seemed very tired. Updike was still sniffing about Wolfe's incorrect use of punctuation, such as spaced dots. Wolfe had won that war; the fifth edition of the *MLA Style Manual* had had to replace "..." with "[...]" as the sign of an ellipsis just because Wolfe and other writers had made using it expressively so common.

Whatever the other grand old men of fiction were saying, Wolfe was once again attracting attention. He was also once more being showered with honors. After a period when he seemed to be pointedly passed over for election to the American Academy of Arts and Letters—which only underscored his self-identification with Balzac, who had never been elected to the French Academy, despite his dominance of French literature for a generation—he was named to that august body in 1999. That same year he received recognition from Britain: he was awarded the London *Sunday Times* Award for literary excellence. His special place in American culture was shown again when he was awarded an honorary degree by Boston University. The university was often associated with conservative ideologies, but it departed from traditions when honoring Tom Wolfe. In place of the red gown it usually presents to new doctors of humane letters, it robed him in a specially made gown—all white, to match Wolfe's suit.

In 1999 Wolfe published the commentary in an art book presenting the work of Frederick Hart, the Atlanta-born sculptor who created the figures at the Vietnam Veteran's memorial in Washington and many of the sculptures at Washington National Cathedral. Wolfe's admiration for Hart was natural. Hart's work is representational and the product of great skill. It is, in that, a great contrast with the Wall, the section of the Vietnam memorial that Maya Linn designed, which, moving as it is, is almost entirely a concept—a black wall receding in a city of white monuments rising—rather than a product of the artist's mastery of craft. (The workmanship of the wall is not Linn's own, after all.) Wolfe's championing of Hart—he also wrote a moving obituary for the sculptor after his death—was part of his continuing quarrel with the artistic establishment, but it was also evidence of his willingness to further the work of artists he admires. He has contributed forewords to a number of books, including a collection of satirical art, an art book on decorative buttons, and a photographic history of his home city, Richmond, Virginia.

The year 2000 saw Wolfe still playing the role of enfant terrible as much as grand old man. He was still pleased to question the received wisdom in every field. *Hooking Up*, a collection that brought together both Wolfe's uncollected pieces from the 1980s and 1990s and the *New Yorker* pieces from the 1960s, received mixed reviews but showed that Wolfe could still entertain by presenting new parts of the American culture. (The subjects range from the sexual habits of teenagers to neuroscience.) He could also still annoy people by suggesting that things were good in America (Bonca). His next project may be a novel on academia—he spent part of 1999 at Stanford doing research—or the big book on status that he has imagined doing for years (Gray 96). His place in American literature—and the culture he had chronicled—might be summed up in an appearance he made late in the year, just as *Hooking Up* was appearing. He spoke at the Association of Literary Scholars and Critics, the association conservative literary critics had created as an alternative to the trendy and left-wing Modern Language Association. Wolfe had been to the hotel where it met before. He had interviewed "the king of the status drop-outs" there when it was the Playboy Mansion. And the girlie magazine publisher's status had risen in Chicago. The street in front of the hotel had recently been renamed "Hugh Hefner Way" by what would once have been called the city fathers. Wolfe was still right in the middle of a changing culture, and very much enjoying it, even while he argued with the values it was adopting.

2

Tom Wolfe's Place in Contemporary Literature

My task . . . is, before all, to make you *see*."

—Joseph Conrad

Tom Wolfe's place in American literature is controversial. In part that is because Wolfe has sought out controversy over and over again. He has never shied away from literary quarrels; indeed, he has sometimes gone out of his way to pick them. He has also deliberately tweaked many of the most influential figures in the world of writing and the arts. Establishment figures in fields from journalism to architecture to literature itself have replied by questioning Wolfe's credentials. The resulting publicity has been good for Wolfe's career as a publishing writer, if not for his reputation in the academy, but it masks his more important role in the literary controversies of the time. During the second half of the twentieth century, the literary world experienced a great anxiety over the relationship of the written word and world at large. Some academic critics went so far as to say that there was *no* relationship between the two. Some journalists held to the idea that reality could be represented only if writers avoided using most of the tools language gave them. Wolfe, in both theory and practice, makes the case that literature can represent the world—and that it does so best when it uses the widest range of possible techniques.

To understand Wolfe's place in the literary world, it is important to

understand the different traditions he took part in. Part of his achievement was that he was able to rejoin elements of literature that had become separated from each other in American culture. He tried to erase,
and certainly blurred, the distinction between journalism and literature
and demonstrated that a writer could be at once interested in matters of
fact and matters of style. Together with the other writers in the movement known as the New Journalism he changed the way literary nonfiction was written and prepared the way for later generations of "literary
journalists." If he has not been able to change the writing of fiction in
the same way, he has at least made novelists and critics question the
assumption that the novel in this era must be personal (about the novelist) or even self-referential (about the fictional text itself).

JOURNALISM, OLD AND NEW

Many of the great names of the American literary tradition are journalists. Mark Twain, Jack London, Frank Norris, Theodore Dreiser, Stephen Crane, and Ernest Hemingway were newspapermen. William Dean
Howells edited the *Atlantic Monthly*, and Willa Cather ran *McClure's*. All
went on to gain fame as novelists, but other writers achieved renown
for their nonfictional work. Some, like Melville, whose first books were
narratives of his experiences in the South Seas, later became novelists.
Others, such as Richard Henry Dana of *Two Years Before the Mast* or
Francis Parkman of *The Oregon Trail*, achieved their place in the literary
world on the strength of their nonfiction alone. By the middle of the
twentieth century, however, the worlds of journalism and literature had
become quite separate.

Journalism and other forms of nonfiction began to be seen as secondary genres in the years during which literature became more and more
closely identified with the fictional. At one time the place of fiction itself
in the literary world had not been particularly high. In the eighteenth
century, for example, the most respected authors were poets, such as
Alexander Pope, or great writers of essays, biographies, and other sorts
of nonfiction, such as Samuel Johnson. But by the middle of the next
century, the novel became the most read and most influential form of
writing. The appearance of a novel by a writer like Charles Dickens was
often a major cultural event, and it would create the same sort of excitement that the appearance of a "blockbuster" movie does now. Journalism, and other forms of nonfiction, began to take the second place that
the novel had formerly occupied. But novels were not seen as high art.

Indeed, part of their appeal was that they reported on parts of the world the reader might never see. What is more, nonfiction was still very much a part of literature, and writers such as Ralph Waldo Emerson, Thomas Carlyle, and John Ruskin were among the foremost writers of their time even though they wrote no important fiction.

Once the novel achieved preeminence, writers like Gustave Flaubert (1821–1880) in France and Henry James (1843–1916) in the English-speaking world began discussing fiction more as a self-enclosed art and less as a representation of the world. Its links to journalism, therefore, were neglected. By the 1950s, one of the most influential literary critics of the time, Northrop Frye, would say that what made literary works literature were all the elements that did not refer to the world outside. So far as a text did refer to the world, it was not literature. Only the self-referential elements, such as style and structure, made writing art. Viewed in that light, most journalism was not literature. And that was especially true because journalism had abandoned many of the stylistic elements it had had access to in the past.

Until the late nineteenth century, journalism was not viewed as a profession and still less as one that had any professional standards. Writers simply wrote, and they did things that no modern newspapers would consider doing. (Samuel Johnson simply made up the speeches reported from the British Parliament based on no more information than the names of the speakers who took each side in the debate.) They were openly partisan. They did not conceal either their personal opinions or their own participation in events. (William Russell became famous for being himself present at the battles he covered.) And there were no limits on the style a journalist might employ.

All that began to change, especially in America. The late nineteenth century saw the rise of professional organizations of journalists, schools of journalism, and a new ideal of what the journalist should be. That ideal was objectivity. The partisan and the personal became taboo in journalism. Journalism also acquired a dominant style, one that to some extent persists in newspaper news reporting to this day. That style is bare and unadorned. It avoids adjectives and evocative descriptions to a great extent. It can seem stripped-down or telegraphic—indeed, it was created as much to save words in telegraphed stories as to create the impression of "just the facts" objectivity. Stylistic flourishes remained possible in some areas of newspaper writing—the gossip column or the sports page, for example—but restraint became the badge of serious journalism. Along with the new professionalism, a sort of hard-boiled, tough-guy ethos grew up in newspaper journalism, which can be seen embodied in texts like Ben Hecht's and Charles MacArthur's 1928 play, *The Front Page*, and that too gave preference to the terse and laconic rather than the florid and evocative.

A different kind of nonfiction developed in American magazines as well, less telegraphic but still marked by restraint. This genre of nonfiction is best represented by the writers associated with the *New Yorker*, the magazine founded by Harold Ross in 1925 and edited for many years by William Shawn. Style was indeed a central concern but only style of a very classical sort, one that avoided rhetorical decorations or flourishes. E.B. White, one of the best of the *New Yorker* writers, makes clear that restraint is the ideal in *The Elements of Style*, the manual he revised. The first of the rules he quotes from his old teacher is "Omit needless words." Simplicity and clarity, not decoration, are what *New Yorker* writers aimed for. They could be merciless in their lampoons of publications that went in for the florid, such as Henry Luce's *Time* and *Life*. (Wolcott Gibbs's profile, "TIME . . . FORTUNE . . . LIFE . . . LUCE," made Luce look bad, but the parody of the style was more devastating than any details about the man.)

The *New Yorker's* own style might lead some to admire it as urbane or dismiss it as genteel. The magazine, however, was in many ways an innovator in American journalism. It created the form known as the "profile"—and even copyrighted the term. "Profiles" by writers such as Lillian Ross became models for the character studies the "New Journalists" would create, albeit in a more adventurous style. The magazine gave space to several sorts of nonfiction. Indeed, the long, nonfictional narrative became one of its hallmarks. It published book-length pieces, such as John Hersey's *Hiroshima* (1946) and Rachel Carson's *Silent Spring* (1962), that became classics of literary nonfiction.

The group of writers who became known as the New Journalists in the mid-1960s developed the long form still further. That was in part because they needed scope for their effects and in part because none of their innovations ever gained much ground in the news pages of respectable American papers. When writing for newspapers, they moved toward "feature writing," as opposed to what would later be called "hard news," and often published in the newspaper's "Sunday supplements" or magazines, which were not held to the same stylistic standards as the news sections—and which lacked journalistic respectability. When writing for magazines, most were more likely to publish in *Esquire*, with its mixed heritage of good writing and pin-up pictures, than in the more purebred *New Yorker*.

The New Journalists were a diverse group, and most of them quickly got tired of the term. Two characteristics mark most of their work, however. First, the New Journalists abandoned the traditional journalistic conventions—except, they would all certainly add, that of telling only the truth. (Their critics, on the other hand, accused them of letting that most important standard go first of all.) Second, they began using the techniques of realistic fiction.

PARTICIPATING IN THE STORY

A convention that many abandoned was that nonfiction be impersonal. Writers in the new form began taking the stage in their work, instead of simply, as Wolfe put it "describing from the grandstand." At times, they took part as actual participants, rather than as pure observers. Some journalists, especially war correspondents like Ernie Pyle, had always done this to some extent, but they still reported as if they were primarily objective observers. New Journalists made their own experience a central part of the action, and, still more important, reported from their own consciousness rather than from an objective point of view. The purest examples of the New Journalist's new involvement in the stories they covered come from those writers who immersed themselves in an event from start to finish. George Plimpton, for example, trained with the Detroit Lions football team and even took the field with them during an exhibition game. He then wrote a book, *Paper Lion* (1966), describing what it is like to be a writer taking part in this very different world. John Sack did much the same in a more serious milieu, joining an infantry company and staying with it through training into battle in Vietnam. He recounted his experiences in *M* (1967), a book named after the army company he had covered. Works like these, which would became much more common, were a great contrast with much earlier nonfiction, even that recounting personal experience. In classic travel writing or memoir, the author primarily recounts only his experiences. In these new works, authors combine accounts of their own experience with reportage. The fusion of the journalistic search for fact and the personal was what made this new form different, exciting—and threatening to some who thought the distinction between fact and fiction was being eroded.

Even when they were covering events that they were not themselves part of, New Journalists abandoned traditional standards of objectivity. These works were subjective, not in the sense that they were partisan or prejudiced, but in the sense that they clearly came from an individual consciousness. The point of view is not that of "a fly on the wall," as it is in traditional newspaper reporting, but of a specific person with an individual sensibility. Joan Didion, for example, does not enter the stories she recounts much as a participant; her sensibility and her style, however, are present everywhere. Throughout the pieces collected in *Slouching toward Bethlehem* (1968) and *The White Album* (1979), the reader knows how Didion experienced life in California during the 1960s and 1970s. Her reactions are as important as her subjects', whether they are crimes or record albums or the Santa Ana winds.

Other works by "New Journalists" are so subjective that the writer's perhaps disturbed mind becomes the focus. In Hunter Thompson's "The Kentucky Derby Is Decadent and Depraved," for instance, the author's increasingly ill-tempered and foul-mouthed reactions to the race are central. The reader learns fairly little about the Derby itself; he learns a great deal about Thompson, and through him, about the crisis in American culture in the 1960s. This style is taken to a still greater extreme in *Fear and Loathing in Las Vegas: A Savage Journey Into the Heart of the American Dream* (1971). There the author's drug-induced visions, which are recounted in a frantic style, full of expletives and exclamation marks, are central, and the accounts of the "square" world, which is suggested to be still more bizarre than the drugged one, are secondary. Thompson could also write more restrained prose, carefully constructed and built on sustained research. His *Hell's Angels: A Strange and Terrible Saga* (1966) draws on both reporting and personal experience, and makes the biker world terribly vivid without using the extravagant style that Thompson later called "Gonzo Journalism." Wolfe learned from some of Thompson's stylistics experiments, but never, like Thompson, made self-expression the main focus of even his fiction.

ADOPTING FICTION'S TECHNIQUES

Subjectivity and style were only part of the experiments in nonfiction that began in the 1960s. The New Journalism and the creative nonfiction that followed it were clearly not just reactions to older forms of journalism. They were also the journalist's response to the novel. Even more important than breaking the conventions of journalism, writers of nonfiction began to adopt the techniques of the novel and short story. It is important to distinguish here between fact and fiction and their literary styles. While the essential distinction between the two is that one claims to be true and the other does not, each has been associated with certain conventions. Fiction could be written like a lab report, with every sentence in the passive voice, though it is not likely that anyone would want to read it. The writers of the New Journalism or the nonfiction novel realized that they could write factual narratives with the techniques of fiction—and they certainly made many want to read them.

Wolfe became a spokesperson for the group as a result of the controversy over his attacks on the bastion of the older forms of nonfiction, the *New Yorker* (see chapter 1). Several of the responses to Wolfe's piece attacked the whole form, and Wolfe responded to them with a defense of the thing itself rather than of his own articles. In part that was because the genre as a whole could more easily be defended than could the two individual pieces. It was also because Wolfe was still enough of an American Studies Ph.D. to wish to justify his practice with theory. He published a number of essays in *New York* and *Esquire* and elsewhere in which he attempted to place the new form into the history of European and American literature. These grew into the introduction to *The New Journalism*, the anthology of writing in the new form that Wolfe and E.W. Johnson published in 1972. In these manifestos, Wolfe not only defends the New Journalism, he claims for it a status equal to the novel, which was at the time very much the dominant and most prestigious literary form.

In his introduction to *The New Journalism*, Wolfe describes the techniques of realistic fiction. It is significant that he describes realism as a technique, rather than a new subject matter. It might easily be argued that the birth of realistic fiction in the eighteenth century, the period usually associated with the "rise of the novel," was mostly a change in subject. Authors began writing more and more about the contemporary middle and lower classes rather than about knights and damsels of long ago and far away. Earlier works of prose fiction, such as Sir Thomas Malory's *Morte D'Arthur* or Sir Philip Sidney's *Arcadia*, are usually called "romances" rather than novels because of their subjects. But there are indeed literary devices that make realistic fiction different from the sagas and chronicles and romances that came before. Wolfe identifies four important devices. He may overstate his case when claiming that these techniques are unique to realistic fiction, since some of them were employed in earlier literature, from the classic epics on. But he is surely right that they are what give a literary work "immediacy" and make it "gripping" or "absorbing," and that they are more characteristic of realistic fiction than of any other form.

The first is scene-by-scene construction. Here journalists were in fact heeding the advice commonly given to fiction writers by the New Critics. That is, they were learning to "show" rather than "tell," to render rather than report. (In order to do this in nonfiction, of course, the writer has to know what things looked like, what each character's gestures and actions were, and what exactly was said.) This technique gives the New Journalism its immediacy. As much as possible, the reader is in a specific time and place, seeing what happens rather than hearing a bare recitation of events.

The second, related device is realistic dialogue. The reader is to hear the characters themselves speaking. The ways in which the characters speak define their personalities more effectively than anything else does.

The third device Wolfe mentions is the manipulation of point of view. Traditional journalism ignores point of view almost entirely. The point of view is objective or it is that of the reporter. New Journalists felt free to write from the point of view of any of the participants in the action they were describing. To see a writer claiming to be inside the head of a real person, recounting what he thought and felt as well as what he did, was a shock for the first readers of the New Journalism. The question was always, "How does he know that?" The writers who used the device had a ready answer: One can find out what people were thinking or feeling at a particular time and place by asking them about it later, just as you can find out what they did on some previous occasion. The thoughts and feelings can be reported as factually as the action—and doing so gives the readers the impression of living the real character's life for a moment, just as he feels he is living the lives of fictional characters when he sees through their eyes.

The last of the devices Wolfe lists is the recording of everyday details symbolic of "status life." In describing the objects that people gather around them and use and, especially, wear, a writer can make clear a character's place in society, or, to put it another way, the sort of person he or she is. Any American, for example, gets a clearer idea of what a person is like and where he fits into our status system by hearing what sort of car he drives—a Volvo, a Mustang, a Cadillac, an SUV, a minivan—than they would from any abstract label like "middle class." Clothes and possessions can have the same symbolic value. Wolfe notices that a man's polished black leather shoes, which are one of the badges of adulthood and respectability in some settings, can make him a despised outsider in others.

It is in making use of these "techniques of realism," still more than in any stylistic innovations, that the New Journalism differs not only from traditional journalism but also from such traditional nonfictional forms as essay and autobiography. Those forms can display great wit or analytical power, but they can only very rarely use the manipulation of point of view, dialogue, or a wealth of status details to create immediacy, because they are not built on the reporting that makes the use of those techniques possible.

Despite their origins in fiction, there is nothing that makes any of these techniques inherently less appropriate for nonfiction than for the novel. They do, however, require the writer to amass a stock of details—thoughts, feelings, utterances, status details—to be able to choose the ones that will give the reader the novelistic impression of living the story. That requires research. Whatever conventions of journalism the new form breaks, it makes its essential activity—reporting—ever more important. To excel in the new form, writers had to be willing to do the legwork. Only after that could they experiment with style and structure.

Reactions to the new form of writing were, unfortunately, often confused with reactions to Wolfe's attack on the *New Yorker*. Dwight MacDonald and John Hersey essentially argued that New Journalism was not the presentation of facts with the techniques of realism but the mixing of facts with things that were just made up (see chapter 1). But as the years went by the controversy faded, and more and more highly praised work in the form appeared. The vogue for the term "New Journalism" disappeared, but the popularity and academic respectability of the thing did not.

WRITERS IN THE NEW FORMS

Among those who explored this new form were several writers who got their start, as Wolfe did, writing feature articles for newspapers. Gay Talese wrote for the *New York Times* when Wolfe was at the rival *New York Herald-Tribune*, and both wrote for *Esquire*. In the introduction to *The New Journalism*, Wolfe singles out Talese's *Esquire* profile of the boxer Joe Louis as one of the first models of the new kind of nonfictional writing he had encountered. In describing the former heavyweight champion, Talese uses all of the techniques of realism Wolfe would later pick out, especially dialogue. Talese applied those techniques—and exhaustive reporting—at length in books such as *Honor Thy Father* (1971), in which he describes life in a Mafia family.

Other practitioners of the nonfiction novel had had careers as novelists before turning to the new form. Truman Capote's *In Cold Blood* (1966) was perhaps the most influential "nonfiction novel" (the term Capote preferred) of its time. It describes the murder of a Kansas farm family and the arrest, trial, and execution of the killers. Capote describes the events in vivid detail, always from the point of view of the participants. Capote had been associated with the *New Yorker* for years, and *In Cold Blood* was serialized in that magazine. But his work in the new form effectively ended his relationship with the magazine. (The *New Yorker*'s editor, William Shawn, later said he regretted having published the non-fiction novel in the first place [Yagoda 348]). Capote himself said that he was drawn to an experimental form of journalism because he wanted to produce something that would have "the credibility of fact, the imme-diacy of film, the depth and freedom of prose, and the precision of po-etry" (xv). By applying fictional techniques to the narration of a real event, he did just that.

Norman Mailer also began his career with traditional fiction. *The Naked and the Dead* (1948) was one of the first novels to attempt to capture the experience of soldiers during World War II. None of his later fictional works, however, were as successful. When he turned to nonfiction nar-ratives, however, his career revived. He had earlier lamented Capote's defection from the world of fiction, but he left it himself in *Armies of the Night* (1968). That book, which is subtitled *History as a Novel, the Novel as History*, recounts Mailer's involvement in an antiwar protest march on the Pentagon. Mailer used both traditional autobiographical techniques—adopting, for example, the convention of writing about himself in the third person from *The Education of Henry Adams*—and techniques more like the New Journalism. In the succeeding decades, Mailer wrote both fiction, much of it based on a great deal of research, and nonfiction. What was undoubtedly his most successful work after his first novel, however, was *The Executioner's Song* (1980), which describes the life and execution of Garry Gilmore, the first man put to death in America after an eleven-year hiatus in executions. The book was sold as a "true-life novel" and won the Pulitzer Prize for fiction. What those blurrings of genre-boundaries showed was that whatever the form was called—New Jour-nalism, nonfiction novel, literary journalism—the techniques of realism could indeed make fact as involving as fiction.

Mailer was certainly not imitating Wolfe in his nonfiction novels, and Capote had begun work on *In Cold Blood* before Wolfe's vogue began, but all of them were part of the same movement. Only Wolfe, however, offered a literary theory to justify their common enterprise. Almost every younger writer of nonfiction, however, did have Wolfe as an important influence.

In the last decades of the twentieth century, Creative Nonfiction or Literary Journalism became an established genre. The *New Yorker* went on producing long form nonfiction, though after Tina Brown became editor in 1992, it lost some of its most distinctive voices, such as Ved Mehta. Some of the best books of the era were literary journalism, including Michael Herr's *Dispatches* (1976), a collection of his reports the war in Vietnam; John McPhee's account of life in Alaska, *Coming Into the Country* (1977); and Dennis Covington's *Salvation on Sand Mountain* (1995), a sympathetic account of the Southern Christians who take up venomous serpents as part of their worship services. By 2000, literary journalism was no longer new—and no longer needed any defense.

REALISM AND OTHER FORMS OF FICTION

When Wolfe graduated from college, the great modern American novelists including Ernest Hemingway, William Faulkner, and John Steinbeck were still writing. Their best work was behind them, but American novelists still worked in the shadows of these writers formed by the First World War and the literary experimentation championed by T.S. Eliot, Ezra Pound, and, most important for fiction, James Joyce. Many of these writers had been exciting because of their technical experiments. Hemingway created a stripped-down, easily imitated, and very powerful prose style. Faulkner used stream-of-consciousness techniques and also followed Joyce in structuring his novels with patterns of allusion to biblical or classical stories. John Dos Passos fragmented his narrative into many different units that the reader had to reassemble. They were, nevertheless, all in the tradition of literary realism, as were such stylistically less avant-garde writers as Steinbeck and Willa Cather. They sought to convey some part of the world to the reader—Spain during the Civil War, California after the influx of refugees from the Dust Bowl, the South. Especially in the work of Faulkner, Steinbeck, and Dos Passos, there was an attempt to capture the breadth of American society as well as to probe personal experience.

Where fiction was going with the passing of this generation was an open question. The novel as the modernists left it was a very different thing than it had been a hundred years before, when it was still possible to write sprawling multi-plot novels with intrusive, commenting narrators. (The works of the English novelists Charles Dickens, George Eliot, and Anthony Trollope are good examples of that form.) But with modernism came what has been called "the death of the author." From about the time of Henry James, novelists began to resist the impulse to comment on the characters they described or the events they narrated. It became an accepted truth that novelists would convey meaning to the reader only by what the reader could see and hear. Whatever turn fiction took, it was not going to be away from this new convention.

Generally, in fact, fiction writers turned still further away from the model of the panoramic novel that showed, as one of Trollope's titles put it, *The Way We Live Now*. The trend was away from the realistic social novel, even as Steinbeck or Dos Passos wrote it, and toward the personal, the psychological, or the fabulous. Among the novels that emerged from World War II, for example, the best known are probably Mailer's *The Naked and the Dead* (1948), James Jones's *From Here to Eternity* (1951), Joseph Heller's *Catch-22* (1961), and Kurt Vonnegut's *Slaughterhouse-Five* (1969). The first two are largely realistic in form; the others full of elements either of satiric exaggeration in Heller's case or the fantastic in Vonnegut's. But all are based largely on personal experience. They do not attempt to capture the sort of sweeping view of a society convulsed by war found in the works of such earlier writers as Thackeray in *Vanity Fair* or Tolstoy in *War and Peace*.

Other important groups of American writers were also turning away from the large, social novel. The school of fiction associated with the *New Yorker* in the 1950s and 1960s and perhaps best exemplified by John Cheever rarely took on large, social questions. Rather, this sort of writing, which might be called the "school of suburban adultery," dealt with the private lives of the middle classes. Other writers who began in this mode, such as John Updike, later widened their social canvas. They also adopted elements of the fabulous, though remaining grounded in the techniques of realism.

In many areas, the personal became the primary subject for serious literature. That became so true in poetry that the "confessional" became the standard for quite some time. It was also true, to a large extent, in fiction. For many years the standard "first novel" was a slightly fictionalized account of the author's life.

There was, of course, great variety in American fiction at the time Wolfe began work. The writers of the "Beat Generation" had tried to capture personal experience by writing it down almost without mediation, and produced interesting, though wordy and unpolished, works such as Jack Kerouac's *On the Road* (1957). Other writers were producing finely crafted stories that both showed the details of contemporary life and suggested something beyond it. The best example of this kind of writer is Flannery O'Connor, whose work was informed by both her Catholic theology and her keen eye for the particulars of Southern life. And writers like Eudora Welty explored how the individual consciousness is always isolated but can nevertheless take part in a larger community. The sweeping social novel, however, was not common in literary fiction, and realism itself, which had been the dominant form in prose fiction for more than a century, was being questioned.

In many cases, authors attempting to capture some of the feeling of absurdity produced by the war and succeeding social upheavals mixed realism with some element of the mythic or fabulous. The model for many postwar literary works was Franz Kafka (1883–1924), the Czech novelist whose stories and novels, especially "The Metamorphosis" and *The Trial*, show people trapped in circumstances they cannot understand, much less control. The traditional forms of realism suggest that, bad as things may be, the situation may be understood. Kafka's work, in which a man may wake up having been turned into a beetle or await trial endlessly without even knowing what he is charged with, suggests that the predicament cannot even be understood. Heller, in parts of *Catch-22*, was clearly a disciple of Kafka. His airmen, who cannot escape the war by pleading madness because wanting to do so would show they are sane, feel they are as trapped as Kafka's characters. Many American writers imitated Kafka in an attempt to capture the feelings of absurdity produced by the threat of nuclear annihilation or the social upheavals of the 1960s.

Most of Kafka's works lack any social setting. They are fables, where the things that make for realistic fiction, such as the details of social status, do not matter. The same is true of many of the works of a later fabulist who deeply influenced American writing in the 1960s, the Argentine writer Jorge Luis Borges (1899–1986). Borges's works rarely try to represent the world. Rather, they often question the very idea of a reality that can be understood or communicated. In one, a man discovers that he is himself imaginary. In another, a condemned poet is miraculously given a year to complete his verse play—and then shot before he can share it with anyone. Many American writers such as Donald Barthelme created similar works, which have more in common with the myth or the fairy story than with realistic fiction.

Modernist writers had sometimes structured their otherwise realistic narratives with allusions to myth or Scripture or fable—and some postwar writers, among them Updike in *The Centaur* (1963), continued to do so. In the postwar years, a number of writers began to make the mythic or fabulous story not a framework with which to give structure to a realistic narrative, but the primary element in their work. Perhaps the best example of this group is John Barth, who declared in his influential essay of 1967, "The Literature of Exhaustion" that realism was a "used up" tradition. In novels such as *The Sot-Weed Factor* (1960), a parodic historical novel, and *Giles Goat-Boy* (1966), which mixed biblical and mythic elements with a vision of a vast computer-controlled university, he abandoned the realistic novel for a collage of elements, fantastic and realistic. Another of the New Fabulists was John Gardner, whose most successful work, *Grendel* (1971), retells *Beowulf* from the monster's perspective.

From about 1960 on, many American fiction writers employed an element of "metafiction" in their work. In this form, the text itself calls attention to the fact that it is a fiction, a made-up verbal artifact, not a work of history or an unmediated "slice of life." Realistic novelists hide the fact that the story is made up; writers of metafiction call attention to it. Earlier novelists, including writers firmly in the tradition of the realistic novel, such as Jane Austen and Trollope, had occasionally used metafiction, but only as a passing joke, not as the central trope of their work. American writers like the Russian-born Valdimir Nabokov made it central. In reading Nabokov's *Pale Fire*, for example, the reader is constantly asking himself not only what is going on but reexamining what it means to know what is going on in a novel, since there is not, as in a history book or a real work of scholarship, any appeal to what "really" happened. In their search for verisimilitude, the Realist and Naturalist writers of the late nineteenth century completely avoided metafiction. In an attempt to question the whole idea of representation, many recent writers have used it frequently.

The writers called postmodernist combine elements of metafiction, fantasy, realism, and other literary forms in an attempt to question the possibility of representing the world. Donald Barthelme builds on—or parodies—fairy tales in *Snow White* (1967) and his many short stories, such as "The Indian Uprising" mix all sorts of elements, so that it is difficult to tell exactly what the work is about, though the passing fragments are often amusing. Other postmodernist writers include Thomas Pynchon and Don DeLillo. Pynchon's stories and novels, most notably *The Crying of Lot 49* (1966) and *Gravity's Rainbow* (1973), mix images and information from the sciences and the arts with both realistic and fantastic narratives to create a vision of an American society that is at once winding down through entropy and, perhaps, controlled by a vast conspiracy. DeLillo's novels mix images from popular culture and American politics with elements of fantasy. This vision is often, like Pychon's, Kafkaesque but set in the recognizable popular culture of America rather than in the indeterminate landscape of fable.

Another departure from traditional realism based on a foreign model is the school of "magical realism." That term is usually associated with

Latin American authors, particularly Gabriel García Márquez. His most influential novel, *One Hundred Years of Solitude* (1967), mixes a chronicle of family in a war-torn South American country with elements of the fantastic. The most important American member of this school of fiction is Nobel prizewinner Toni Morrison. In novels including *Sula* (1973), *Song of Solomon* (1977), and *Beloved* (1987), she mixes family chronicle, the history of oppression, and elements of the mythic and the fantastic.

Many authors, of course, continued to write more or less traditional realistic fiction, despite new fashions. Those who did, however, were not for the most part those most celebrated in academic and critical circles. What is more, when realists again won critical acclaim, they were not the ones who wrote large, social novels but the "minimalists." The most important member of this group was Raymond Carver. Carver's *What We Talk About When We Talk About Love* (1981) depicts the woes of mostly inarticulate working-class people in chiseled miniatures, short stories that are spare not only in style, but in action. Even the novelists in the minimalist school avoid the large canvas of the social novel.

American fiction turned away from the large social novel for many reasons. One was simply fashion. No literary form remains dominant permanently. There were also critical and academic reasons that realism fell out of fashion. From the 1960s through the 1980s, American academia was inundated with a series of European critical theories, grouped variously under the labels structuralism, deconstruction, post-structuralism, and postmodernism. What all these theories had in common was the idea that the literary text is an independent artifact. In their most extreme form, they even argue that the text had no relationship with the world beyond it. Few critics could hold that extreme position for very long, but some form of these ideas were, and continue to be, very influential. Like the ideas Frye presented in the 1950s, they assume that literature is art insofar as it is self-referential. Therefore metafiction and similar forms seemed to exemplify what was on the cutting edge of literary theory as well as being avant-garde in themselves. Furthermore, deconstruction and the postmodernist theories that succeeded it suggest that meaning in a text is never stable, because the meaning of any sign or symbol always exists only in a shifting pattern of relationships with other signs and symbols. Any representation of the world is thus tentative at best. By juxtaposing clashing systems of meaning—realistic narrative, myth, and popular culture—postmodernist works seemed to be themselves illustrations of the latest continental theories, and they were valued for it.

The critical bias against realism, however, was in place long before the critical theories associated with Roland Barthes (structuralism) and

Jacques Derrida (deconstruction) came into vogue in America. While their work questioned the very possibility of representation, Anglo-American critical schools had already suggested that representation was what was least important in literature. Northrop Frye's devaluation of the referential is mentioned above. One sees the seeds of the same assumption in the work of many members of the critical school known as the New Critics. In works stretching back to Percy Lubbock's *The Craft of Fiction* (1929), critics began arguing that fiction was an art of its own with its own rules, separate from representation. (While that suggestion was obviously true in itself, the rules the critics drew tended to suggest that every novel should be more like those of Henry James.) By the 1950s, when classic New Critical textbooks such as Cleanth Brooks and Robert Penn Warren's *Understanding Fiction* (1943) and Caroline Gordon and Allen Tate's *The House of Fiction* (1950) appeared, the critical assumption seemed to be that fiction writing was a matter of solving structural and stylistic problems, rather than of representing the world.

American fiction was also moved in the direction first of the formal and the personal and later on to the fabulous and the postmodernist because of the rise of creative writing programs. Until about the 1930s the idea that a creative writer needed separate training was unheard of. Writers got their training by writing—for newspapers, for magazines, or for the desk drawer—until someone took their work. If a writer needed a "day job," it was unlikely to be in a university or college, though some academics wrote fiction or poetry. After World War II, however, it became increasingly common for aspiring writers not only to take "creative writing" classes but to attend graduate school, seeking an M.F.A. as their credential as a fiction writer or poet. The bias of a creative writing program is, inevitably, toward the structural and the stylistic. That can be captured in a textbook, discussed by an instructor, and critiqued in a workshop. The representation of reality, especially of large sections of society, is not so easy to bring into the creative writing program, since it requires extensive reporting before the writing can begin.

UPHOLDING THE REALISTIC SOCIAL NOVEL

Just as Tom Wolfe rejected the reigning conventions in journalism, he attacked the dominant trends in the world of fiction, particularly its devaluation of the large, realistic, social novel. In the 1960s and 1970s, he pointed out the retreat of the novel from the representation of social reality in order to argue that its place had been taken by the New Journalism. He claimed that a shift in literary hierarchies was taking place, one much like the one that had raised the novel to the status of dominant genre in the first place. It is sometimes hard for contemporary readers to imagine a world in which the word "writer" did not mean primarily "novelist." But that was the case until, with what Wolfe would call the discovery of the techniques of realism, the novel edged out the history, the verse tragedy, and the moral essay for the position as dominant genre. Wolfe noted that the novel was dismissed in almost the same terms that the New Journalism would be: It was " 'superficial', 'ephemeral,' 'mere entertainment,' 'morally irresponsible' " (*New Journalism* 37). The very uneasiness shown by the literary establishment toward the new form showed that a shift in literary hierarchies was taking place.

Wolfe sometimes comes close to admitting that the New Journalism was, in part, the new top genre by default. He describes himself wondering when the novel doing justice to the diversity of life in New York in the 1960s—and still more, of California during that era—would come out and swamp nonfiction works like *The Electric Kool-Aid Acid Test*, but they never appeared. The novelists were not using the techniques of realism to paint on a large, social canvas, so readers had turned to nonfiction to see "the way we live now." In his 1972 *Esquire* piece, "Why They Aren't Writing the Great American Novel Anymore," which was later incorporated into the introduction to *The New Journalism*, Wolfe describes the turn away from realism and the social novel and toward the New Fabulism and what would later be called postmodernism. To him, this change is not just a shift in literary fashion, for, he argues, the realistic novel became dominant not just because of the shifts of fashion but also because the techniques of realism allow the reader to become involved in the text in a way that is possible in no other literary form. Readers would always want that involvement, once it had been discovered to be possible. They would therefore turn to the New Journalism, find their involvement in the text heightened by the knowledge that "this actually happened, and await the return of the realistic, social novel.

Later, he sought to re-create the realistic novel himself in *The Bonfire of the Vanities* and *A Man in Full*. What is more, he wrote critical manifestos that built on the theories he had advanced in *The New Journalism*. Wolfe also rejected the idea that realism is just a technique like any other. Rather, he argued that in discovering the techniques of realism, fiction writers had discovered a basic new way of understanding human life. In abandoning it for more purely "literary" forms, novelists were hobbling themselves, much as if engineers decided that electricity had had its day and it was time to go back to working only with the level and the screw.

Part of his argument was that reporting was part of novel writing. In "Literary Technique in the Last Quarter of the Twentieth Century" (1978), he claims that it is, in fact, the most important of the novelist's techniques. The idea that novels involved reporting at all was a bit shocking. The idea that the novel was a matter of creation rather than reportage had become widely entrenched. Many writers had romantic visions of having to live life before writing but not of doing a reporter's legwork. Creative writing programs only taught technique, and writers working in the fabulous or postmodernist mode hardly needed reporting. They made books out of other books—or out of texts from popular culture—not from observed reality.

Wolfe's theory is the antithesis of postmodernism as a literary theory. Rather than positing, as literary theorists would have it, that the world is unknowable and that, to quote Derrida, "there is nothing outside the text," Wolfe claims that the world can be known. His critical writings essentially dare writers to do the research that will allow them to put the world, in all its complexity, into fiction. He argues that literature is primarily representation. The postmodernists argue that it is primarily something else, since the very possibility of representation is, at best, questionable. It is interesting that this declaration that material is the most important thing in great literature comes from someone known so much for his style, for his verbal pyrotechnics. Wolfe is, in fact, arguing that in both fiction and nonfiction, a writer needs to both capture the reader's interest—through stylistic bravura as well as through the techniques of realism—and show the world to him.

Wolfe makes all these points again in "Stalking the Billion-Footed Beast," which appeared in *Harpers* in 1989. It is in some ways a summary of all his theoretical writing from *The New Journalism* on. He defends the realistic tradition and celebrates research. He laments again that writers since World War II have chosen to limit themselves to the never-never land of the fable or the claustrophobic isolation of minimalism. He still calls the new forms of nonfiction "the most important experiment in American literature in the second half of the twentieth century," but he also explains what attracts him to fiction, despite his defenses of factual narrative. It is that fiction allows him to bring together the parts of society that segregate themselves from each other in real life, so that it is hard to report a scene at which they appear together. The freedom of fiction allows the writer to bring them together.

Wolfe chooses an interesting group of models for his enterprise. One group includes the American Realist and Naturalist novelists who were out of fashion when modernism was the latest thing. They never quite regained their place in the literary pantheon but neither did they lose their place in a corner of the literary canon. These include Theodore Dreiser, Frank Norris, Upton Sinclair, and Sinclair Lewis. He admires Sinclair Lewis especially for living in the world of the revivalists before writing his satirical attack on it, *Elmer Gantry* (1927). He also celebrates their European analogues, especially the French novelists Balzac and Zola. He recounts incidents in which each of them, when writing a novel, did reporting. In describing how Zola descended to the bottom of coal mines so that he could render them in his novel *Germinal*, Wolfe makes him a sort of hero as realistic novelist. Wolfe also claims the mantle of the Victorian masters of the sprawling, serialized, social novel, especially Dickens and Thackeray, writers who themselves began their careers as journalists.

WOLFE'S PLACE IN THE LITERARY WORLD

Tom Wolfe has become an inescapable character in the American cultural landscape—and he has become one without ceasing to be primarily a writer. Magazines put him on their covers. Radio programs seek to interview him. Newspapers quote him. But most important, his books stay in print and people go on reading them. He has, nevertheless, always remained something of an outsider. The outsider, of course, is not an uncommon role for an American writer to play. Many play it in exactly the same way, however. (The rebel creative writer who wears only black has become a cliché by now.) Wolfe has found genuinely new ways to play the role.

Despite the strong narrative element in his work, he has always been a critic, in the sense of one who analyzes social and artistic phenomena. He stresses the importance of reporting in part because it gives the writer material toward which he can then direct his critical intelligence. He has questioned the assumptions underlying the established way of thinking in journalism, in the art world, in what might be called the self-congratulatory left, in the New York literary establishment, and in academe. He is probably the only writer in America daring enough to ask in public if the co-ed dorm, which became almost universal in American colleges in his lifetime, was a good idea, after all. He also explores themes, such as the nature of heroism or the positive qualities embodied in traditional masculine roles, that few other writers examine.

Wolfe's attacks on various establishments, and his sometimes conservative political positions, have kept him an outsider. His works on art still draw angry responses from professional critics, and the old fights over his attack on the *New Yorker* are still echoing. His most recent novel, *A Man in Full*, drew mostly positive reviews, but the attacks on it in the *New Yorker* and the *New York Review of Books* became news events in themselves. Again, the very level of the opposition it provokes shows the importance of Wolfe's work.

Wolfe's two novels, *Bonfire of the Vanities* and *A Man in Full*, have been major events. They have not, however, sparked a major turn back to the large social novel. There is no "school of Wolfe" in fiction. That may be because many have already adopted Wolfe's views on the novel. His manifestos may have been a bit behind the trend of history in this area. The vogue for the New Fabulist writers, such as Barthelme and Barth, has been fading for some time. In the very decades that Wolfe was writing about a primarily masculine tradition that had abandoned realism for fabulism—and was attacked in return by defensive male authors—a largely realistic body of fiction was created by women. Gender aside, the novels that have gained the most critical and popular acclaim in recent years have more often than not been realistic works based on a great deal of research, such as Charles Frazier's historical novel of the Civil War, *Cold Mountain* (1997).

In nonfiction it is also hard to identify a school of Wolfe, but that is because the whole growing field of literary journalism owes so much to him, both as a pioneer and a theorist, that his influence is everywhere.

3

Short Stories: *The Kandy-Kolored Tangerine-Flake Streamline Baby* (1965) and *The Pump House Gang* (1968)

Perfect journalism would deal constantly with one subject: Status. And every article would be devoted to discovering and defining some new status.

—Tom Wolfe (Dundy 9)

The covers of the paperback editions of *The Kandy-Kolored Tangerine-Flake Streamline Baby* have changed in many ways over the last thirty-five years. The earliest, for instance, directs the bookseller to shelve it in "sociology," while the latest provides no such advice on the tacit assumption that the book will now take its place with all the matching Tom Wolfe titles in "literature." They are, however, all headed by the same quotation from Kurt Vonnegut: "Verdict: Excellent book by a genius." But the newer, more dignified edition, which no longer shows the author's trademark white suit and tie changed to stripes and polka-dots with a felt pen, omits the second half of Vonnegut's verdict: "who will do anything to get attention." Vonnegut proved to be right not just in recognizing Wolfe's powers but in seeing that he would use any means of attracting an audience for them. Wolfe's early collections show him trying anything, especially the things people writing for serious newspapers, much less for books to be shelved in sociology, are simply not supposed to do.

In publishing *The Kandy-Kolored Tangerine-Flake Streamline Baby* and *The Pump House Gang*, Wolfe used all sorts of stunts and gimmicks to attract attention. The eccentric spelling and the unusual titles—titles that give you no idea what the books are about—were only the beginning. The very day of publication chosen for *The Pump House Gang*—the same day Wolfe's third book, *The Electric-Kool-Aid Acid Test* appeared—was meant to send a message, to get people talking about the young writer who had just brought out two new and very different books. The reader finds still more tricks, gimmicks, and stunts in the various pieces in the two books. Wolfe keeps surprising the reader and demanding that he pay attention. The vocabulary veers from the hip to the scientific and back within the sentence. The point of view shifts and shifts again within a paragraph. Italics, capital letters, and exclamation points—sometimes lots of them—demand that attention be paid to this or that right now. The sounds of the street and the casino break into the quiet world of type, and onomatopoeia blasts everything from the Las Vegas croupier's call of "HERNia, hernia, hernia" to the "Dum-da-dum-dum" of the *Dragnet* theme into the reader's ear. Wolfe always brings a sense of immediacy to his work that most writing on the state of society so noticeably lacks.

These two books are hard to categorize as anything but miscellanies. They collect an assortment of the work Wolfe published in various newspapers and magazines in the earlier years of his career. The pieces take a wide variety of forms. Along with sketches of several sorts—some in pen-and-ink drawings and some in words—there are essays that describe this or that social type, profiles of the famous or notorious, and descriptions of various parts of American or British culture. While some are simply vignettes, or static descriptions of a situation, most have a narrative element and something in common with the fictional short story as well as the newspaper story.

What the pieces share is Wolfe's recurring interest in several subjects: status, culture, form, and style. Wolfe was one of the first to recognize that the collapse of the old status hierarchies did not mean that the culture was no longer concerned with status. Rather, different groups were creating their own, independent hierarchies, hierarchies that even the members of the older elite would have to reckon with. In the same way, he saw that the decreasing relevancy of "high culture," especially as embodied in the New York art world, did not mean that interest in art, especially in its purest sense as an interest in form, had disappeared. Rather, that interest in form was expressing itself in unexpected places, such as Las Vegas with its extravagant architecture and Southern California with its "custom car culture," where the automobile became a work of art rather than a means of transportation. Wherever Wolfe looks, he finds an irony. The desire for beauty, form, style, and even ritual has appeared where the cultured would not expect it. The anxiety over status, privilege, and membership in (or exclusion from) an elite or in-group reappears in just the place from which the bohemian or egalitarian think they have banished it. In the subjects of his essays, as much as in the style, Wolfe gives the reader endless surprises.

PLOT

Few of the pieces in *The Kandy-Kolored Tangerine-Flake Streamline Baby* and *The Pump House Gang* have the sort of plot one would expect in a fictional short story or that Wolfe would be able to develop in his later nonfictional narratives. All the same, none of them is static. In each one, something happens, either to a character, or to the narrator, or to American culture itself. Wolfe's introduction to the volume is a story like those that follow. He describes how he came write the title piece—and in the process stumbles on a new way of writing journalism—and then goes on to mention the changes in American life that he will focus on.

"Las Vegas (What?) Las Vegas (Can't Hear You! Too Noisy) Las Vegas!!!!" describes the culture of Las Vegas, which was in the early 1960s much more remote from that of the rest of the country than it has since become. (Most states have since legalized some kind of gambling, and Las Vegas has tried to attract family groups as well as dedicated gamblers.) Wolfe captures the spirit of the city by describing a number of characters and evoking several settings: the casino, the neon-sign factory, the mental hospital. Along the way we see a tourist on the verge of flipping out at the craps table, not so much because of "pep pills" as of the sensory overload. Visitors to Las Vegas are constantly bombarded with overblown sights and sounds. Everywhere there is the call of the croupier, the ring of the slot machine, and an ever present background of Musak. Inside the casinos the decoration is gaudy and baroque and the costumes provocatively sexual; outside, signs of fantastic design rise ten stories above one-story buildings.

Those huge signs allow Wolfe to make the point that Las Vegas, the embodiment of what America's cultural elites would have seen as tacky, was in fact a hotbed of artistic innovation. The designers whom Wolfe visits at the Young Electric Sign Company are, in fact, more avant-garde than are the architects celebrated by the art world. They have created something the world of art history has not yet created a vocabulary for. Wolfe sees in Las Vegas "one of those historic combinations of nature and art that creates an epoch" and tells the story of the man who made that combination possible. Starting in 1945, the gangster Bugsy Siegel poured millions of dollars from organized crime into what had been a sleepy, Western town, creating the wild, multicolored "Miami modern" Flamingo Hotel. By the time of his murder in 1947, he had created what amounted to an artistic movement. Clustering around his hotel, other buildings grew, all of them adopting some form of the wild, pastel-colored, space-age architecture that was becoming the city's dominant style.

Several other pieces also make the point that new art forms are being developed far from the centers of high culture. "Clean Fun at Riverhead" describes the creation of the Demolition Derby. "The Fifth Beatle" and "The First Tycoon of Teen" profile important figures in the world of rock music, disc jockey Murray the K and record producer Phil Spector. "The Kandy-Kolored Tangerine-Flake Streamline Baby" describes a whole artistic movement. Wolfe visits a "Teen Fair" in Burbank, California, and discovers that what he is really attending is a celebration of art and of art created by people devoted to form. Wolfe sees in every detail, from the hairdos to the styles of clothing, something that recalls the Baroque, the period in Western art that rejoiced in complex forms and extravagant ornamentation. The embodiment of this new, American Baroque art movement is the custom car. Since Baroque art often tried to bring a sense of motion into everything—painting, sculpture, and even architecture—that is strangely fitting. The new art has been largely ignored, because it has welled up from far outside the artistic establishment of the East Coast. In fact, it has come from where it might be least expected, the teen culture of working-class California. The styles created there, however, are being adopted elsewhere, and despite the vulgarity of much they create, the artists here, like the artists of other great centers of the Baroque—the Versailles of the French kings, St. Mark's Square of Venice, and Regency England—have both a "slavish devotion to form" and plenty of money to support it.

Two men dominate Wolfe's account of the car culture—George Barris, who takes customizing in the direction of pure art, and Ed Roth, who keeps more of its outlaw flavor, even when finding himself joining the bourgeoisie. Both now have studios—Roth's refers to his as that; Barris calls his "Kustom City"—and both are now sought after for design advice by the Detroit automakers. Their roots, however, are in the teen car culture of the 1940s. Barris has been working with models and then real cars since the age of ten, always working toward a sort of perfectly "streamlined" design that the carmakers of Detroit shy away from. Coming to Los Angeles in 1943, he finds the first real teen culture growing.

The war has both disrupted family life, giving young people more independence than they have had before, and made a great deal of money available. Through the 40s and the years that follow, Barris takes part in the teen car culture of drive-ins, hot rods, and drag races. The cars he customizes make him famous in that world, but his interests turn more and more to the car as an art object, rather than as something that can win a race. Gatherings devoted to showing the cars, not racing them, are organized, and people flock to them. He creates his own line of brightly shiny metallic paints, the "Kandy-Kolors," including "Tangerine-Flake." Starting with very little, he becomes like the old master painter of the Renaissance. He is widely imitated and he attracts disciples who come to his atelier/garage to learn his art. Barris, whose training in design goes little beyond drafting and "free art," becomes the consultant sought after by the carmakers. The art created far from the centers of design becomes the standard, and Barris becomes a happy, middle-class success on the basis of it.

Ed Roth attains the same sort of success, but he resists becoming too much like those outside the teenage car-culture. He still wants to shock the bourgeoisie—and in matters of more than form. Barris is happy to use his Kandy-Kolored paints at a car show to transform the bouffant hairdos of visiting girls into the same sort of baroque streamline sculptures as the bodies of his cars. Roth uses his skill with the airbrush to create not just shocking pictures on his cars but the Weirdo line of T-shirts. All the same, the skills he learns as a craftsman in the subculture of cars make him successful, sought after, and completely a member of the middle class. Instead of living in a house evoking the extravagance of his automobile art, he occupies the sort of suburban home that is the emblem of respectability.

In "The Last American Hero," the piece many think the strongest in *The Kandy-Kolored Tangerine-Flake Streamline Baby*, Wolfe again deals with a part of American culture in which the automobile has become the embodiment of people's values and aspirations. The title character is Junior Johnson, one of the pioneers of stock-car racing. In the course of the piece, Wolfe describes the day of a NASCAR race at the North Wilkesboro Speedway (one Johnson does not win), the social history of the South, and Johnson's career. Shifting back and forth between these three strands, Wolfe makes Johnson the emblem of how the South has changed since the end of World War II and how it has not.

The race day is another example of the new cultural expressions springing up far from the traditional centers of American civilization. The stock-car races draw thousands, and they appeal to a particular class.

They certainly don't appeal to those interested in the elite world of grand prix racing, which has a European orientation even in its terminology. Rather, they attract men and women of the class known as "good old boys," a term Wolfe helped bring to national attention. These are neither the "Southern gentlemen" nor the "white trash" of so much Southern fiction. They are part, Wolfe says, of the status system of their region, but they also seem to have been excluded from it when status was largely based on landownership. With the boom after the war, these people, too, found themselves able to express themselves. The automobile, representing as it did independence and freedom, became for many of them the symbol of their new, assertive presence in society.

For such people, Junior Johnson became a folk hero. The legend is that Johnson developed the skills that made him dominant on the NASCAR circuit while transporting the products from his father's illegal still and outrunning the revenue agents. The legend has its element of truth. Johnson did transport "moonshine whiskey," though he learned his driving skills at dirt track races as well as on the back roads. Even after his first successes in NASCAR, he was arrested at his father's still and sentenced to two years in a federal prison for moonshining. Although he has now become a rich property owner himself on the strength of his NASCAR winnings, some of his fans like to think that Junior Johnson is still out there running whiskey at night, outrunning the revenuers.

In describing Johnson, Wolfe captures a paradox. Johnson has been an outlaw, but he is a very traditional man. Whiskey making, legal or illegal, has been the tradition of his people for centuries, and he simply followed it. What is more, his goal in life is not an escape from the world in which he was born but a deeper investment in it. He uses his newly won wealth to build himself a house not far from his father's and to buy up the surrounding land. He is soft-spoken and speaks with respect of even the law that put him in prison. This combination of rebellion and rootedness is perhaps what makes him a hero to the good old boys. His example says that they can remain who they are and still prosper, that their efforts will not be a fruitless struggle against the authorities, like running whiskey, but a new kind of self-assertion that will win them the respect and attention they deserve. Since the national automakers vie with each other for the chance to have Johnson drive their cars, their hero, at least, is achieving that goal.

Wolfe does not neglect those at the traditional center of American culture in *The Kandy-Kolored Tangerine Flake Streamline Baby*. But here, too, culture is changing, and the forces that change it are not being controlled by the traditional elites. Instead, the elites—or their children, such as

Baby Jane Holzer, the subject of "Girl of the Year"—are being attracted by what is bubbling up from below. Fashionable young women no longer play the old socialite's role of being the first to adopt the new styles that will be imitated by the lower orders of society. Instead, they become the first to pick up whatever dance, or fashion craze, or style of music (the Rolling Stones are a favorite) is coming up from the "underground" and daring the rest of high society to adopt that, as indeed they will. Wolfe points out a similar cultural paradox in several pieces on the New York art world. It claims to be cosmopolitan but is actually small and enclosed. What is more, the great irony of the art world is that the bohemian or avant-garde is not the rebel but the establishment.

The pieces in *The Pump House Gang* follow the same format as those in Wolfe's first book—so much so that one critic refers to it as "something like 'Son of Kandy-Kolored.' " In this collection, however, Wolfe less often celebrates the energy of newly evolving social structures. (His description of a "happiness explosion" in the introduction seems to fit parts of the earlier book better.) Rather, he shows how the collapse of traditional social structures leaves groups and individuals still more isolated or describes how, despite whatever changes have come, the barriers between social groups remain hard to penetrate.

The title piece describes a group of teenage surfers who congregate around a pump house at the beach in La Jolla, California. Theirs is a very tight subculture—or "statusphere"—and they are very clear on what status markers make one an outsider. The first thing we see them do is make a middle-aged couple, hopelessly uncool with their beach equipment and black leather shoes, feel so uncomfortable that they abandon their attempt to use the gang's section of the beach. In leaving the beach to the gang, they are simply playing their part in a larger social pattern, the segregation of society by age. These young people are able in live in a world practically free of adults. They come from good families, and money is never an issue with them, but instead of entering the adult world—or even preparing to enter it—they live in a society of their own.

All of the Pump House Gang seem free from the concerns of adult life. One has just been turned out of the garage he was living in as a squatter, but he, like the others, will soon find somewhere to live, something to drive, and the money for trips and kegs. Unlike the adult world, they feel "immune"; bad things cannot happen to them. They therefore can take risks, such as surfing in heavy seas or even visiting Watts during the riots. The Watts neighborhood during the worst of Los Angeles's race riots was the last place most white youths wanted to be, but for the gang, it was just another party. The group is living a life that is carefree to the point of recklessness. Nevertheless, the gang and other groups of young people interested in little beyond surfing and parties become style setters. The bourgeois adults they despise come to the beach in order to pick up what "surfing styles" they can commercialize.

A few of the entrepreneurs of the surfing culture come from it themselves and use the business as a way of extending their time in *"The Life,"* that is, the sort of life the Pump House Gang is living. Hobbie Alter and Bruce Brown are making surfboards and movies about surfing, but they still live the life the gang relishes as much as possible. Brown is even able to wall out the world that does not live *"The Life"* by buying enough property in the mountains to keep the bourgeois world away. But Wolfe ends his description of the youth surfing statusphere by suggesting there cannot be many Bruce Browns, and that once they are too old for *"The Life"* the gang will not have anywhere to go.

Several pieces describe a very different cluster of statuspheres, those of London in swinging 60s. "The Mid-Atlantic Man" describes a British advertising executive caught between the still very different status systems of London and New York. Others, such as "The Noonday Underground," describe a world of English young people who are much like the Pump House Gang in their separation from adult society—and unlike them in that they come from the working classes rather than the comfortable upper-middle classes.

"The Private Game" can be read as an English version of Wolfe's piece on Las Vegas in *The K-KT-FSB*. Here Wolfe visits a private, and illegal, casino that has been set up in a London townhouse. There are legal casinos in London, run as private clubs, though clubs that anyone can join. Floating, truly private games still exist, however, run by Tony, a man with an upper-class accent and a mysterious background. They attract a more select clientele than the legal ones. Tony rents houses or flats—preferably, large, old elegant ones—brings in gambling tables and high-class liquor, and sets up his operation. He runs it like a gentleman's game, giving the gamblers credit and trusting them to pay. These floating games have none of the associations of American illegal gambling. The atmosphere recalls Regency rakehell aristocrats rather than *Guys and Dolls* mobsters and molls. And while London's legal casinos are being infected with mob influence, the illegal, private games are not. Because they are small, friendly arrangements among people of the same class, the mob cannot use them for what would later be called money laundering.

Las Vegas, of course, is the creation of mobsters, and their intention was to create "American Monte Carlo—without any of the inevitable upper-class baggage of the Riviera casinos" (*K-KT-FSB* 15). They achieved their goal and produced a thriving, noisy city that is also a hotbed of creativity. But class, especially in England, will always reassert its appeal. Tony's private game attracts just those who want the upper-class baggage. The game is quiet, its setting is a moldering old house, and the ethos is an aristocratic contempt for fate rather than any trust in luck. The two ways of gambling embody the two nations' cultures.

Wolfe also profiles iconic cultural figures of the 1960s, such as media theorist Marshall McLuhan, a thinker who has transformed himself into a celebrity. Another cultural icon is Hugh Hefner, the founder of *Playboy* magazine. Wolfe presents him in "King of the Status Dropouts" not as one of the pioneers of the sexual revolution or as a prosperous pornographer but as a recluse. Hefner boasts that he does not leave his huge mansion for weeks at a time. We first see him kneeling on his revolving bed, manipulating the controls on the headboard. Showing an almost childish joy in gadgets, he shows his visitors how he can spin the bed so as to see the "hi-fi" area, the living area, or the "conversation area," which is dominated by a huge TV camera. The spinning bed almost hits a set of earphones and an object like a "clear fiberglass helmet" that is evidently used to treat head colds. The implication is clearly that Hefner's isolation can be almost total.

Wolfe contrasts the world Hefner has created, in which everything comes to him in his mansion, with older forms of society. In society it was once important to be seen in the right places, such as the opera, and to dress the part for the occasion. Being seen to play a part in society, as much as mere wealth, determined status. Hefner, however, is outside the traditional status structure. His undistinguished family background and his state university education tell against him, but the tainted source of his wealth—the "skin magazine" and "bunny clubs"—is what would really exclude him from "society." Hefner, however, is not trying to enter society. He has created his own separate statusphere, with himself at its center. Rather than going out into society and dressing to be seen, he dresses as he pleases and lets several circles look in on him, first his visitors, then the employees whose work is directed from the house, and then the readers of his magazine. Wolfe argues that the fantasy Hefner creates for his readers is not just one of sex but also of "a potentate's control of the environment." In Hefner's mansion, and in the "*Playboy* pads" described in the magazine, a man can imagine himself in the center of things, at the controls, and responsible to no person or society outside.

CHARACTERS

What is most interesting about the characters in Wolfe's first two books is that the reader does experience them as characters. In much nonfiction by other writers, the real people described seem like stick figures. They do and say things, but because the reader is never privy to their thoughts, they never seem as real as the characters in fiction. Wolfe takes the reader that extra step, always claiming that he does it without compromising the factual accuracy of his work. He knows what people think and feel in a given moment because he has asked them about it and they have told him. That is, after all, how journalists discover much of what people say and do. So when, in "The First Tycoon of Teen," we are inside Phil Spector's head and he looks at the raindrops moving sideways across the airliner's window and feels worse and worse about the coming flight, Wolfe wants us to believe that he knows what he felt because Spector later told him. Readers, however, can ignore any factual basis for the account and follow the character's thoughts and actions just as they would follow those of one who was completely made up.

In describing Junior Johnson, for example, Wolfe uses several techniques to make the character come alive. The reader first hears about him from the outside, as a sort of legend. Once he enters the story, however, the reader sees a great deal of it from his point of view, and knows what he is like by what elements of reality his mind picks out. Wolfe often reveals important aspects of character simply by the details he narrates. He does not say that, despite his lack of formal education and country accent, Junior Johnson is quite intelligent. He describes how Johnson wins the Daytona 500 in 1960 even though other cars prove faster than his in all the trials. Johnson figures out that by "drafting"—using the vacuum created by the car ahead of him—he can make his car go faster than it ever has before. He uses that technique to "hitch rides" through most of the race, and finally wins not just because of his courage and his luck, but also because of his brains.

The characters Wolfe evokes with these various techniques fall into several groups. Many might be called outsider artists. Barris and Roth with their custom cars, the designers of the mammoth signs in Las Vegas, the surf millionaires with their streamline boards and *Endless Summer* movies, and even the creators of cultural forms such as Demolition Derby and stockcar racing have much in common. They are all working in what are almost entirely aesthetic forms. A concern for the practical is secondary for these creators—even making money seems secondary to many of them. They are also almost completely cut off from the world of high art (though not totally ignorant of it), for that world does not recognize art that arises from the working classes instead of from a sort of tame bohemia. But whether they are creating cars or signs—or driving stock cars, for that matter—they show an artist's devotion to the craft, to finding the way to get the thing done right.

Another group of characters is also unexpectedly creative. These are the self-promoters. They make their own public images, images that become larger than any achievement they are based on. Murray the K becomes almost as famous as the Beatles. Cassius Clay, whom Wolfe profiles in "The Marvelous Mouth," uses a combination of bravado and verbal fluency to make himself much more than a boxer. Carol Doda, of "The Put-Together Girl," achieves fame for being among the first strippers to have her breasts enhanced with silicone injections. She literally sculpts a public persona that allows her to be famous for being famous. There is also an element of the self-promoter in some of the thinkers Wolfe profiles. Marshall McLuhan is a thinker, but he is also creating a public image as an oracle, one who will have a profound, if impenetrable, comment on any social phenomenon that attracts his attention.

Hugh Hefner is certainly a self-promoter. He is also, as the title of Wolfe's piece on him suggests, one of the many "status dropouts" who appear in these books. He has made what seems a conscious decision not to move in the traditional status system. Many of Wolfe's other characters make the same choice, often creating their own status communities. Sometimes, as in "The Pump House Gang" and "The Noonday Underground," they define their world by age, and sometimes, as in "The Last American Hero," by class. But their defining characteristic is often their obliviousness to society's traditional status makers. Other Wolfe characters are very much a part of that traditional status system and are shaped by their efforts to change their places in it. The title characters in "Bob and Spike" and the central figure in "The Mid-Atlantic Man" are obvious examples, but there are many others. A number of Wolfe's characters, such as Bob in "The Secret Vice," find they cannot stop thinking about class makers, such as real buttonholes on jacket sleeves, once they become aware of them.

One of the things that makes Wolfe's work in these books different from much nonfiction is that he is willing to create characters through whose eyes readers see for perhaps half a sentence and who then disappear. Many of these are, of course, versions of Wolfe himself at different points in his life. When describing McLuhan's background in English literature, for example, Wolfe describes the life of a graduate student in his library carrel "hunched over in silence with only the far-off sound of Maggie, a Girl of the Stacks, a townie who puts books back on the shelves—now she is all right, a little lower-class-puffy in the nose, you understand, but . . . —only the sound of her to inject some stray, *sport* thought into this intensely isolated regimen." Within a sentence the reader sees a character who is isolated, well read, class conscious, and sexually frustrated—and then he disappears.

THEMES

   Art, culture, class, status, and the ways in which those issues are related to each other thematically dominate Wolfe's first two books. Wolfe finds art almost everywhere he looks, as much in the ignored activities of undergrounds as in the "art world" itself. The human desire for expression will manifest itself whenever it finds an opportunity, whether that is in a culturally approved venue or not. What is more, the ideal of an "avant-garde" art, one in which the artist leads society to fresh discoveries rather than expressing society's existing values, is not to be found among the "avant-garde" artists patronized by institutions such as the Museum of Modern Art. Rather, it is to be found among custom car enthusiasts, the makers of neon signs, rock 'n' roll musicians, and teenagers doing dances like the Twist and the Jerk.

   The way America has been transformed by its postwar affluence is another of Wolfe's themes. Many of the social phenomena he describes are only possible because money is more plentiful than it has ever been. The newfound wealth makes it possible for whole social classes to assert themselves. The "good old boys" who follow NASCAR are a rising element in southern society, rather than a despondent underclass. The car customizers can create their own, separate world of art, and others can create things like the demolition derby. And money makes possible a whole range of other cultural phenomena, ranging from the new or renovated museums in New York whose openings Wolfe describes to the temples to self-indulgence he finds in Las Vegas and the *Playboy* mansion. Wealth has also allowed teenagers to break out of the culture of their parents and even to form little societies of their own.

   The ability of some groups to drop out of the larger society provides the focus for many of Wolfe's pieces. That the old status structures are under siege does not, however, mean that status is no longer important. New groups can be just as exclusive as old ones. Various groups do relate to each other in surprising ways. In the world Wolfe describes, the lower classes no longer take their cue from their "betters." Rather the upper classes tend to imitate styles of dress, dances, and even modes of speech from the newly wealthy working class or of the teenage subculture that has sprung from it.

Whatever level of society he is describing, Wolfe sees an interest in form reasserting itself. In later books, *The Painted Word* (1975) and *From Bauhaus to Our House* (1981), Wolfe attacks the world of high art for slighting art for theory. He is especially repelled by the dogmas of mid-century architecture that require every building, whatever its function, to be an undecorated box. The underground artists, however, have never lost their love of form and decoration. The custom cars, the Las Vegas signs, the dances, the hairdos—all are celebrations of form. The unboxlike streamline styles in cars and signs and bouffants show that a love of form will win out wherever money will make it possible and a theory imposed from above does not prevent it.

POINT OF VIEW

That point of view is an issue in the pieces in Wolfe's first two books in itself makes them different from most earlier nonfiction. As chapter 2 points out, most traditional journalism uses only an objective point of view. Wolfe uses any point of view that might make the story vivid, and he will shift the point of view not just within an essay, but within a paragraph or sentence. The reader has to keep asking, not just "Who is talking here?" but "Who is seeing this?" In "The Voices in Village Square," the point of view is first that of the young man surprised to hear his name called. Then it is the observer who knows that he is being put on. Later we see things from the point of view of the girls in the House of Detention—we are looking down at the square. In "First Tycoon of Teen" much of the story is told through Phil Spector's eyes. What we first hear is not a description of him but his thoughts during the beginning of a few bad moments on an airplane. Objective descriptions are mixed with Spector's subjective perception. Wolfe uses a similar strategy in "The Pump House Gang." The reader sees many things first through the eyes and in the voice of the gang, things whose meaning only becomes clear after passages told from an objective point of view make clear where the narrator is and what is going on.

In "The Last American Hero" Wolfe makes another sort of experiment in point of view. He tells part of the story from his own and part of it from Junior Johnson's. When he gives general information on a subject Johnson would know about, such as running a still, he writes from what might be called an objective point of view but in something like John-son's regional dialect. It at least gives the impression that we are seeing Johnson's world through Johnson's eyes.

A RHETORICAL READING: THE END OF GOOD GRAY JOURNALISM

Probably the best-known anecdote about how a text came to be written concerns Samuel Taylor Coleridge, the English poet. He published his poem "Kubla Khan" with a note describing how it had come to him in a dream after he had taken an "anodyne" (opium). The poem, complete with the story Coleridge attached, was a manifesto for a new kind of writing, one more related to the unconscious, visionary parts of the mind than to the rational. It was part of the conscious rebellion of Coleridge's generation, "the Romantics," against their eighteenth-century "neo-classic" predecessors. Coleridge and his circle would not write rational verse essays in heroic couplets. They would write poems in varied forms embodying whatever welled up from the imagination.

Like "Kubla Kahn," Tom Wolfe's *Kandy-Kolored Tangerine-Flake Stream-line Baby* begins an account of how the text came to be. After becoming interested in the world of custom cars, Wolfe persuades *Esquire* magazine to send him to California to meet people like George Barris and Ed Roth. After returning to New York, he finds he cannot write the story. *Esquire* needs to run some sort of piece, since a picture to go with it is already in production. Byron Dobell, the managing editor, tells Wolfe just to type up his notes so someone else can write it. Wolfe begins a memorandum "Dear Byron" and types away furiously all night, recording everything he can recall, and the next morning he sends the forty-nine pages he has produced to *Esquire*. At four that afternoon Dobell calls. He is striking "Dear Byron" and running the rest of Wolfe's memo as it stands. It be-comes "The Kandy-Kolored Tangerine-Flake Streamline Baby." The piece, with the story of its conception, is also a manifesto for a new kind of writing. Wolfe is declaring his independence from the standards that had shaped journalism, and indeed most non-fiction, for decades.

It is likely that neither Coleridge nor Wolfe is telling the whole truth in these stories. Like all good writers, they probably revised their work before presenting it to the public. (Wolfe mentions editing beyond the cutting of "Dear Byron" in an interview he recorded at the Smithsonian Institution.) But both have claimed for writers of their sort the right not to follow the conventions that have been dominant, to get experience on paper in new and different ways.

Rhetoric is, among other things, the study of how language can be used to influence and persuade. A rhetorical reading of a literary work will concentrate on the tools an author uses to move the reader. Those tools can be purely verbal, involving such things as diction (word choice) and syntax (sentence structure). They include, however, many other devices an author may use to provoke or persuade the reader, including imagery and the manipulation of point of view. Wolfe's work invites a rhetorical reading because he employed the tools of language in new and different ways.

Wolfe made a splash with *The Kandy-Kolored Tangerine-Flake Streamline Baby* not because of his subjects, new and interesting as they often were. What was exciting, and, to some, infuriating, was his rejection of journalistic conventions described in chapter 2. He was willing to use every weapon in the writer's rhetorical arsenal, not just the few with which journalists had learned to make do. His freedom in manipulating point of view has already been discussed. He was also happy to enter his stories instead of simply observing. When he was a participant in a story, he did not hide it. Still more important, he created a narrator who was free to express opinions, to comment on the action, even to address the reader directly.

Wolfe does not limit himself to the dry language of traditional journalism. Instead, he uses language of every kind. Sometimes he is conversational, and he uses the sorts of expressions that one does when just talking to friends. (One can tire of his saying things like, "and so forth," but even tags like that add to the immediacy of the stories.) He will also bring in many other kinds of language. Much of it is clinical. When Wolfe describes the human body, he can sound like *Gray's Anatomy*, giving every muscle its Latin name. He will also use medical terms metaphorically: lots of old people are "sclerotic." He will use vulgar language and then switch to elevated diction. He will use commercial language, calling products by brand names. He uses the slang of every sub-culture, high and low, British and American. He uses onomatopoeia, something serious journalists never employed, so parodies of him often include a "VAROOM" or a *thraggggh*. Even in terms of type, he uses every possible resource, including capitals, italics, and exclamation points. Sometimes he uses all of them at once.

Still more important, he describes as many of the details as he can— occasionally the furniture, like his nineteenth-century predecessors, but more often hairdos, clothes, cars, voices. In the introduction of *The*

K-KT-FSB, he reports that recording all the details "made me see what was happening." The new form of writing he unwittingly embarked on in his memo to Byron has, in other words, changed the way he understands the world. A spare description of the traditional journalistic sort might have missed what is most important, because the details of form, the things conveyed in the adjectives (like those piled up in the title of Wolfe's first book), are what matter most. And that is, again, the growing celebration of style, of form, where it is least expected in America.

Wolfe seems to be describing the emergence of a new common style in American culture and finding the rhetorical devices he needs to describe it. He will take some terms from California shop classes or from architecture or from engineering: it is free form, it is streamline. He will also take terms from high culture. For example, he brings together two sets of contrasting terms to help make clear what is happening in the custom car world. One is Nietzsche's placing in opposition the Dionysian and the Apollonian, one referring to the creative-intuitive power, the other to the critical-rational power. (They come from the names Dionysus and Apollo, the Greek gods of wine and of poetry.) The other is Wolfe's own contrast of Mondrian (after Piet Mondrian, the modern painter whose works are almost all perpendicular lines) and Brancusi (after Constantin Brancusi, the modern sculptor whose works are almost all curves.) The new forms created in the custom car world are all Dionysian and Brancusi. They are energetic, expressive, decorated—streamline. The establishment, whether it is the Detroit automakers or the New York modern art world—or the guardians of the standards of traditional journalism, for that matter—are Apollonian and Mondrian.

Wolfe's own prose can easily be classified as Dionysian Brancusi. Is certainly not restrained and classical. The shifts in point of view, the variety of diction, the tricks with onomatopoeia and typography make it, instead, ornate, highly decorated, and full of motion. It fits, in other words, its subject. It is the rhetoric to describe a Baroque age.

4

The Electric Kool-Aid Acid Test
(1968)

You're either on the bus . . . or off the bus.
—Ken Kesey (EK-AAT 83)

Wolfe's first full-length book became, with Truman Capote's *In Cold Blood* and Norman Mailer's *The Executioner's Song*, one of the premier examples of the new form of "nonfiction novel." Its success, however, was as much a matter of its subject as its form. In the mid-1960s American society was terribly agitated by the emerging counterculture and "hippie" movements, which were associated with illicit drugs and especially the psychedelics, such as LSD, that had just come on the scene. These movements seemed to reject many of the traditional values of American society, and in this they were very different from the other great movements of the '60s, the political ones. The national Civil Rights movement, the Berkeley "Free Speech" movement, and even the antiwar movement, at least to begin with, invoked the values that the culture supported, even when railing against the corruption into which it had fallen. The protesters tended to wear coats and ties, wave the flag, and sing the hymns and anthems that were part of the common, national heritage. The hippies, on the other hand, seemed to reject all traditional values from top to bottom. Their clothes were a deliberate hodge-podge that could not be read to reveal any traditional status details. They were more likely to wear American flags as shirts or trousers than to wave them. They seemed to deliberately flout every convention of law, morality, manners, and even hygiene. The ideals they invoked were more likely to be taken from Eastern sources (though in a thoroughly Americanized form) than from any part of the Western tradition. It was this threatening new world from which Wolfe reported.

The nation's anxiety over the issue of drugs began in earnest in the spring of 1963. Two Harvard psychologists, Richard Alpert and Timothy Leary, were dismissed from their academic posts amid charges that LSD was being given to students. Up to that time, drug use was mostly limited to socially marginalized subcultures, such as jazz musicians and some minority groups, and the drugs used were marijuana, opiates such as heroin, and cocaine. With Alpert and Leary, drug use was clearly moving into the intellectual and social elites. What was truly disturbing, however, was that the experimenters, Leary especially, were totally unashamed. These were not back alley pushers; they were Ph.D.'s.—and at that point, they were not breaking the law, since LSD had not yet been banned. They claimed that drugs, especially psychedelics, were not life-destroying poisons but the means of transcendence. They even asserted, in what could only sound like blasphemy or madness, that drug experiences were "indistinguishable from, if not identical with," profound religious experiences (Lee and Shlain 76).

That new attitude toward drug use expanded in the culture and began to attract, alarmingly, the children of the upper and middle classes. Many of them did think that humanity might be on the threshold of a new level of awareness and that psychedelics might be the key to achieving it. What might be called the traditional drug culture quickly merged with the new: once the taboo was broken, all forms of mind expansion were embraced and all restraints cast aside. The press and the media became fascinated with the new phenomenon and with the styles in music, art, and clothing that were associated with it. While the dream of transcendence through chemicals has receded from the culture and the intractable problem of addiction has taken its place, American culture was indeed shaped by the counterculture of the 1960s, and *The Electric Kool-Aid Acid Test* is the best firsthand report on it and its West Coast leader, Ken Kesey.

Wolfe's book has been especially important because the psychedelic culture has not been especially good at chronicling itself—at least not in prose. The music and graphic designs of Haight-Ashbury are still present in the culture, but the hippies did not produce important books. That was even true of Wolfe's immediate subject, the Merry Pranksters, even though they were led by a major novelist. The Pranksters' books (*On the*

Bus by Paul Perry and Ken Babbs [1990] and Ken Kesey's own *The Fur-ther Inquiry* [1991]) would not appear for decades, and when they did, they were essentially collages, as much picture books as narratives. Tom Wolfe reported the experience at the time—and found a form of prose to convey it.

STRUCTURE AND POINT OF VIEW

The structure and point of view of *The Electric Kool-Aid Acid Test* are complex, and they present the reader with issues different from those presented by traditional novels or traditional forms of nonfictional nar-rative. In a novel, the author has free rein to use whatever point of view seems best to suit his purposes. He can tell the novel from a single point of view; he can move in and out of the minds of several characters; or he can speak in the voice of an omniscient, all-knowing narrator. In tra-ditional nonfiction, the author either speaks in his own voice, reporting what he has seen and heard in the first person, or takes an objective stance, drawing on his research to recount the historical events. The au-thor of the nonfiction novel brings some of the flexibility of fiction to his subject, but his choices are limited by the facts of his research. He cannot report what he does not know and that limits his choices as to point of view. The narrator cannot tell what is going on in someone's mind if that person has not reported what he or she was thinking.

While these limitations mean that the narrators in nonfiction cannot do all that fictional narrators can, they bring an advantage of their own. They allow the reader to know the source of the information by follow-ing shifts in the point of view. A point of view that suggests any knowl-edge of the interior life of a character tells the reader that that character is one of the sources of the author's information. The blending of points of view in a single scene means that the author can say, in effect, this is what A tells me it felt like, and this is what B tells me it felt like, while melding the testimony of both A and B into a single involving narrative. The shifts in point of view act almost like footnotes, pointing the careful reader to the original source.

The structure of *The Electric Kool-Aid Acid Test* is also related to the facts of Wolfe's research. The book begins and ends in the present of 1966, when Wolfe was in San Francisco covering the story. The body of the narrative, however, is a long flashback, chronicling the whole of Kesey's life up to that point. The first and last sections are mostly in the present tense; the body of the book in the past. Wolfe is again drawing the reader's attention to what he has seen firsthand and what he is reporting on the basis of research, though without the traditional scholarly apparatus. (Wolfe's sources included not only interviews he himself conducted but also the films and tapes made by the Pranksters during their adventures, and later reports, written or taped, by both participants and other writers, including Robert Stone and Hunter S. Thompson.) In another sense, the narrative follows one of the two structures possible for a tale that recounts a journey. Journeys can end with the final arrival at a destination, maybe the intended one, maybe not, or with a return to the place from which the travelers set out. Wolfe's characters seem to end up, literally or figuratively, just about where they started.

PLOT

The narrative begins with Wolfe going to meet the Merry Pranksters in their San Francisco headquarters, the Warehouse, as they await the release of their leader, Ken Kesey, from jail. The place is dominated by a twenty-five-year-old school bus that had been decorated in true hippie fashion, and the Pranksters are preparing a banner reading "*ACID TEST GRADUATION*." The counterculture world is facing a political crisis. It is reported that Kesey has planned to stage a gathering of all involved in the counterculture, where he will tell them to go "beyond acid." The idea that one of the leaders of the lifestyle created around LSD would now denounce the drug has people worried.

Wolfe has already met Kesey in the San Meteo County jail. He now gets to know the group whose members can only be called Kesey's disciples, for Wolfe quickly realizes that he is in the presence of a new religious movement. Kesey is clearly the prophet. Once he arrives, he is the center of attention and is encircled not only by his followers but also by his wife, Faye, another woman, and the children he has had with both of them. People hang on his words, but like other prophets, he often speaks in aphorisms and parables. Among those gathered is Neil Cassady, who seems to play the role of Kesey's forerunner, his John-the-Baptist. Cassady is always speaking his own version of the new vision and serves as a link to the earlier version of the movement for some sort of liberation through transgression. As the "Dean Moriarty" of Jack Kerouac's *On the Road*, he is one of the great figures of the "Beat Generation."

Wolfe begins tracing how Kesey came to be in the center of a great cultural shift. An "all-American boy" from rural Oregon, Kesey does not come from any elite background, but he wants to write and in 1958 enters Stanford University with a creative writing fellowship. While in Palo Alto, he enters a traditional bohemian group, centered on Perry Lane, where he and many others connected with the university live inexpensively. Welcoming the "searching hick" shows the Perry Lane bohemians how cool they are, how indifferent to social boundaries. Kesey, however, is breaking boundaries for real. Vic Lovell, a psychology graduate student, gets Kesey involved in "psychomimetic" drug experiments at a veterans' administration (VA) hospital. Kesey and Lovell soon find that some of the drugs being tested vastly increase their perceptions or lead to fascinating visions. Before long they begin taking drugs outside the clinical context. The drug use worries some of the Perry Lane bohemians, both because real outlawry seems to be on hand and because the social focus of the little community is shifting to Kesey.

While taking peyote, Kesey has the inspiration that shapes the novel he is writing, *One Flew Over the Cuckoo's Nest*, though he also does real research. His novel is set in a mental hospital; he gets a job working in one as a night attendant. A central action in the book is an electroshock treatment; he undergoes one himself. The publication of *Cuckoo's Nest* to the best possible reviews in 1961 validates for many Kesey's drug experiments. A group begins to gather around him when he returns to Perry Lane after a stay in Oregon. The group includes Cassady, novelist Robert Stone, Carl Lehmann-Haupt, and Richard Alpert.

When a developer buys the Perry Lane area, Kesey moves to a property in La Honda, California, that backs up on a redwood forest. There is a Wild West feel to the place: the locals invoke the memory of the gunslingers hiding out in the town long ago. Kesey uses the property as the site for "experiments in conscious," only some related to drugs. He fills the area with audio and video equipment and begins to create the sort of collagelike multimedia pieces that will come to characterize the psychedelic movement. Much of what is played over the speakers are recordings, perhaps looped and rerecorded, of Kesey and the group "rapping"—that is, improvising often surreal monologues. The group is growing. It soon includes Carl Lehmann-Haupt's brother Sandy, a twenty-two-year-old with a mastery of electronics and a history of mental illness; Kenneth Babbs, a former Marine helicopter pilot; and Mike Hagen, an old Oregon friend. Others, however, are put off, because Kesey is more and more organizing people's "trips." As the group grows they begin the pranks, the "public put-ons," that give the group its name. Their life together seems to involve many earnest discussions not unlike group therapy, and the rapping develops into something not so different from the call-and-response dialogue that characterizes worship in some American churches.

The Merry Pranksters now prepare their biggest Prank, a journey to the East. (They are beginning to see their experience reflected in the books that are becoming the canon of the counterculture: Hermann Hesse's, *Journey to the East*, Arthur C. Clarke's *Childhood's End*, and Robert Heinlein's *Stranger in a Strange Land*.) The group acquires a 1939 International Harvester school bus, which has already been refitted as a kind of camper, with bunks and a refrigerator and a sink. The Pranksters install a sound system and repaint it in a hodge-podge of brightly colored and mostly very sloppy artwork. They also change the destination panel on the front to read "Furthur" and add a warning sign in the back saying, "Caution: Weird Load."

After a test trip, they set out across the country. Cassady is usually at the wheel—and driving fast. The sound system is always operating, and all is being filmed. Kesey treats the trip as an allegory of life, and though he takes the role of "Non-Navigator," he is clearly in control. Sandy begins to notice both that Kesey is also controlling the drugs and that there seems to be an inner circle and an outer, determined by closeness to Kesey. As in many religious communities, people take on new names. Steve Lambrecht becomes Zonker, Cassady becomes Speed Limit, Ron Brevitt becomes Hassler, and Paula Sundersten becomes Gretchen Fetchin. The trip includes not just drugs and rock 'n' roll but also sex. Kesey and Babbs vie for Gretchen, even as George Walker, rather than Kesey, is calling Faye back in La Honda.

The ride is not a comfortable one, and unable to sleep, they try alternating drugs—speed, marijuana, LSD. Some, especially Sandy, begin to long to get off the bus for a while. The stops, while offering the Pranksters the pleasure of shocking gas station owners by bringing their dayglo madness into their nice clean bathrooms, seem far too short. But Kesey makes the issue part of the allegory: "There are going to be times [. . .] when we can't wait for somebody. Now, you're either on the bus or off the bus. If you're on the bus, and you get left behind, then you'll find it again. If you're off the bus in the first place—then it won't make a damn" (*EK-AAT* 83). They head to Houston to visit Larry McMurtry. Along the way one of the young women has taken to wearing nothing but a blanket and been christened Stark Naked. When they arrive at McMurtry's, she, still naked, rushes out in into his front yard and picks up his son, convinced he is her own, and they realize she has gone mad. She ends up in the local psychiatric ward.

With Stark Naked off the bus, they continue through the South, shock-ing the populace and getting past any encounters with the police by behaving so bizarrely—playing out the "cop movie"—that the bewil-dered officers back off rather than dealing with them. In the course of the drive and the drug trips, some of them feel thoroughly one with each other. In New York, the day-glo bus with speakers blaring makes people stop and stare. Kesey meets with the heroes of the Beat movement, in-cluding Allen Ginsberg and Jack Kerouac himself, and as his second novel, *Sometimes a Great Notion*, appears, heads back toward the West.

The first stop is in Millbrook, New York, where Timothy Leary has his own community, the League of Spiritual Discovery. The Pranksters expect a warm welcome, but the reception is surprisingly frosty, so they move on, preferring their loud, American brand of transcendence through drugs to the quiet, Eastern, tomblike one the Learyites have created. They travel back through the West of the cowboys, flouting every convention imaginable wherever they go—picking up underage girls in Calgary, driving the day-glo bus through a funeral in Boisie—before returning home to La Honda.

Once there, Kesey begins organizing new activities for his followers. Others begin to seek him out as a guru. He is invited to lead a seminar at Esalen, a retreat created by Gestalt psychologist Fritz Perls. Some of his own Pranksters, however, are not doing so well. Sandy, especially, is becoming paranoiac, craving Kesey's attention and fearing all around him. Kesey and the Pranksters see his need and try to cater to him, even arranging of sort of ceremony at Esalen to show their love for him. He, however, interprets it as some bizarre attack and runs off, ending up in the hands of the police. When his brother arrives at the jail to take him to a mental hospital, Kesey appears, trying to get him back to the Prank-sters.

The feeling among the Pranksters is getting more and more mystical, and still more people arrive to join the community. Among them are Mountain Girl, who will quickly enter Kesey's inner circle, and the Her-mit, a local youth who begins living in a cave on the property. Kesey begins holding weekly "briefings" at which he presents, essentially, his own teachings and discusses them with the group. The main point seems to be living in the moment, not just watching the movie of your life but writing it.

The neighbors view the community with growing alarm. Beyond the rumors of drug use, there is the noise and the redwoods painted in day-glo colors. The Pranksters are put under surveillance—something that they treat as a big joke. Finally, they get warning that their place will be raided. They respond both by putting up signs to freak out the cops and by clearing the place of drugs. When the raid comes, there are nevertheless arrests. Kesey and twelve others are charged with marijuana possession, resisting arrest, and impairing the morals of minors, since Mountain Girl and the Hermit are underage. All the charges are quickly dropped, except for one count each of marijuana possession against Kesey and Page Browning. The furor over the arrest simply makes Kesey a more important and sought after public figure.

Kesey's circle soon attracts other outlaws. He meets some of the Hell's Angels, the notorious motorcycle gang, through Hunter S. Thompson, and invites the whole group to visit. The neighbors are soon passing a huge sign saying "The Merry Pranksters Welcome the Hell's Angels." When the Angels arrive, others are there to welcome them, including poet Allen Ginsberg and Richard Alpert. The Angels, much like the Pranksters, spend much of their time "testing people's cool," though the response they seek includes "naked terror" as well as shock. The Pranksters, however, are shockproof, and despite the police hovering in the vicinity, the two groups get along fine, with lots of LSD and beer, and even one of the "gang bangs" (consensual, in this case) for which the Angels became notorious. The Pranksters are soon invited to take part in the annual conference of the California Unitarian Church at Asilomar. Their antics shock some of the participants but delight others, who treat Kesey as a prophet. Kesey himself is becoming fascinated by the idea of "Control": he finds he can shape events by drawing others into the Pranksters "movie," even if they planned to follow a completely different script.

He is not always immediately successful, however. The new sign, "The Merry Pranksters Welcome the Beatles," does not actually bring about a visit from the world's most famous rock band. And when the Pranksters take the bus to a Beatles concert, they are unable to bring all the screaming teenagers into their movie. In fact, they seem to experience a "bad trip" in every sense of the word. On the other hand, the Beatles do soon start experimenting with LSD and adopting psychedelic styles, so perhaps they do bring them into their movie, if only at one remove.

The Pranksters are much more successful during their next outing, which takes them to a major rally against the Vietnam War in Berkeley. They prepare for the demonstration by painting the bus blood red and building a gun turret atop it with two mock cannons. Kesey puts on a uniform of sorts: an orange highway worker's coat with epaulets on the shoulders and hash marks on the sleeves and an orange-painted World War I helmet. He is the next-to-last speaker, and his performance could not contrast more with the earnest rhetoric that has come before. He tells the crowd that their activity is pointless. Like the girls screaming at the Beatles concert, Kesey says the protesters are really just crying "ME! ME! ME! ME!" and the cry of the ego is itself the cause of war. The only thing that will help is just to look at the war and turn your back to it. Kesey's speech lets the air out of the rally and begins a period when the fashion of Northern California bohemia will turn from genuine political action to self-exploration.

The Pranksters are now trying to share their experience with others through large, semipublic gatherings where many take LSD and all experience the rest of the things that become associated with psychedelics: rock music—Jerry Garcia and the Grateful Dead play at some of them—strobe lights, multimedia projections, people rapping over microphones, and bizarre decorations. The Pranksters publicize them with handbills reading "Can you Pass the Acid Test?" and even some who are not using drugs feel a "contact high" in the charged atmosphere. Kesey is still experimenting with control: he can manipulate the crowds through the strobe light and the rest of his electronic equipment. The "acid tests"—which the police are powerless to do much about, since LSD is still legal—set many of the styles in popular art and music for the rest of the decade and beyond.

In January of 1966, Kesey is both preparing for an appearance at the Trips Festival, a grand celebration of the counterculture in San Francisco that will culminate in another Acid Test, and facing the marijuana charges in San Mateo County. He is sentenced to six months in jail and three on probation. While still out on bail and just days before the festival, he and Mountain Girl are arrested for possession of marijuana in San Francisco. The arrest is great publicity for the festival, but it also means that Kesey faces five years in jail without parole. The festival goes on as planned, with Kesey dressed up in a space suit atop a tower of equipment in the center of the hall.

Rather than stay to face the charges, Kesey decides to flee the country. He first plans one last prank, a faked suicide by drowning in the Pacific. (The police are not fooled.) Kesey goes to Mexico, and the Pranksters try to carry on without him. In fact, they carry out their greatest prank, the Electric Kool-Aid Acid Test itself, while he is out of the country. Kenneth Babbs, Cassady, and others put on an Acid Test in Los Angeles in February, and Hugh Romney arranges to serve LSD-spiked Kool-Aid. While some who drink the stuff realize what is in it, others do not. Disagreements over having people take drugs unknowingly exacerbate divisions in the group, which now splits into Babbs and anti-Babbs factions.

Meanwhile Kesey has made his way to Puerto Vallarta via Mazatlan. He has followed Cassidy's example and begun to take amphetamines—speed—heavily, and they have helped push him into paranoia. He fears that he is about to be arrested and spends days and nights hiding in the jungle, rather than in the house with his friends and Black Maria, a new recruit to Pranksterism. His whereabouts are known; there have been stories placing him in Puerto Vallarta in the American newspapers, but before the Mexican authorities seek him out there, he returns to Mazatlan. There he rendezvouses with more of the Pranksters, who have come down in the bus. Among them are Faye and children; Mountain Girl, who has been let off lightly on the drug charge, in part because she is now eight months pregnant with Kesey's child; and Kenneth Babbs. They set up housekeeping in the coastal town of Manzanillo. Kesey begins thinking of the group as a biblical tribe, and people start taking on the names of figures from Genesis. Kesey is certainly living as the Old Testament patriarchs lived, with their several wives and concubines sharing a household. Kesey comes to a new realization. He thinks that they need to move "beyond acid," to "make this thing permanent inside of you."

After some brushes with Mexican law, Kesey decides to stop running, playing the cops and robbers game, and to make it once more the Prankster movie by going home. Kesey returns to the Bay Area and begins popping up in public as a way of tweaking the authorities. He swings from paranoia to utter disregard for his own security. He appears at an Acid Test with the Rolling Stones at San Francisco State University, as many people inspired by the Pranksters pour into the Haight-Asbury district of the city to take part in the new scene. The rest of the Pranksters are soon there, too, living in the Warehouse, a hotel garage lent to them by another communal group. Kesey appears at the Love Festival held on October 7 as a response to the law that goes into effect that day outlawing LSD. He is interviewed for the newspapers and says he wants to stay in the country as a fugitive, "as salt in [FBI Director] J. Edgar Hoover's wounds." He is even interviewed by a TV station. He plans to appear at another Acid Test, one that will be a masked ball, deliver his message of the way "beyond acid," and then escape before the police can apprehend him. But before that can happen, he is caught.

Kesey appears in court, and his lawyers make a plea for leniency. He has returned, they say, to denounce LSD use. Despite more charges, including a federal one of flight to avoid prosecution, he is out of jail after only five days—and Wolfe is now on hand to report what happens. Kesey and the Pranksters plan the Acid Test Graduation, and both the authorities and the drug culture are worried about exactly what he is going to say. He appears on a TV show, where he is expected to discuss "The Dangers of LSD," but he does not. He talks about moving on the "next step." Some think that at the Graduation he will not denounce LSD; instead, he will pull another prank that will bring about a real crackdown on the drug scene. At first it looks as if the Graduation will come off as planned. But politics of several sorts are disturbing the counterculture world, and when the producer they are working with pulls out, the Pranksters lose their chance to have their event in a large hall. They fall back on holding it in the warehouse. The event there is like the earlier Acid Tests but with lots of press coverage. When Kesey finally speaks there is neither a prank nor a real renunciation of drugs. Instead there is, early in the morning, after the curious have given up on the event, another celebration of the unity the Pranksters feel.

After the Graduation, other groups take center stage in the counterculture. There is no going back to La Honda, so many of the Pranksters move to Babbs's place outside of Santa Cruz. Near there, at a bar called the Barn, they have another one of their parties, with their speakers and amplifiers, but the music they make just drives people away, including even some Pranksters, and the atmosphere is like a wake. Kesey and Babbs begin rapping, in the old call-and-response pattern, but after a time Babbs's only response to Kesey's surreal visions is, "We Blew It!"

In an epilogue Wolfe describes the Pranksters scattering. Kesey serves five months at a work farm very near La Honda, and then he and Faye and their children go to live on his brother's farm in Oregon. Mountain Girl joins the Grateful Dead's group, and others join other communes. Other Pranksters follow Kesey to Oregon and find the bus parked beside his house. Neil Cassady is found dead beside a railroad track in Mexico, where he has been using speed heavily and may have mixed alcohol and barbiturates.

CHARACTER DEVELOPMENT

The central figure is, of course, Ken Kesey. He remains, nevertheless, something of an enigma, and his appeal to so many is mysterious. He has attained fame as a novelist, but during the period recounted in *The Electric Kool-Aid Acid Test*, he has renounced fiction. What he is doing now is sharing his vision directly and through the events he creates. He is, nevertheless, not exactly what one would expect of the guru of a counterculture movement. One of the things that seems to appeal to Wolfe about Kesey is that he has kept in touch with his authentic American roots, even in the midst of a cultural movement that largely rejects the whole culture that makes the movement possible. He has not moved away entirely from the values and ideals of his rural childhood. Even when he is living among a self-conscious intelligentsia, he preserves the signs of belonging to other classes. He keeps his "soft country accent" and moves like an athlete. And he takes his ideals as much from the American popular culture as from any foreign literary or intellectual authorities. The free life of teenagers with cars and even the dreams of transcendent personal power offered by superhero comic books mean as much to him as do Jungian psychology or Eastern religions, though he can discuss them, too.

Kesey is, in his strange way, a figure of integrity. The world he moves in is full of people playing the role of outlaw. Kesey adopts it for real, and that is what makes him frightening to many. The Perry Lane bohemians reject society's values and seek self-fulfillment but only in their own safe and genteel way. Kesey rejects them whole-heartedly, breaking the law and taking new and unpredictable drugs. The citizens of La Honda cherish the memory of gunslingers' visits to their town and give their businesses Wild West themes. Kesey makes friends with the Hell's Angels and invites them to his parties. This quality of real, not pretend, outlawry is part of his attraction—and also part of the danger associated with him. He calls people who are merely dabbling in the rejection of society's values on their pretenses. People who talk to him about being "out there" had better be ready for an invitation to strip naked, board their motorcycles, and roar off up the highway.

No description of him can really capture the charisma—the "aggressive, outgoing charm"—that Kesey displays during the Prankster period, but he clearly has it. He has the ability, displayed by the leaders of many groups, whether they are called cults or religious movements or political organizations, of drawing people to himself and making their primary concern not their own welfare so much as their relationship to the leader. Even his essentially polygamous lifestyle places him in this traditional course, since a long line of American prophets, from Brigham Young to David Koresh, have gathered harems about themselves. (Kesey's women, however, are also free to find other partners of their own.) The focus of Kesey's community is Kesey himself, not any doctrine he preaches.

In this band of free spirits, Kesey is clearly in control. Even when he tells them to be themselves, he is giving the order: "Everybody is going to be what they are" (73). He is, all the same, uneasy in the role of the prophet. He keeps repeating, "Never trust a Prankster," (233) suggesting that he is not the source of all answers. What he does teach is couched in aphorisms, many of them as inscrutable as the koans of Zen Buddhism ("What is the sound of one hand clapping?"). Kesey's include "You're either on the bus or . . . off the bus," "See with your ears and hear with your eyes," and "What did the mirror say? It's done with people" (126). None of them are easily translated into something like a religious doctrine or a philosophy, but they somehow provide, for those already attracted to Kesey and in tune with the experience his community offers, a summing up of the insight they have already gained.

Kesey's wild, joyous, outlaw, profoundly American version of mind expansion is a clear contrast to the sepulchral, Orientalist version associated with Timothy Leary. (Leary and Alpert emphasize a calm and tranquil "set and setting" for the use of psychedelics rather than the multimedia bacchanals the Prankster favor.) Another character links him with an earlier generation that merged the figures of the outlaw and the seeker—and that looked to the East for its spirituality. That character is Neil Cassady. By the time he joins Kesey's band, he is already famous, thanks to his portrayal in Kerouac's *On the Road* as the embodiment of transcendental rebellion. He is almost a generation older than the rest of the Pranksters and is a veteran not just of the incessant, aimless travel that Kerouac chronicled, but also of the intellectual explorations of the Beat generation. Like the Pranksters, the beats sometimes turned to Eastern philosophy for inspiration, rejected conventional morality, and saw something holy in their very outcast state. (Kerouac describes Dean Moriarty, Cassady's alter ego, as something like a saint.) Kesey sometimes offers Cassady as a model for the other Pranksters, since he seems truly to live in the moment.

Cassidy is certainly always full of manic energy. He talks constantly, punctuating all he says with the repeating phrase, "you understand," which is ironic, since he, too, speaks in cryptic aphorisms and instantly allegorizes whatever occurs. And most of the times we see him, he is repeatedly throwing a sledgehammer up in the air and catching it. He is at the wheel of the bus during the Pranksters' outings, and he drives with abandon, usually at top speed—hence the name Speed Limit. All that, however, may be as much the result of his heavy use of speed as his ability to live in the moment. Certainly the news of his death and the report of his having become despondent over the prospect of growing old cast a pall over the account of this youth rebellion.

Perhaps the greatest contrast to Cassady among the Pranksters is Sandy Lehmann-Haupt. While Cassady has reached the point where he "doesn't have to think anymore," Sandy is thinking constantly. He is always unsure of his place in the group and on the verge of lapsing back into real mental illness. He is never sure of his relationship with Kesey or the others—or whether he belongs with them or not. During the bus trip, he leaves and returns so often that he acquires the name Dismount. Later the Pranksters notice his anxiety about his place in the group and try to reassure him, but he runs away in panic. Reunited with them again in Mexico, he leaves once more, and when he leaves this time his reassertion of his private ownership of a piece of the sound system suggests that he is also rejecting the Pranksters' communal lifestyle. He exemplifies both the tensions caused by the group's clear but unmentioned hierarchies and the dangerous possibilities in its quest for mind expansion.

If Sandy is a contrast to Cassady, other characters are Cassady's rivals. Kenneth Babbs, for instance, goes so far as to "prank" Cassady while Kesey is off in Mexico. When Cassady and some of the others are being photographed for *Life* magazine, Babbs refuses to participate—and then drives off with the bus, leaving them stranded. His only motive seems to be the desire to control the group in Kesey's absence, and to be, therefore, closer to Kesey than the rest. With his military background, Babbs shares Kesey's macho alienation from genteel bohemia. He seems always to be Kesey's favorite and right-hand man. Like the other inner-circle Pranksters, including Hassler and Zonker, he aids Kesey in pressing their adventures further. (The original pranks are, in fact, Babbs's idea.) But without Kesey present to keep them together, the rest fall out with each other.

Beyond the inner circle, of course, there are many who seem tolerated by the group rather than a real part of it. Some innocents, including the Hermit, simply seem to appear and then stay on. Others, like some of the Perry Lane crowd, are just regular visitors. And still others are ostracized. An obnoxious kid named Pancho Pillow never returns after Kesey asks him, "Why should I share your bad trip?" The inner circle and the outer group also become clear at the final Acid Test, where the ecstatic moment of unity comes only after the outsiders have left.

The fact that there is a Prankster hierarchy is not lost on the women in the group. *The Electric Kool-Aid Acid Test* certainly provides evidence to support the idea that the 1960s counterculture was very much a men's movement in which women were marginalized. Women, like men, seem to need Kesey's attention and approval, but for them the attention is sexual as well as intellectual and emotional. Kesey's wife Faye is cast in the role of mother, in a sense, to the whole group, the "beatific country wife," who, intelligent as she may be, speaks little. The other important woman in his life, is the eighteen-year-old called Mountain Girl, whose real name is Carolyn Adams. She seems very attuned to both Kesey's ideas and to his style. She is "completely out front" and, despite a middle-class upbringing in Poughkeepsie, New York, country in her style. She arrives on a motorcycle and sprinkles her speech with "git" and "gonna." She is with Kesey when he is arrested the second time and, of course, bears his child. And she feels lonely and isolated among the Pranksters. Black Maria, a young American woman who joins Kesey's group in Mexico, also comes to feel lonely in what she realizes is a "Prankster hierarchy. [. . .] Right now, among the women, Mountain Girl was first, closest to Kesey, and Faye was second, or was it really vice versa, and Black Maria was maybe third, but actually so remote it didn't matter" (330). Other women in the group suffer treatment still worse than Black Maria's. Stark Naked is, after all, simply abandoned after her experiences on the bus have left her genuinely insane. The Prankster world, like the world of Dean Moriarty in *On the Road*, is one where some women are always there to come home to and others can be abandoned at will.

Observing all these characters is Wolfe himself. While Wolfe does not show himself doing a great deal in the course of the narrative, he does appear at the beginning and the end, and he is important as a character. He is very much not on the bus. He wears all the badges of the world against which the Pranksters have set themselves. He wears a coat. He wears a tie. Still worse, he does not wear huarache sandals or hiking boots, but "shiny FBI shoes," the kind that the Pranksters associate with the straightest of the straight. His presence makes it clear that one need not join the group in order to understand it.

LITERARY DEVICES

In the course of *The Electric Kool-Aid Acid Test*, Wolfe uses a number of literary devices to involve the reader in the narrative and capture the flavor of the Pranksters' lives. Just as they create multimedia scenes with both visual and aural elements taken from disparate sources brought together, Wolfe brings together many different sorts of writing in his account of them. Some parts of the book do read like an earnest, factual account of a social movement. But much of the rest of the book is in other voices. In places Wolfe abandons prose altogether and writes in a loosely rhyming sort of free verse, perhaps invoking the Prankster's own raps. In other places he adopts the style of one of his characters. For example, he presents the most notorious of the Pranksters' actions in the flat and earnest voice of Clair Bush, one of those who unknowingly takes

LSD in the form of Electric Kool-Aid. Her very style captures the outlook of the young attracted to the "beautiful people" better than any objective description could.

Wolfe adopts a number of voices in the course of his story, and indeed at times they interrupt each other. For example, several times the flow of the narrative is broken by a voice that might be called the Jain disciple. Some word that might be taken as cosmically significant, such as "accident," is repeated, as a question directed to the master: "*Accident, Mahavira?*" Mahavira, founder of the Jain religion, gathered a band of disciples around him, much as Buddha did—and, by implication, as Kesey does. And of course, in telling much of the story from the point of view of his informants, Wolfe also adopts their language.

Another device Wolfe uses to give immediacy to his description is to directly address his characters. The very first sentence of the book— "That's good thinking there, Cool Breeze"—is a good example. Instead of telling the reader first what the scene looks like from the outside, he takes us into the mind of one of the characters—himself, in this case— and shows his reaction to what is going on. (How, he wonders, can this young man talk about not attracting the notice of the police when he is decked out in full Prankster regalia and riding up the street on the back of a truck with a woman who is drawing a bead on passersby with a very realistic looking cap pistol?) Later on voices address Kesey directly. The chapter titled "The Fugitive" begins, "Haul ass, Kesey. Move. *Scram. Split, Flee, Hide, Vanish, Disintegrate.* Like *run.*"

That string of imperatives also illustrates the sort of diction Wolfe uses to convey not just the Pranksters' actions but also the atmosphere around them. He mixes every level of diction, from the most vulgar to the fairly elevated, and he draws his language from several fields. The vocabulary of every sort of discourse—from Eastern religions to anatomy to popular science fiction—provides words for him, and the reader has to be ready to deal with *satori* (illumination in Buddhism), *orbicularis oris* (a muscle that controls the lips), and *grok* (to understand totally and intuitively, from Heinlein's *Stranger in a Strange Land*). The extravagant vocabulary is matched with creative punctuation, with many dots, repeated colons, and exclamation points. Wolfe even fits the punctuation to the country he is writing about. When describing scenes in Mexico, he sometimes punctuates in the Spanish style, with opening exclamation points as well as closing ones—"¡Diablo!" or "¡Take Me to Eat Alley!"

MAJOR THEMES

Wolfe's major theme is that the Merry Pranksters were indeed a religious movement. That idea may strike many as strange, since they are hardly interested in questions of ethics or morality at all, and many middle-class Americans consider religion primarily a means of making people morally better. That is not, however, the only possible purpose for religion, much less the impulse that led to the creation of the major religions that now do make ethics a large part of their doctrines. While some great religious leaders are, in part at least, ethical teachers, as Jesus and Moses are, many are not. Rather, they are what Max Weber calls *"exemplary* prophets," who present themselves and their own connection with the divine as examples to their followers. Jesus, of course, also fits into this category, as does Buddha. For the Pranksters, Kesey clearly plays the role of someone who has received some sort of illumination, which they want to share.

Religions (and religious revivals) tend to begin not with calm deliberations about doctrine, but with moments of ecstasy. Buddha receives illumination. St. Paul is struck down on the road to Damascus. Zoroaster meets the Archangel Vohu Mano. And the ecstasies described sound like what LSD takers report: the separation between the isolated ego, the I, and the vast impersonal world in which it is trapped disappears. The visionary feels part of the "divine All-one" and in touch with the whole universe. The identification of religious ecstasy and a drug high may seem shocking, but it is not a new phenomenon in the history of religion. What the Zoroastrians called "haoma water" and the Hindus "soma" was a drug, and may have been the basis of their visions. Even in early Christianity, wine played such an important role that St. Paul has to warn against excesses. Peyote, a drug Kesey himself used, still plays a role in Native American religion. The Pranksters simply re-create an old pattern using a powerful new substance.

The ecstatic experience also shapes the group as a social unit. Those who have had the new experience and are committed to seeing the world in a new way feel united with each other and separate from the rest of the world, from those who remain "unaware." There is a deep separation between the initiate and the outsider: "You're either on the bus or you're off the bus." There is also, however, a desire to spread the experience to the rest of the world. And that is why Kesey and his followers do not simply "do their own thing" in La Honda; they try to share it with the rest of the world, first by shocking people out of their complacency and then by offering the experience directly at the Acid Tests. In other words, after the ecstasy, they go out to proselytize.

With the Pranksters' drug taking and their group therapy-like "briefings," their ecstatic experience may seem very different from most American religious movements. But in fact it has a lot in common with several sorts of revivals that had already taken place in American Christianity. The whole Pentecostal movement, with its speaking in tongues and feelings of having received the Spirit directly, came from just that sort of revival, where with music and clapping and lack of sleep people were brought to emotional levels that allowed them to feel themselves truly in touch with a power outside themselves. The same is true, with the added element of danger, in the American sects known as snake handlers, who, taking literally the biblical promise that Christians will be able to take up serpents, dance while holding poisonous snakes. Even in the world of the Acid Tests, drug use was not the only key to ecstasy: the "contact highs" experienced by those who had not taken anything showed that just being with others seeking ecstasy was enough to communicate the experience.

The Pranksters do not only feel that they are especially in tune with ultimate reality when they are experiencing a drug-induced high. Rather, they are constantly feeling that they have grasped the patterns of the universe. Wolfe uses psychologist Karl Jung's term synchronicity to describe their feeling (140). What may seem to be coincidences are not, to them. Rather they are glimpses of the archetypal patterns that elude the conscious mind. (In Jung's view, all people shared a "collective unconscious" stocked with "archetypes," that is, images of the great psychological realities.) At times the Pranksters seem to feel they are the darlings of Providence, that the universe is looking out for them. At one point they drive up a little mountain road in the High Sierras and run out of gas. Almost immediately, and much to their surprise, a Chevron gas tanker arrives. They take it as a sort of sign. While they eschew any sort of traditional religious language, they clearly feel they are in touch with something greater than themselves—"Cosmo" or "the Management." They feel the currents of the universe and so can say, "Go with the Flow."

Another theme Wolfe explores is the pretense of bohemianism. Some of the Pranksters, like Kesey himself, are presented as real rebels. But others are simply playing at rebellion and are always able to fall back on the middle-class values that sustained them. (Early on, Wolfe notes that Hassler, who is living with the rest of the group in an old hotel garage that does not even have its own toilet, has a toothbrush in his pocket, so he can go up to the gas station and brush after every meal.) The Perry Lane crowd are mostly playing at being rebels, and many of the youth of the counterculture are, too. And when they meet real outlaws, such as the Hell's Angels, they do not always like them.

Wolfe notes, however, that the dream of leaving the safety of the middle class has grown, especially among those nourished in the comforts of that class. He observes that the psychedelic lifestyle attracts few blacks, both because LSD breaks the "in-control" aura of "cool" black culture then celebrated and because few blacks felt any *nostalgie de la boue*—literally, longing for the mud—which often means the desire to play at being poor. Those who have been brought up with money and comfort, however, do enjoy shocking their parents by running off to some distant place to live in squalor with a group of "beautiful people." For the white middle-class youth the psychedelic lifestyle is an attractive pose, for it offers a way of creating a statusphere with one's contemporaries while rejecting that of one's parents.

That world has its status hierarchy, however, just as the world of the corporation and the country club does. Those who come to the Pranksters seek a place in a status system. The first question is whether they will be let in at all. For, while there are no formal admission procedures and no one can be officially blackballed, those who do wander into the group feel themselves on trial for a while before they are either accepted or given the idea that it is time to leave. Once in, they compete for status in the form of closeness to Kesey. And the whole group seems to be in a struggle to maintain their leadership in the larger counterculture. The political struggles—Who will get the Grateful Dead to play at their event? Will the Pranksters be allowed to use a large public hall?—show them vying with other rebels to shape a growing movement. Such struggles are not surprising anywhere, but here they have a certain irony. The Pranksters worry about status even while rejecting it, just as they struggle for leadership even when their leader, the "non-Navigator," claims he is not one.

Another theme is the game. Kesey and his group reject the games of society, by which they mean all the conventional patterns of behavior. Kesey's solution to the problem of war is to just stop playing that game: do not fight, do not protest, just drop the whole business. And he is trying not to play the cops and robbers game, the conventional pattern into which police and criminals fall, each knowing their assigned role. Sometimes he and the others are able to shock or foil those used to following a certain script by not playing their parts. Rather than act like frightened drug users when stopped by the police, they act like outrageous show people, and so confuse the officers that they are let go. They discover, of course, that they cannot simply opt out of some of society's patterns, such as the law. More important, they create their own games. Besides forming social customs as a group, the Pranksters also play "Power," an allegorical game of Kesey's creation. They are not so much escaping the world of games as playing a slightly different set.

The idea of "game" merges with the idea of the "Movie." The Pranksters are actually at work on a film. They shoot and record hundreds of hours of material. But the idea of the movie also becomes a metaphor for them. It is not just the artwork on which they are working; it is life they are living out. Indeed, for all their talk about living in the moment, the Pranksters are constantly watching themselves do whatever they are doing. There is a real element of self-conscious performance in all they do. After all, they are always in costume. The idea is not to be the movie that society plans for them, but to bring others into the Prankster movie. While on the run in Mexico, Kesey decides that fleeing further will not help: "That's *their* game, the cops-and-robbers game. That's *their* movie and they know it backward and forward and they know how it comes out. [. . .] The only way out is to make it the Prankster movie and imagine [the Mexican agent] into the Prankster movie" (334). Kesey tries to control events by not following a preset script—with mixed results.

A final theme is the danger of real madness for all the seekers Wolfe describes. *The Electric Kool-Aid Acid Test* is neither a celebration of drug taking nor antidrug propaganda. Most of the experimenters with drugs he describes seem to emerge from their experience unharmed. But several of them are in serious straits because of the drug use. Stark Naked is left in the asylum and never heard of again. Sandy becomes paranoiac and has to be hospitalized. Kesey himself is frighteningly paranoid for a time—and in his case, as in Sandy's, Wolfe makes paranoia vivid by describing it from the paranoid's own point of view as well as that of those observing his mad behavior. Neil Cassady ends up dead. The price of ecstasy can be quite high.

ALTERNATE READING: *THE ELECTRIC KOOL-AID ACID TEST* AS PICARESQUE NOVEL

When reading a literary work, it is often useful to think about what kind of work, what literary genre, it falls into. Once we decide that a work is a comedy, a tragedy, a romance, or a member of one of the subgenres, such as the bildungsroman (novel of personal development) or social problem novel, we can think about how it either follows or breaks the conventions of the form. If we think of use of fictional techniques for a true narrative, we would call *The Electric Kool-Aid Acid Test* a nonfiction novel or a work of literary journalism. But if we think of the structure of its plot and the nature of the characters it presents, and that is largely how we classify tragedies, comedies, and romances, it falls into the genre called the picaresque.

The name of the form comes from the Spanish word *pícaro* or rogue. The hero of these tales is not the knight errant who goes through the world fighting for the ideals of courtly love or of Christian chivalry. A parody of that figure dominates Cervantes's *Don Quixote* (1604), which many could call the first modern novel and which builds on the picaresque tradition. Rather he is the knight-errant's serving class counterpart, often one unburdened with ideas of any kind. The classic examples are novels such as the Spanish *Lazarillo de Tormes* (1553) and the French *Gil Blas* by Alain-René Le Sage (1715). The central characters in both those works are servants who both observe and imitate the corrupt actions of a series of masters. The satire, in which the upper classes are always more wicked than their inferiors, goes from one object to the next as the hero moves through the world. The structure is always episodic, with sometimes very little relationship between what goes on in one scene and the next. The picaresque hero is invariably a traveler, and his adventures are determined by the sorts of societies he moves though. With a few exceptions, the form is thoroughly comic.

The main character is often some sort of outlaw—though as often as not someone unjustly on the wrong side of the law. Eighteenth-century English novelist Henry Fielding writes about both sorts of outlaws. *Jonathan Wild the Great* (1743) describes a highwayman who is simply a common criminal. (Fielding based him on a real robber, though the character is also an allegorical portrait of a corrupt prime minister.) In *Joseph Andrews* (1742), which is modeled more on Cervantes, he presents in both Joseph and in Parson Adams innocent characters who nevertheless are persecuted by the forces of the law—sometimes for their very integrity. *Tom Jones* (1749) also shows a mostly innocent character moving through the corrupt world. In Fielding, as in earlier picaresque novels, the very act of travel is a large part of the action, and many events are determined by what passes on the road—or in the coach.

In the hands of a number of writers, the picaresque becomes a vehicle for philosophical investigations. Voltaire's *Candide* and Samuel Johnson's *Rasselas* both show characters who wander through the world, in each case with a tutor or master who is unable to provide the answers to their questions. Both realize, in a religious or secular way, that they are not as innocent as they thought and that the world is not what they imagined it to be. Many more picaresque novels, of course, like many "road" or "buddy" movies in the twentieth century, simply used the form to string together amusing incidents.

The picaresque became very popular in American literature, for the man—and it almost always is a man or boy—traveling alone or with a single trusted friend is one of the defining archetypes of the American tradition. Perhaps the classic American example is Mark Twain's *Adventures of Huckleberry Finn*. In that novel Huck and Jim float through many societies, wary of each because Jim is a runaway slave, and are often appalled by the violence or corruption they see. Herman Melville does much the same thing in *The Confidence Man*, though his central figure is not an innocent boy, like Huck. In the twentieth century the picaresque, both in its purely comic and more philosophic forms, remained a characteristically American form, in fiction, nonfiction, and works that straddled the dividing line between the two. We see genuine rogues in works like Kerouac's *On the Road* and Hunter S. Thompson's *Fear and Loathing in Las Vegas*—though Kerouac builds on Jean Genet's idea that the thief is also a saint. In other works, such as John Steinbeck's *Travels with Charlie* or Robert Pirsig's *Zen and the Art of Motorcycle Maintenance*, authors who seek to understand the state of their country or of their own souls set out to discover it by traveling more or less aimlessly down the road and describing what they meet.

The Electric Kool-Aid Acid Test fits the picaresque form in many ways. It is thoroughly episodic. When the characters are not moving from one setting to another—and they do that both while on the cross-country bus trip and while on the run in Mexico—they create a series of discrete events with different audiences. Even while headquartered in La Honda, they travel out to meet those they wish to shock or enlighten, meeting thoroughly different societies at Esalen, the Unitarian conference, the Beatles concert, and the antiwar rally. They, on the other hand, are a unified little band, united against the world, much like Candide and his several companions or Huck and Jim on their raft. (The bus, of course, takes on a totemic meaning for the tribe of outcasts. It shows both their unity and their separation from the societies they move through, just as Huck and Jim's raft does.)

The traditional picaresque tale satirizes both the roguishness of its heroes and the still more profound corruption of those they meet. (In a couple of places, such as the death of Huck's friend Buck and the murder of Boggs, the old drunk, *Huckleberry Finn* becomes not satiric but tragic.)

In Wolfe's account of the Merry Pranksters, it is hard to tell, often, what the object of satire is, in part because the Pranksters are themselves satirists. They themselves are mocking every convention of dress and behavior they can imagine. When Wolfe's own voice is most present, he indulges in some satirical commentary, as in the initial address to Cool Breeze and when commenting on Hassler's toothbrush. But for the most part, he simply recounts the Pranksters' own satirical activities.

Here again, the Pranksters' self-consciousness sets them apart. Fictional pícaros do not set out to place themselves in the role. Huck Finn simply wants to get away from the women who want to "sivilize" him and the father who abuses him. Joseph Andrews just wants to get home with his chastity intact. Candide would not leave Westphalia if he wasn't thrown out. The Pranksters, however, deliberately set out not just to set themselves against society but also to shock it. In this they are going even further than their immediate models, Kerouac and the other Beats, who also deliberately set out to become pícaros. They want not only to detach themselves from every society they move through, but also to make sure society notices. Traditionally, picaresque heroes try to avoid attention. They do not court it by driving painted buses with loudspeakers down the streets of Manhattan or aiming toy guns at businessmen climbing the hills of San Francisco.

The object of the Pranksters' satire is often clear. It is the "games" they find society plays. They mock the "cops and robbers" game by posting signs addressing the federal agent investigating them—"We're Clean, Willie!"—rather than pretending not to notice that they are being watched. They mock the "war" game by turning their bus into a mock tank and refusing to treat the war as the profoundly serious thing both its advocates and its protesters think it is. But the most successful satire is, perhaps, not of the straight world but of their fellow bohemians.

Part of the bohemian pose for almost two centuries has been the project of shocking the rest of society. The motto has been *épater les bourgeois*—shock the middle classes. And the Pranksters attempt to do that, without any question. They also, however, prove that other groups who set themselves against the traditional values of society are, in fact, still bourgeois themselves. The Unitarians reject all dogmas and invite all to seek in their own ways; but Kesey and his group are enough to split their convention in years to come. The war protesters are against the authorities and all those in control, but they do not want joking; they want decorum, since rebellion itself is serious business. The leaders of the San Francisco counterculture want everyone to let it all hang out— but they do not want Kesey to say anything in front of a big crowd that might get the cops really mad at them. The Pranksters are able to show that all the bohemians are just playing at non-conformity. They test their cool, and most fail the test. Of course, they themselves find their own cool tested and found wanting when they try their act at a segregated beach and run up against the great American divide—race.

If the Pranksters usually succeed in shocking both the bourgeoisie and the bohemians, one is still left wondering about the validity of their own pose. What right do they have to be in this genre in the first place? How are they pícaros, rogues, outlaws? They are certainly criminals, in some senses. Kesey is in fact convicted, and the rest of them have violated the drug laws, at least. But they are not outlaws like the traditional picaresque heroes by any means. If they don't have enough to eat, it is because Faye has gone in for serving a macrobiotic diet, not because they cannot get enough food. If they wear rags, it is because they like the effect the rags create, not because they cannot buy new clothes. If they are not clean, it is because they enjoy chanting, "Oh but it's great to be a [Hell's] Angel / And be dirty all the time" (173) not because they lack access to showers and soap. They are not on the run because, like another great American picaresque hero, the narrator of Ralph Ellison's *Invisible Man*, the structures of American society have left them no place else to go. They are "on the bus" because they enjoy the "current fantasy." They are in fact, if not playing the "cops and robbers game," playing at being outlaws, and the state's arbitrary drug laws, like ordinary standards of dress and decorum, simply give them what they most need: a convention to flout in order to validate their outlawry. Even if there is jail time involved, they turn out to be not real outlaws, but merely more posing bohemians.

Picaresque narratives can end in several ways. The hero can reach a place of safety and reasonable contentment, as Candide does once he realizes the best he can do is "tend his garden." Or the narrative can end with some adventures past and more to come: at the end of *Huckleberry Finn*, its hero is ready to "light out for the territory," and in fact he appears in two more books. Or the conclusion can be a homecoming. At the end of *Tom Jones*, the wandering hero is welcomed back to Paradise Hall, and as in *Joseph Andrews*, the picaresque narrative ends with the traditional conclusion of comedy: a wedding. *The Electric Kool-Aid Acid Test* fits none of these patterns perfectly. It ends more or less where it began. Kesey does his time near his place at La Honda and then returns to a family farm back home in Oregon. But the reader may feel that he has not achieved anything on his travels. When Tom Jones arrives back home, he knows much more about himself, including who his parents are, and is compensated for his suffering with the hand of his true love Sophia. By the time the family in *Humphry Clinker* (1771), Tobias Smollett's great picaresque novel, returns home, they have found sons, fathers, husbands, wives, and good health. In all cases, those who went out confused and innocent return happier and more mature. The end of *The Electric Kool-Aid Acid Test* suggests something else. Perhaps the Pranksters did achieve some insight during their journeys and the Acid Tests. Certainly the followers of the Grateful Dead, who sometimes called their twenty years of touring a continuation of what the Pranksters started, thought so. But Wolfe's narrative, ending with the characters back where they started, suggests something else. It suggests that the whole strange trip was really futile, that it did not take anyone anywhere, that people got hurt along the way, and that Babbs is right when he chants, "We Blew It!"

Radical Chic & Mau-Mauing
the Flak-Catchers
(1970)

"Like . . . this is what we want, man. [. . .] We want the same thing
as you, we want peace. We want to come home at night and be with
the family . . . and turn on the TV . . . and smoke a little *weed* . . . you
know? . . . and get a little high . . . you dig? . . . and we'd like to get
into that bag, like anybody else. But we can't do that . . . see . . . because if they send in the pigs to rip us off and brutalize our families,
then we have to fight."
"I couldn't agree with you more!"
—Black Panther Field Marshal Don Cox and
Maestro Leonard Bernstein (66)

When Leonard Bernstein gave a party for the Black Panthers on January
14, 1970, it created a furor. Bernstein was one of the most important of
American composers. He had written both for Broadway (*West Side
Story*) and the classical concert hall ("Chichester Psalms"), and he was
successful in bringing different musical worlds together in pieces with
titles such as "Prelude, Fugue, and Riffs." He was the most famous conductor in the country, leading the New York Philharmonic Orchestra.
He was also an international celebrity, and even, in America, a TV star,
thanks to his Young People's Concerts. In contrast, the Black Panther
Party was, to many, the dark shadow of the Civil Rights movement. The
mainstream Civil Rights movement, associated with Martin Luther King,
Jr., was committed to nonviolence and rooted in the church. It held to

traditional American values and manners and had integration as its goal. The Black Panther Party, on the other hand, advocated violence (in at least some contexts), and rejected both the church and many traditional American ideals. It embraced socialist and even Maoist doctrines, adopted the styles of the counterculture and third-world insurgents, and had as its goal either black separatism or revolution. The Panthers were also thought by many to be simply criminals dressed up as revolutionaries. The spectacle of Bernstein, the representative of high culture—and, thanks to his wealth and fame, of high society, as well—entertaining the most frightening elements of the underclass aroused both disgust and derision.

Tom Wolfe did not start the controversy, though he had arranged to be present for the event. Charlotte Curtis, the women's news editor of the *New York Times*, also attended. (In this period most newspapers covered society news in what were called the "women's pages.") Curtis's report of the event was by no means unfriendly, but it brought a hail of criticism down on the Bernsteins and those who were planning to follow their example. When Wolfe presented his own version of the party a few months later, he was able to describe the event in great detail and reflect on the whole phenomenon which he called "radical chic," and an expanded version of this essay is the first half of Wolfe's fourth book.

The Black Panthers were the most famous of the black radical groups of 1960s, but they were by no means the only one. Wolfe researched some of the others on the West Coast, where the Panthers had also been organized. His description of their interactions, not with high society, but with middle-level bureaucrats, forms the other half of the book. *Mau-Mauing the Flak Catchers* describes how the poverty-program bureaucracy and various pressure groups, some of them little more than street gangs, interact, each in a strange way needing the other in order to maintain its own power base. The ritualized "confrontations" allow the various minority groups to at least seem to be taking a stand against the "Establishment," thus validating their own positions of leadership, while at the same time allowing the bureaucrats to identify minority leaders with whom they can then work.

Both parts of the book frequently use the verb "mau-mau," which Wolfe introduced to the wider language in its contemporary sense of confronting someone, especially a public official, with the intent of gaining concessions or benefits through intimidation. Wolfe took the word from then current street slang, but it has its own grim history. The Mau Mau were the members of the Kikuyu people of Kenya who in the early 1950s rebelled against British colonial rule in their country. Their campaign of sabotage, which included attacks on white civilians, brought a crackdown by the British, and thousands died—including some whites, but more Africans loyal to the British and still more rebels. Jomo Kenyatta, who had been jailed by the British as a Mau Mau leader in 1952, did become the first prime minister of an independent Kenya in 1962, but by that point Mau Mau had become a byword for violence. The issue of the hideous violence in the cause of liberation—"the white child hacked in bed"—gave West Indian poet Derek Walcott the subject for one of his most famous poems, "A Far Cry from Africa" (1962). The Mau Mau entered American popular culture through the 1957 film *Something of Value*, in which Sidney Poitier plays a Mau Mau leader and Rock Hudson his white friend whose little sister and brother are murdered by the rebels. African Americans who go in for mau-mauing are invoking a frightening image of savagery—and also trading on a history not their own. In the contexts Wolfe describes, violence is constantly invoked, but the threat of it is mostly a sham. Instead, violent resistance is mostly a pose struck to gain one's ends through one or another status system.

STRUCTURE AND POINT OF VIEW

Radical Chic & Mau-Mauing the Flak-Catchers comprises, as the title suggests, two separate pieces. Taken together, however, they do form a sort of matched set on the excesses of the late 1960s politics. *Radical Chic* shows the upper classes looking down in dismay on the strife below them; *Mau-Mauing the Flak-Catchers* shows the lower classes pressing up against bureaucracies that hardly know how to deal with them. In both cases, a great deal of the status issue has to do with not being part of the bourgeoisie, the great middle class. The elite wish to maintain their status above it; the activist groups would lose their power if they joined, rather than frightened, it. The book is about social extremes—and about those who are fairly pleased to be at social extremes. The middle classes appear in, perhaps, only two roles: as the servants in the elite's world and the flak catchers in that of the activists.

The pieces are not in the first person, though Wolfe does present his own impressions. For example, he describes in detail the flavor of the hors d'oeuvres served at the Bernsteins' party. For the most part, he describes the events as a neutral observer, or lets observations float freely, as if that is what everyone is thinking. Much of the language is impersonal. Instead of "I" or "they," the narrating voice uses "one" or "you." The focus is thus not on the observer but on the observed. The various status details Wolfe picks out are allowed to speak for themselves and reflect on their owners or wearers, rather than revealing what catches the eye of a dramatized narrator.

In *Radical Chic*, Wolfe moves through the evening at the Bernsteins' and then describes its aftermath sequentially. At several points, however, he focuses on some observed detail and then digresses for several pages in order to place that observation in the context of the general social pattern he is describing. Noticing that the Bernsteins' servants are white, he explores the problems faced by those who wish both to ensure their status by having servants and to appear as tribunes of the lower classes. The announcement that contributions to the defense fund will not be tax deductible leads him explore how political organizations became more chic than purely charitable ones. Other observations lead him to discuss the place of Jews in American society and politics. The discussions of larger social issues, in other words, are sandwiched between sections that illustrate them by describing what is happening in a specific instance.

Mau-Mauing the Flak Catchers has a similar structure. Sections of description alternate with sections of commentary and historical exposition. Here, however, there is no connecting narrative. In *Radical Chic*, the reader is always taken back to what happens next in the story of the party. In *Mau-Mauing the Flak Catchers*, each confrontation is an independent set piece, unrelated to the others. They do build up to a climax, however, in that the importance of the flak catchers increases. We first see a mid-level bureaucrat in shirtsleeves facing a few protestors in the bare anteroom of a poverty office; the piece ends with the mayor of San Francisco meeting a crowd of children and their dashiki-clad leader in the gold and marble "Great Central Court" of City Hall.

PLOT

In *Radical Chic* Leonard and Felicia Bernstein host a party to raise money for a defense fund for several members of the Black Panther Party, a black militant group. The guests come from very different groups. The Black Panthers, some of whom have recently been arrested and are out on bail, are from the revolutionary fringe of the Civil Rights movement. Most of the rest of the guests, however, are firmly in the Establishment, either as members of New York society or as luminaries in the arts. Indeed, the appeal of the event is the idea of real revolutionaries in a palatial Park Avenue apartment.

After the guests are greeted, the Panthers' lawyers talk about the injustice of the recent arrests of black militants, trying to appeal to the Jews and other traditional liberals in the audience by comparing them to Hitler's early actions against the Jews. Pledges of support begin to pour in. When the Panthers themselves speak, however, they soon show a certain amount of anti-Semitism of their own: one of them talks about "donations" from merchants who exploit the black community, and everyone is uncomfortable, since it is clear that the "donations" are extorted and the merchants are Jews. The situation is partly defused when one guest asks whom one should contact to put on a party of one's own, making it clear that the interest is as much social as political.

As the evening continues, the contrast between the Panthers' radical views and the liberal views of their hosts becomes obvious again and again, but disagreements are embarrassing and are mostly glossed over. The Panthers' rhetoric is violent—"The only power we have is the power to destroy," says Don Cox: and their politics are Marxist—Cox wants "the means of production" to be "taken from the businessmen." Film Director Otto Preminger sometimes disagrees, arguing that the United States is a more just society than the Panthers claim and bringing up issues like the plight of Soviet Jewry. Bernstein himself sometimes seems to be trying to turn the event into a group therapy session, while television journalist Barbara Walters, who is frightened by the talk of violence, tries to connect with the Panthers' women as fellow mothers. All is smoothed over, however, and the Bernsteins and Cox go on talking for hours after the party breaks up, not realizing the furor that will ensue when a story about the evening appears in the *New York Times*.

Charlotte Curtis's article is, in fact, rather friendly. But when the story is distributed by the *Times* news service, the reaction from outside New York society is negative. The *Times* itself runs an editorial denouncing the event, using terms including "elegant slumming" and "group therapy" and suggesting that to patronize the Panthers, with their "confusion of Mao-Marxist ideology and Fascist para-militarism," mocked the memory of Martin Luther King. The Bernsteins try to defend the event, but most reaction is still negative. People call Bernstein a masochist for hosting a group that despises him. The Panthers' anti-Semitism has been largely ignored in the intellectual world, but many middle-class Jews find it genuinely threatening. In Miami, Jewish pickets force a movie theater to stop showing a film of Bernstein conducting the Israeli Philharmonic to celebrate Israel's victory in the Six-Day War. United Press International quotes him as calling the Panthers "a bad lot," but he tells the *Times* that he did not actually say that. He does, however, say that he does not support their philosophy, with its advocacy of violence and hostility to Israel. It looks as if the controversy will follow him for some time to come, and other society hosts decide to build their events around less controversial causes.

Mau-Mauing the Flak-Catchers describes how various radical groups use intimidation to achieve first attention and then funding from the poverty programs. These "confrontations" have the advantage of proving that the radical leader can make the white authority figure feel personal fear. (They are thus very different from the "demonstrations" of mainstream Civil Rights groups, which seek to persuade and to bring black and white together in a common purpose.) All the same, there is little real danger in any confrontation; to actually hurt anyone would kill the goose that laid the golden egg. The group leaders Wolfe calls Chaser and Dudley, who are not so different from street gang leaders, become masters at pressing the authorities just far enough to get what they want.

The confrontations, while embarrassing, also serve a purpose for the administrators of the poverty programs. They allow them to determine who the leaders of the ghetto community are, since they are clearly not the essentially middle-class leaders of the traditional Civil Rights groups. The "poverty professionals" are looking for the "natural leaders" and "charismatic figures" in the community, and Chaser and Dudley prove they play that role by mobilizing angry crowds. The events Wolfe describes are essentially rituals through which groups validate themselves to the poverty professionals and thereby receive funding. The funding is more likely to help those running poverty programs than any constituency they claim to serve, but that seems to be a secondary consideration both for the "natural leaders" of the community and for the government officials who want to seem to be doing something about social problems and avoid the embarrassment of having angry crowds in their offices.

CHARACTERS

Radical Chic

Leonard Bernstein, the central figure in *Radical Chic*, seems on top of the world. He is not only at the top of his profession, he also seems as prosperous as can be in other ways. He has achieved great wealth, and his house displays it tastefully. He is surrounded by friends. He seems to be physically flourishing as well. He is a short man, but is "trim" and seems tall. His head is "noble," with just enough gray hair to show that he has achieved a certain maturity while remaining the "wunderkind" of American music. Nevertheless, Wolfe suggests that there is uneasiness in Bernstein's life. Wolfe captures that uneasiness by describing a vision Bernstein had after awaking in the middle of the night on his forty-eighth birthday. He is on stage trying to deliver an antiwar message, but all that comes out is "I love." A black man appears and, speaking like a radio announcer, says, "The audience is curiously embarrassed." After another failure, Bernstein get his message out. He thinks about delivering such a speech in real life but rejects the idea and is left wondering who the black man announcing that Bernstein is making a fool of himself can be.

That may be in part because he is trying to move his influence beyond the musical and into the wider culture. He would like to take the celebrity he has and use it to improve the world around him, to speak out against the war in Vietnam and injustice at home. But there he is much less sure of his audience. In a political debate, he is not in control as he is before his orchestra. What is more, it is unclear exactly what his position is. Socially, that instability is revealed even by the mix of status markers in his clothes, even though he carries them off well. The blue blazer and Black Watch tartan slacks say establishment, the black turtleneck and medallion say, if not radical, a least "swinger," and the mixture of the two roles is unstable. (There is, on the other hand, no question of what role the maestro is playing when he is in white tie and tails.) Bernstein is also not clear on whether he is a partisan of the Black Panthers or a free, inquiring intellectual. The latter role is clearly the one in which he is more comfortable. He would like to turn the evening at his apartment into a free, open, and exciting conversation—with himself at its center, to be sure. He therefore brings up many of the issues the Black Panthers would have to discuss in an open debate. But he does not press any of those issues, since to question even the Panthers' most extreme views seems to be somehow in bad taste in this society, and so he falls back on agreeing with their statements again and again.

Bernstein is finally frustrated because the new political role he tries to play leads people to question the sorts of moral authority he had gained already. Pressing forward to assist the dubious fringes of the "black power" movement leads people to suspect his loyalty to the Jews. Such attacks are particularly galling because his own Judaism is something he asserts, rather than downplays—"Bern-STEIN, not—steen"—and because of his active support for Israel. And his real concern for the poor (mixed as it may be with other motives) is turned into a source of mirth by the middlebrow press. It all suggests that while he is secure in his material position, the social eminence is precarious.

Felicia Bernstein seems free of her husband's anxieties. She handles both the flare-ups at the party and the aftermath much more calmly than Bernstein himself does. She seems to have the more intense political interests. It is, in fact, her party for the Panthers, one at which Bernstein jokingly refers to himself as a guest while making his pledge. Felicia, more than anyone else, controls the events of the evening, either in her own voice of through her assistant. (Bernstein, on the other hand, seems almost a loose cannon that she has to quiet at one point.) She seems very much a part of the elegant setting he has created. She is described as a sort of timeless beauty, with a classic sense of style and a "theatrical voice." She greets all her guests, whether they are in the Panthers' paramilitary garb or evening dress with the same style. She is clearly secure in her status.

Other characters are not. There are women who, despite their wealth, too closely ape the styles of the poor, which seems an error in this setting. And there are those who are too eager to exploit the cause for social advancement. Richard Feigen, a recent arrival from Chicago, has just entered the New York art world, and he is moving to establish his position rapidly. He looks like one already secure in his position. At the Bernsteins' party he is not only in a tuxedo, he is wearing it and his "Eaton Square hair" like a "replica 1927 Yale man." His early question, "Who do you call to give a party?" shows that all that matters to him is that there is a new avenue for social advancement, a political complement to the one that leads through the arts.

Other figures are so secure in their social position that they can rock the boat by questioning the Panthers, at least for a moment. Otto Preminger, the film director and actor, quickly joins in the conversation Bernstein starts. Like Bernstein, of course, he is accustomed to being the center of attention. Wolfe renders the thick accent that helped make him such a popular guest on TV talk shows and that had, despite his Jewish background, made him a popular choice for Nazi characters in movies, such as the prison camp commandant in *Stalag 17*. He is willing to demand answers to his questions and to contradict some of the Panthers' more extreme assertions. Nevertheless, he also wants to show his essential agreement with the cause, and we last see him giving Cox a "grip of goodwill and brotherhood." Barbara Walters is also secure enough in her status as a celebrity to question the Panthers. Rather than telling them that what they say is not true, as Preminger does, she tries to connect with them, and especially their wives, as a mother.

Most of the other guests are part of the Bernsteins' own status system, but several are not. The lawyers for the Black Panthers, for example, fall into the despised middle classes and therefore are not as warmly received as their lower class clients. Their language is the language of the Old Left, which has lost much of its resonance and romance. Leon Quat and Gerald Lefcourt still invoke the old struggle with Fascism, over for many years by then. The Black Panthers, on the other hand, invoke contemporary revolutionaries and, more important, a genuine lower class.

The Black Panthers' style is a large part of their appeal, and they adopt that style from third-world revolutionaries. The beret, for example, invokes Che Guevara, the hero of the Cuban revolution killed in 1967 while trying to extend Fidel Castro's revolution to South America. His bereted image became an icon of the counterculture, and the Panthers build on it. They invoke the Cuban revolution and other Communist insurgencies, including that of the Viet Cong, in their language as well as their clothes. The titles in their organization are partly those of a Communist party, partly those of an army, and partly those of an established government— they have a "central committee," a "field marshal," and a "minister of defense"—and they are deliberately not those used by the corresponding American institutions. But the Panthers blend Third-World revolutionaries' styles with inner-city hip. Rather than Che's battle fatigues, which many white radicals affected at the time, they wear tightly fitted pants and leather jackets. They are projecting not just an aura of radicalism but one of dangerous masculinity.

The Panther Wolfe focuses on is Don Cox. He is physically imposing and his style is impressive. His speech is a mixture of memorized rhetoric, complete with elaborate titles, and street language. While his presence captivates his hearers—and opens their wallets—there is little real connection when the dialogue begins. He seems not to be acquainted with the ideas and events they cite (Preminger suggests he does not read) and the white guests prefer to pass over the truly radical implications of what he does say. It is almost as if he is present not as an interlocutor but as an exhibit. The other Panthers at the event, and the wives of their imprisoned comrades, seem to be there more as props than as participants.

Besides the patrons and the black militants, the narrative also includes the journalists. Charlotte Curtis is always present with her notebook open. When she jots down her last notes, the party is over. Her story, however, is what brings about the controversy, a controversy that she, at least, handles with aplomb. The other journalist, Wolfe himself, is present only by implication.

Mau-Mauing the Flak Catchers

The characters in *Mau-Mauing the Flak Catchers* are all presented superficially. We see them in their public performances and never see any part of their interior lives. For the most part we are told only their street names or their job titles, not their real names. That method of presentation is appropriate, for Wolfe's point is that mau-mauing is largely a performance, a ritual in which the characters play established roles. There is, all the same, some variety among them.

Chaser is more the radical organizer along the lines of the Black Panthers, though without their genuine violence. He dresses in a beret and a dashiki—the African-inspired loose-fitting garment that entered American culture about 1968. He talks constantly and plans everything. He controls his group, and intimidates the authorities, through confrontational displays of masculinity. He keeps his members active by questioning the virility of the lax, and with his two main men, puts on a show of power. One of them talks like a Southern preacher, while the other is simply a physical presence, dressed in a dashiki and tight pants and always bracing his muscles to display his physique.

Dudley, on the other hand, does not go in for masculine display. The style he and his associates prefer is not neo-African but street pimp. He is a powerful man, and he has grown a wild Afro, but the rest of his outfit is the sort of "spurious aristocrat" finery that characterizes the style. Rather than emphasizing his masculinity by flexing his muscles, he does it by not needing to flex them, by being "so cool, so languid, [that he is] almost feminine." The veneer of cool is just that, of course, since he can calmly recess a meeting to hand out a real beating. He is able to work the system with ease, since it seems like just another hustle.

The last of the organizers Wolfe describes brings a sort of Prankster frivolity into the serious business of winning recognition from the authorities. When this leader goes to City Hall, he transforms himself from something like Bill Jackson into Jomo Yarumba, in an elegant dashiki and leopard-skin fez. Unlike his peers, he intimidates not through intimations of violence but through equally powerful ones of embarrassment, creating visions, not of beatings but of melting snow cones in a marble hall.

Yarumba's—or Jackson's—tactics are so creative that he gets to meet Mayor Alioto himself. Most of those going in for mau-mauing, however, confront the nameless "flak catcher." The one that Wolfe describes most closely bears status details that put him firmly in the middle class, such as short-sleeved white shirts with several pens in the pockets. He is not in charge, and once the protestors appear, he is not in any sort of control. They are testing his cool and his masculinity—and he fails the test. When they ask impertinent questions, such as what his salary is, he responds. He does all this, clearly, to keep any situation from escalating into something worse. He has no true power. He is not even a paper tiger. He is the sacrificial lamb for his superiors.

MAJOR THEMES

Several of the themes Wolfe explores in earlier books reappear in new forms in *Radical Chic & Mau-Mauing the Flak Catchers*. The most important of these is status. Here it is presented with double irony, because both pieces in the book describe radical groups that should, in theory, be free of status concerns but are nevertheless thoroughly bound up in them. The Black Panthers themselves have created a status hierarchy with titles to rival an imperial court. They also use a number of status markers from the larger culture, including both their clothing, which is hip and sharp, and their language, which mixes the physically intimidating language of the street and the intellectually intimidating language of the New Left. They themselves are used as status markers by an entirely different section of society. The whole idea of radical chic is that patronizing the politically outré raises a socialite's status in a way that patronizing a hospital or a museum does not.

A related theme is the *nostalgie de la boue* Wolfe also explores in *The Electric Kool-Aid Acid Test*. The attraction of those of the middle or upper classes to a romanticized version of the lower classes is the basis of bohemia in every age—and has also been the affectation of the great and powerful in many periods. Those rejecting middle-class values—the rebellious children of that class in *Acid Test* and the upper classes in *Radical Chic*—imitate the lower classes, the lower and more different the better, both because doing so shocks the bourgeoisie and because there is no danger of their actually being mistaken for a member of that class. It is an act that does not endanger one's real position in the status hierarchy and, in fact, may strengthen it. Another advantage of patronizing those socially or geographically distant—and for New York society, the Oakland-based Panthers are both—is that the new dependents will not be uncomfortably "underfoot." In *Bleak House* Dickens shows a starving English boy resting on the steps of the Society of the Propagation of the Gospel in Foreign Parts; Wolfe makes a similar point by showing the wealthy of New York entertaining the "field marshals" and "ministers of defense" of a group playing at revolution in a city full of genuine poor people.

Among the problems with *nostalgie de la boue* is that it romanticizes poverty. The poor are treated as noble savages—but as savages nonetheless. The stance suggests that the standards of people from the middle and upper classes cannot be expected of those born lower on the social scale. The group gathered in the Bernstein apartment would doubtless blanch at any suggestion of violence—or even of the stockpiling of firearms—by members of their own classes and would be appalled if such suggestions came from white ethnics. Yet violence is almost expected of this black group; it gives them part of their thrill. The cultural expectations are as low as the social and moral ones. Much of Bernstein's work was, laudably, intended to bring high culture to everyone. That was the purpose of the Young People's Concerts and the television appearances. Yet when Cox presents watching TV and smoking weed as his people's vision of happiness, Bernstein claims he agrees entirely. It suggests that he envisions a very different level of development, in every way, for the people he is supposedly celebrating. (That conflict will be the burden of much of the criticism against him, with its contrast of the bourgeois Civil Rights leader Martin Luther King and these outlaw representatives of "black power.")

Bernstein and his friends are not led into these lowered expectations for some blacks simply because of the cult of the noble savage or an unspoken racism, though both may indeed be at work. Rather they are led to espouse dubious positions by "liberal guilt," which is another of Wolfe's major themes. Liberal guilt is, like noblesse oblige, an impulse of those in positions of wealth and power toward those less fortunate. The traditional form of patronage assumes that class divisions are just and that they give those at high levels a duty they must responsibly carry out toward the less fortunate. It tends, of course, to be paternalistic and can imply the ongoing dependency of the poor upon their "betters." The new form, on the other hand, assumes that class divisions are unjust. Wealth and privilege do not place one in a position of responsibility that carries with it duties; they place one in a position of guilt that demands atonement. Since many of society's structures are inevitably unjust, some such feeling may be natural, but it also places one in the paradoxical position of at once occupying a position and deploring it. (There is no conservative guilt because the conservative thinks his place in society, earned or inherited, to be his rightful one.) Bernstein lives in a lovely apartment and talks about how angry it must make Cox to enter it. The question of responsibility also becomes confused for the sufferer from liberal guilt. The old-fashioned philanthropist can feel secure in thinking his very position shows that he knows best. But having first adopted the idea that he is in the wrong, the guilty liberal cannot continue to act from a position of either intellectual or moral superiority; rather, he forfeits that position to the object of his compassion. If the patron's place in society is ill-gotten, the disenfranchised, however they manifest themselves, have the moral authority. That leads to a certain moral hesitancy or irrationality on the part of the patron. He hesitates to question any idea or program advanced by those who wear the badge of the oppressed. In this case, many at the Bernsteins' party are reluctant to question the violence advocated by the Panthers.

The guilty liberal faces another problem, which is the scorn that may be heaped on him by those who find his position not just paradoxical but hypocritical. Bernstein faces that derision from the middlebrow press, such as the *Times* with its comment about "elegant slumming." The problem is exacerbated by ethnic rivalries, which are another of Wolfe's themes. He describes in passing how the "radical chic" host advancing the cause of the Panthers or farm workers may feel scorn from his white servants, who will despise him as a "limousine liberal," someone ready to help distant blacks and browns but dead to the problems of impoverished whites. Most of his attention to group rivalries, however, is focused on Jews, to the point that Wolfe has been accused of showing a tinge of anti-Semitism in the piece. (Wolfe's wife, Sheila Berger, is herself Jewish.) Bernstein finds that the middle-class Jewish community turns on him because it is unwilling to adopt a posture of guilt to any other group, especially ones that attack it. Part of the pose of the guilty liberal is accepting any charge of injustice made by oppressed groups, especially blacks, but middle-class Jews, seeing themselves as an endangered group, are unwilling to accept such slights. The tensions Wolfe describes had just begun to show in the years after the great alliance of blacks and Jews in the Civil Rights movement—and were thus especially uncomfortable for many to read about—but they have become only more obvious as the years have gone by, years during which black leaders both extremist (such as Louis Farrakhan) and mainstream (such as Jesse Jackson) have made more or less vicious anti-Semitic remarks.

Another theme Wolfe raises is the futility of much of the activity so earnestly carried on by both philanthropists and poverty workers. The question is, do the movements that so dramatically gain money from the establishment advance their stated causes or do they only advance the prosperity of their leaders? In *Mau-Mauing the Flak Catchers*, the implication is that neither the poverty programs nor the pressure groups do much good—except as employment programs for those who run them. Certainly the leaders Wolfe describes are out to create their own little empires and ensure their own continuing stream of dollars either from philanthropists or from the poverty programs. While there doubtless were community organizers who were truly committed to their neighborhoods and who may even have used the mau-mauing tactics Wolfe describes for altruistic ends, it is certainly true that many were just as venal as Wolfe suggests. In later years leaders of groups Wolfe mentions, including the Black Panthers and the Blackstone Rangers, were convicted of fraud in the misappropriation of the funds they had received from the government—and, indeed, leaders of both groups also became involved in the drug trade (Chicago Crime Commission 15; Pearson 312). The confrontations they staged certainly put money in the leaders' pockets, whether or not it produced any other results.

A final major theme, masculinity and intimidation, will be explored in the next section.

GENDER, RACE, AND CLASS: A FEMINIST READING OF *RADICAL CHIC & MAU-MAUING THE FLAK CATCHERS*

The major concerns of much contemporary criticism are gender, race, and class. *Radical Chic & Mau-Mauing the Flak Catchers* is about just those issues, but it is particularly interesting to consider the book from the perspective of gender, because the racial and class issues are more overt. Feminist criticism takes many forms, but it always seeks to understand how literature describes or embodies the roles culturally prescribed for women, roles that often leave women powerless.

Critics working from a feminist perspective will be quick to notice that the central interest of many of the male characters is their masculinity— as perceived primarily by other men—and that women are consistently marginalized even in the setting of liberation movements. The very titles of *Radical Chic* and *Mau-Mauing the Flak Catchers* bring up the confrontation of different races and different strata of society, but those confrontations are, in every case, conditioned by the gender roles the participants are playing. Another way in which the two pieces collected in the book are pendants is that one describes the traditionally feminine sphere, the social world, and one the traditionally masculine sphere, the world of work and politics. In each, however, power is related to gender and the assertion of gender roles is related to power and dominance.

In *Radical Chic* the forum is the traditionally feminine sphere. The setting is the living room, not the workplace or a public area, and that is traditionally the domain of the woman. The Bernsteins play out the social convention that the wife is the director of a couple's social life. (In traditional etiquette, the wife handled all social correspondence, issuing all invitations and receiving all replies.) This party, despite its ostensible serious public purpose, follows that convention. Officially, it is Felicia Bernstein's party. She has arranged it, and Bernstein even presents himself as a guest. The very decoration of the room is feminine—Chinese yellow walls with sconces and family photos in silver frames rather than, say, wood paneling and hunting prints.

Into this feminine area comes a strong, masculine presence, and the intrusion of that assertive masculinity is as titillating as the transgressions of political and class boundaries that go along with it. In traditional society, men entering the social sphere are to some extent feminized. They, like women in many settings beyond the social, wear constricting clothing with many unnecessary accoutrements that serve no purpose except the very important one of acting as status markers. The white or black ties, the vests or cummerbunds, the studs and cufflinks and suspenders, all can be read as symbolic restraints as well as markers of high status for the man entering the feminine sphere. In the social sphere men also traditionally restrain their speech. The social setting is supposed, at least, to be the woman's territory, though it can of course be read as simply the stage on which she is most obviously displayed to the male gaze.

In any case, the Black Panthers enter this traditional feminine sphere with no restraints on their masculine display, while most of the white men present are either in formal wear or some almost equally restrained attire. The Panthers' clothes call attention to their bodies. (Traditional male formal wear is usually thought to direct all attention to the face.) Their pants and turtlenecks are tight. Their leather jackets associate them with danger and daring—either the aviator or the motorcycle gang. Their language, in some cases, is that of the gutter. They project an aura of sexual danger.

In projecting such an aura, they are building on several strands of American culture. First, the lower classes in general are usually presented in American popular culture as sexually vibrant, while the upper classes are shown as stuffy and frigid. Movie stars of the lower classes, first Irish, then Italian, and later black and Latino have made careers on that image. (It is an image, of course, that can easily be understood as oppressive, as it romanticizes the exclusion of groups from the classes that hold the real power.) Second, the sexuality of black men was suppressed for centuries. Black men were not allowed to display assertive masculine roles—or even to be called a man rather than a boy. Third, black male sexuality was all the same considered dangerous. Black men were often thought of as predators preying on white women, an idea used to justify America's shameful tradition of lynching. As a corollary to the fear of the black rapist, there was a widespread fantasy of the black lover desired by white women.

In the 1960s, many black men were aggressively casting off any restraints on the display of their sexuality. Certainly part of the appeal of the Panthers was that they were confidently masculine. They did not follow the middle-class standards of the traditional Civil Rights leaders, much less the infantalizing role laid out for Blacks in the Jim Crow South. One of the guests at a party for the Panthers says it explicitly: "These are no civil-rights *Negroes* wearing gray suits three sizes too big—these are *real men*" (54). The same feeling is present at the Bernsteins' party, where "[t]he idea of them, these real revolutionaries, who actually put their lives on the line, runs through Lenny's duplex like a rogue hormone" (6).

It is, of course, significant that what gets the hormones moving is the idea of violence. The willingness to embrace violence both separates the Panthers from the traditional civil rights leaders and, once again, asserts their masculinity. The contrast there is not just with the middle-class black leaders but with the men they are addressing at the Bernsteins'. When Cox asserts that everyone present would defend their families, "every woman in the room thinks of her husband . . . with his cocoa-butter jowls and Dior Men's boutique pajamas . . . ducking into the bathroom and locking the door and turning the shower on, so he can say later he didn't hear a thing" (23). The Panthers win the game of masculine display without a contest.

During the discussion, some men are perhaps cowed by the Panthers' virility. What is still more significant is how thoroughly the discussion is dominated by men—even in this feminine sphere. The women who do speak either do so through male mouthpieces, or are told in effect to return to traditional feminine roles, or try to gain some authority by speaking from traditional feminine roles. The men who speak, on the other hand, especially those who are used to command—Bernstein the conductor and Preminger the director—do so freely. They also feel free to interrupt and restrain themselves only when it seems they have offended their male guest.

It is Felicia's party and her special cause. She, however, says very little in her own voice. Even when playing her social role as the "manager" of the event, she speaks through the little gray man who assists her. When the discussion seems to be going out of control and she does intervene, she does not do it in her own voice. Rather, she reads a letter written by a man. A male voice is the only voice of authority, and to make her point, she must adopt one.

The "ash-blond girl" who tries to join the discussion is not treated as a serious participant. The fact that she is nameless underscores that. She asks what someone without a lot of money can practically do, if there is perhaps a committee she can join. The unattributed voice that silently answers her reduces her to a mere sex object: "Well, baby, if you really—" (59). Moments later, Rick Haynes responds to her by suggesting, in effect, that politics is men's work. In a voice dripping with sarcasm, he infantalizes her: "This *lovely young lady* here was asking about *what she could do.* [. . .] Well, I suggest that this lovely young lady get someone like her *daddy*, who just might have a little more *pull* than she does, to call up the *Wall Street Journal*" (62–63). And Cox rewards that comment with a "right on."

The women who do get a hearing are those who speak primarily in their traditional roles. At an earlier party, the wife of Lee Berry, a Panther seized by the police from his hospital room, speaks as a wife, even introducing herself, in her "small quiet voice," as such: "I am a Panther Wife." Barbara Walters, though she is a journalist and a celebrity, does not join the conversation as such. Rather, she speaks in the traditional female role of mother. She begins by talking about her conversation with one of the Panthers' wives, with whom she made contact saying, "You have a child, and I have a child" and explored the question of violence based on that shared role. Later in the discussion, she addresses, not the whole group, but Mrs. Lee Berry. When Bernstein asks what they have said, the issue has again been seen through the lens of motherhood. Mrs. Berry has said that Walters sounds afraid, and she has responded, "I'm not afraid of you, [. . .] but maybe I am about the idea of the death of my children" (75). Even when the subject is violent revolution, she only speaks from the perspective of the personal, the sphere that is traditionally allotted to women.

When the furor over the party breaks out, part of Bernstein's embarrassment is that he has been forced into the feminine sphere. He is not on a news page but the society page, the "women's section." He has not had a "meeting," which is business, men's work, but a "party," which is society, women's work. And he has been covered, not by a famous man, but only by a well-known woman. Charlotte Curtis has turned out to be as big a challenge to Bernstein's masculinity as the Panthers themselves.

The spectacle of black men and other minorities challenging the masculinity of white men is only a sidelight in *Radical Chic*, since it turns out that even the Panthers are restrained in a social setting, but it is the central subject of *Mau-Mauing the Flak Catchers*. If women are silenced or relegated to traditional female roles in the first piece, they are almost entirely absent from the second, which is set in the traditional masculine spheres of work and politics. Where women do appear, it is sometimes only to show a man using them to play on other men's concerns about their masculinity. Chaser, for example, tells the women in his group not to have anything to do with men who are not contributing to the cause. Even when addressing the women, his real audience is the men, whose masculinity he is challenging. Of course, challenging his own followers' masculinity is merely a prelude to the main event, which is to destroy that of the flak catcher.

The imagery of these confrontations constantly calls attention to the fact that they are essentially ritual displays of masculinity, much like the contests of bulls or stags or peacocks fighting for dominance. The Samoans who visit the poverty agency carry Tiki canes, which serve no purpose except as phallic images and threats of phallic violence. The other groups are dressed up in garb that also announces their status as dangerous men. Even the Flak Catcher, the underling at the poverty agency who must deal with this invasion, tries to prove that he is at least one of the boys and not one to primly cross his legs and look as if he fears immediate castration. Instead he "sits down on [a chair] backwards [. . .] like the head foreman in a bunkhouse" (109).

Part of the purpose of the confrontation is to take away from the authority figure the dignity he expects will be accorded to him. The response of the bureaucrat is not a counter-assertion of dominance but a sign of submission, a smile. "When some bad dude is challenging your manhood, your smile just proves that he is right" (112). As the confrontation goes on, and the Flak Catcher gives way, it is clear who has won this struggle for dominance. The leaders of the confrontation have their images of masculinity bolstered; the bureaucrat has seen his effaced. His efforts to keep some shred of it are pitiful. "The way he [talks], you can tell the man is trying to get back a little corner of his manhood. He tries to take a tone that says, 'You haven't really been in here for the past fifteen minutes intimidating me and burying my nuts in the sand and humiliating me . . . ' " (117). On the other hand, it is only the Flak Catcher, not the authority itself, who has been humiliated. "And even the Flak Catcher himself wasn't losing much. He wasn't losing his manhood. He gave that up a long time ago, the day he became a lifer..." (118–119). The set-piece struggle for validation as the alpha male in the pack really does not mean a thing, since the real alpha male is not disposed to come down to scrap with the mongrels.

This form of confrontation, with all its overtones of masculine struggles for dominance, is another result of the strange history of sexuality in American race relations. The threat of violence—the literal violence of lynching—had suppressed expressions of black masculinity and elevated white. "The *Man* was the white man. He was the only *man*. And now, when you got up close to him and growled, this all-powerful superior animal turned out to be terrified." In fact, "The white man, particularly the educated white man, the leadership, had a deep dark Tarzan mumbo jungle voodoo fear of the black man's masculinity" (119). Different styles of black masculinity, the radical style, the almost feminine "pimp" style, are just different ways of intimidating the former oppressor.

The feminist reader will note that, at least as presented here, all these styles are games played among men, black and white, with women present only as props. What is more, they are just games. Little changes except who gets to enjoy the spoils based on the confrontations. And even those are rigged. The poverty money will go to someone, and the men in charge do not much mind if their subordinates suffer a little embarrassment in the process of deciding who is enough of an authentic leader—a good enough master of the art of confrontation—to get it. The many real issues women might bring up, be it equal pay or enforceable child support or domestic violence, are ignored, while the males in power, both in the halls of government and in the streets, play their little game of dominance.

The world of *Radical Chic & Mau-Mauing the Flak Catchers* has little room for women, especially active women, and its men are obsessed with proving their own masculinity by intimidating other men. Since Wolfe's interests have always focused on both masculinity and status, it is not surprising that he would depict such a world—though one could hardly suggest that such a world was not already there for him to describe. A feminist critic might add that a world in which men make social arrangements by displays of ferocity like those of rutting deer and women must either keep silent or appear only as wives, mothers, or sex objects is one that needs to be changed—and that in some areas, thankfully, already has been. Since feminists do, in fact, tend to have a good sense of humor, he or she might also add that Wolfe's depiction of that world as it was is still very funny.

6

The Right Stuff
(1979)

Yea!!!!
—Spontaneous reaction of a restaurant full of baby boomers in St. Louis when a television announced that 77-year-old John Glenn had once again been safely launched into space

During the 1960s there was probably no group of Americans more genuinely admired and subjected to less critical scrutiny than the astronauts of the Mercury, Gemini, and Apollo programs. In the midst of an unpopular war, racial strife, and bewildering social changes, the Space Program was the one area where America seemed not only to be doing something unquestionably good but also doing it right. The romance of exploration was part of the aura that enveloped the astronauts. But that aura included several other elements as well. One was sheer admiration of bravery. They were literally willing "to boldly go where no man has gone before," as *Star Trek* put it. Another was admiration of technical prowess. That the nation could put a man in space showed that it was not, as it sometimes seemed, an aging power that had seen its best days. Finally, the astronauts seemed to be the nation's champions in the Cold War. While success in that struggle seemed dubious in other arenas, such as the proxy war in Vietnam, in the "space race" America came from behind and triumphed. The astronauts became universally known and almost revered as the embodiment of so many good things.

The astronauts might seem an odd choice of subject for Tom Wolfe.

Up to this point, much of his work had been about pretense—the bohemian pose, the radical pose. In *The Right Stuff*, he wrote about the real
thing, the qualities he genuinely admired. He is, nonetheless, exploring
some of the issues that have always interested him, only now as epic
rather than farce—although there is still a good deal of farce in his narrative. He is dealing with his constant theme of status, only here status
is achieved not through purely symbolic things like clothing but by skill
and action. Status is again associated with a certain conception of manhood. (That the Space Program could be seen as a test of manhood was
not lost on anyone who thought about it: poets as diverse as W.H. Auden
and C.S. Lewis had seen the rocket as an image of phallic power.)

The astronauts and test pilots, it turns out, have something in common
not just with Junior Johnson but also with Neil Cassady, Ken Kesey, and
the Hell's Angels—and that is not only that they all think they are masters of any vehicle on wheels. Rather, like these outlaws, there is something real about the astronauts, something proved through a willingness
to face danger. They are not just posing. They have a rare authenticity.
These men, however, are as authentic when acting like Boy Scouts as
they are when acting like outlaws—and they do both. That there was an
outlaw appeal to the life of the military flier would not have surprised
even the Hell's Angels. They, after all, took their name from Howard
Hughes's *Hell's Angels* (1930), a film Wolfe mentions in *The Right Stuff*.
Even the language sometimes echoes the earlier books. When Gus Grissom meets the squadron he will fly with in Korea, all the men who have
not been shot at by a MiG have to stand up. By the next day, Grissom
is sitting down: he has sought out a fight with a Chinese fighter "just so
he could have a seat on the bus" (42). Wolfe is using Ken Kesey's most
famous maxim to describe a world very different from that of the Merry
Pranksters.

Wolfe's immediate audience knew the story of the space program in
a way that later readers may not, and that influenced the way the book
was read—and written. Wolfe is telling a story that his readers know,
so while he describes scenes in new detail, he also can count on many
references being evocative. The reader who lived through the 60s would
know not just that Neil Armstrong would go on to be the first man to
walk on the moon, but that Pete Conrad became a Gemini astronaut and
traveled to the moon on Apollo XII, that Deke Slayton finally made it
into space years after being grounded during Project Mercury, and that
Gus Grissom died in a launch pad fire while preparing for the first
Apollo flight. The book, in fact, ends with the recognition that the days
when the names of the Original Seven Astronauts were household words

are fading. Wolfe chronicles a special time, when people really did feel a deep personal investment in men who seemed to be risking all in a truly glorious cause.

PLOT

Wolfe begins the story of the astronauts by describing the culture that produced them. He follows a group of navy test pilots and their wives, particularly Pete and Jane Conrad, through their training and first assignments in the mid 1950s. Many of Pete's comrades are killed in flying accidents, and waiting for news of a missing pilot and attending funerals become regular parts of their lives. These young men are clearly different from the other young men of their generation. On entering flight training, they have joined a new culture and are shaped by its values. The competition to excel as fliers has given them a different view of danger and success: being at the top of the profession is more important than any consideration of risk. And the man at the top of the profession is air force test pilot Chuck Yeager.

As Wolfe presents it, Yeager helped create the whole ethos of test flying while working at Muroc Field, later Edwards Air Force Base, in the Mojave Desert. In 1947, while still only twenty-four, he is selected to try to "break the sound barrier," that is, to fly a plane faster than Mach 1, the speed of sound. Some consider the feat impossible, and a civilian pilot has turned down the project because the air force will not pay him a bonus to face the danger. Yeager, however, takes the task in stride and carries on the usual life of a test pilot as the date for the attempt approaches. He injures himself during a midnight horseback ride just before the flight but does not let his broken ribs deter him from finding a way to operate the X-1 rocket plane. The attempt is a success, and the horseback riding injuries just provide another example of Yeager's apparent ability to handle any problem, whether a malfunctioning machine or a fellow pilot delirious from lack of oxygen. Yeager does not immediately achieve the public acclaim he deserves—when a film called *Breaking the Sound Barrier* is produced, it recounts and embellishes the life of a British test pilot, not Yeager's accomplishment—but he is renowned among his fellow pilots.

The whole country looks to the fraternity of test pilots a few years later, while the Soviet Union launches Sputnik, the first artificial satellite, in 1957. The United States is locked in the Cold War with the Soviet Union, especially since the Soviets developed a nuclear bomb, and leaders such as House Majority Leader Lyndon Johnson declare that whoever controls "the high ground" of space will control the world. The test pilots know the United States is on track to put not just satellites but manned vehicles in space. They assume the first Americans in space will come from the Edwards test pilots and will fly vehicles that build on the X-series planes that Yeager and others have tested and that these vehicles will be propelled by rockets planned for production in the next two to three years. The nation's political leaders, however, want immediate action. They want to make sure the first man in space will be American, so they choose to take a "quick and dirty approach," using existing Redstone and Atlas rockets. The vehicle launched will not be a ship flown by a pilot but a capsule or pod occupied by a passenger or research subject who cannot control its movements. The endeavor, which is called Project Mercury, is put in the hands of NASA, the National Aeronautics and Space Administration.

Test pilots are not at first part of the plan, since the astronauts will be less "star voyagers," which is what the word means, and more guinea pigs subject to endless medical tests and unable to take control of the vessel. (The plan is, in fact, for the capsule to be occupied by a chimpanzee for the first fights.) President Eisenhower, however, decrees that the pool of applicants for astronaut positions be restricted to test pilots. It is not certain that many will apply. The commander at Edwards tells his top pilots that the astronaut job would be a waste of their abilities: they would not be flying; they would just be "Spam in a can." Many pilots do wonder whether Project Mercury will advance or sidetrack their careers. Most who are invited to apply, however, do so. The project, which is supposed to be dangerous and volunteer-only, looks like the equivalent of a combat mission, and that is something they have been trained never to refuse. Besides, since the pilot can control the "attitude" of the capsule in case of malfunctions, there may be something like real flying involved in it after all.

Pilots including Pete Conrad, Wally Schirra, and Alan Shepard undergo extensive testing first at the Lovelace Clinic in Albuquerque and then at Wright-Patterson Air Force Base in Ohio. The tests are often humiliating and seem to have little to do with flying. Pete Conrad rebels, protesting to the commander and playing jokes on the staff. Others play along with program, and John Glenn and Scott Carpenter take all the tests seriously, especially the physical ones, and they excel at them. Their plan turns out to be the more prudent, since they are selected and Conrad is not.

The introduction of the seven Mercury astronauts is a great media event. John Glenn is perfectly at ease before the cameras and happy to talk about his patriotism, his Presbyterian faith, and his happy home life. Talking about things like that makes most of the other astronauts uncomfortable, but they recognize that Glenn really means what he says. They are troubled when they are asked if they are confident of "coming back from outer space," since it suggests that the press and public think of them not as skilled pilots but as daring boys going on a suicide mission for God and country. Others think the same thing: when asked about the astronauts, Yeager remarks that there is little flying in Project Mercury and adds that "a monkey's gonna make the first flight" (127). Such doubts do not diminish the public adulation the astronauts receive. They are given a lucrative deal with *Life* magazine that also ensures they are protected from the rest of the press, and soon first the astronauts and then their wives are featured on the magazine's cover.

The image presented of them is thoroughly sanitized. While some, like John Glenn, are straight arrows, others keep up the old pilots' tradition of testing themselves through Drinking & Driving and so forth. Especially when far from their wives while training at Cape Canaveral or making visits of encouragement to the plants fabricating their equipment, some enjoy the sexual attentions of aviation groupies. John Glenn rebukes his colleagues for endangering their reputations and thus the mission itself through sexual indiscretions. The dressing-down from a colleague irks some of them, especially Alan Shepard, though most agree that Glenn has a point. Their conflicts are not reported and do not disrupt their training.

The training is not like flight training. Rather than learning to do things, they are learning what things will feel like by repeating every part of the planned missions in simulators, including some in centrifuges that simulate G-forces and planes that create moments of weightlessness. The astronauts, however, work to change the mission so that they will be more than test subjects, in part because they are irked by comments made about them by their colleagues at Edwards. They are able to force NASA to redesign the capsules so that they can, if need be, guide the booster rocket on liftoff and handle re-entry entirely manually.

For a time it looks as if the program is in trouble. The Edwards pilots taking the X-15 up to the borders of space are making progress, while Project Mercury seems to be failing: test rockets are blowing up on the pad. The astronauts fear that, after all the adulation, they will in the end accomplish nothing. They are also dealing with competition among themselves to pilot the first mission. Glenn seems to be the front-runner, but then the project's director decides to make the selection by a peer vote among the astronauts. Alan Shepard is selected as the prime pilot, with Glenn and Grissom as backups. Glenn is appalled, especially because NASA announces only that one of the three will make the first flight, and the press continues to treat him as if he will be the first man into space.

That man turns out to be none of the Mercury astronauts, but Yuri Gagarin, a Soviet cosmonaut. Project Mercury still presses ahead. Alan Shepard makes a successful sub-orbital flight and becomes a genuine national hero. Gus Grissom makes a similarly successful flight, but after splashdown his capsule's hatch opens and although he is rescued, the spacecraft fills with water and sinks. Many suspect that he opened it himself out of panic, but he denies that, and his career seems unaffected. The Soviets have by this point put a man in orbit, so the other sub-orbital Mercury missions are canceled. John Glenn becomes the first American to orbit the Earth. In the course of his flight, it becomes clear that ground control is concerned about something. The heat shield may not be firmly in place, and if it is lost during reentry, the capsule will burn up in the atmosphere. Glenn is troubled that ground control will not tell him, the pilot, about the problem directly, but he accomplishes all the tasks the new situation requires. He splashes down safely and finds himself receiving even more adulation than Shepard did. The astronauts are now part of President Kennedy's circle, and thanks to their success, Kennedy commits the United States to putting a man on the moon by 1970.

Project Mercury is losing some of its pioneer feeling as the program moves into extensive new quarters in Houston. What is more, a philosophical split is developing between those, like Glenn and Scott Carpenter, who are interested in the scientific aspects of the project and those who take a purely "operational" view of it, thinking that a test pilot's job is to get the ship working correctly, not to collect data about other subjects. The next flight, by Carpenter, seems to bolster the "operational" side's arguments. He spends much of the flight investigating an interesting phenomenon that Glenn had noticed, and in doing so uses too much of the fuel needed to prepare the ship for reentry. For a time it is feared that his ship has been lost, but he splashes down safely, albeit 250 miles beyond the target area. Despite the hero's welcome he receives, he begins to feel a cold shoulder from some of his colleagues, and flight director Chris Craft says he will never fly again. The pilots of the final two Mercury missions, Wally Schirra and Gordon Cooper, make their flights purely operational, cutting all the distracting experiments they can. Cooper also proves beyond doubt that the astronauts are real pilots, since he brings his craft down manually after several of its instruments have malfunctioned. The great era of the Edwards test pilots, on the other hand, is nearing its end. Several of them have joined NASA's astronaut corps. Chuck Yeager is commanding a new school at Edwards that is both part of the Air Force's plan to create a separate military space program using "lifting bodies" and a means of preparing Air Force pilot's for the NASA astronaut corps. On the same day that the secretary of defense announces the end of the X-20 program, and thus of all prospects of a military space program, Yeager dramatically bails out of a plane he is preparing to use for a new altitude record. Despite severe injuries, he returns to duty and flies many combat missions in Southeast Asia. The days of the rivalry between the astronauts and the Edwards test pilots are over. And quite soon, the era in which the astronauts are true national heroes fades away as well, since with the creation of the hotline and the test ban treaty, the most dangerous phase of the Cold War has ended. Astronauts now, however admired they may be, will not provoke the tears of gratitude they once did.

STRUCTURE AND POINT OF VIEW

The structure of *The Right Stuff* reflects Wolfe's belief that the story of the Mercury astronauts began long before the space program was conceived. In Wolfe's view, the astronauts were not just amazing individuals. They were the products of a specific culture—a particular "statusphere": that of the military test pilot. He therefore describes that culture before going on to chronicle Project Mercury. That culture includes not just the pilots but also their families. Throughout the book, the point of view shifts from that of the wives of the fliers waiting for news to that of the fliers themselves. Wolfe also alternates sections describing the new breed of pilots, the astronauts, with the old breed, the pilots out at Edwards Air Force Base. (The men are actually the same age.) By the end of the book, the astronauts have met the standards of the test pilot fraternity, and the glory days of test flight are over.

As in *The Electric Kool-Aid Acid Test*, the point of view is sometimes determined by Wolfe's sources, and paying attention to point of view allows the reader to determine where Wolfe gets his information. The reader can tell that Bill Bridgeman is a source when Wolfe says, "it didn't dawn on him until years later" that Yeager, a younger man, had called him son (67). What Bridgeman realized is something only he could report. The reader can also tell that Jane Conrad and Betty Grissom are sources, since we hear what they are thinking. All that remains in doubt is whether Wolfe's information comes from interviews or their published writing. Once again, careful use of point of view takes the place of a scholarly apparatus.

CHARACTERS

While most of the characters were well known to the American public at the time *The Right Stuff* was published, the fame of one of the most important had already been eclipsed. Chuck Yeager, the man who broke the sound barrier, never achieved the sort of universal adulation that went to the Mercury astronauts. Yet Wolfe sees him as the model for many American fliers, including the astronauts. He begins his description of Yeager by describing his style of speech. The soft Appalachian drawl that passengers often hear from the airline cockpit, the one with a self-assured calm that suggests everything is under control, even as it reports some problem that must be dealt with, has spread through the whole of American aviation, and Yeager is its source. His voice reported on the behavior of the newest and most dangerous of experimental aircraft, and it became the model first for other test pilots, and then for the rest of the profession.

Yeager comes from Lincoln County, West Virginia, and after high school he is headed for the gas drilling business in which the rest of his family works. But with war in sight, he enlists in the army air corps in 1941. In his first eight missions over France and Germany, Yeager shoots down two German fighters. On his next mission, he is shot down over France. Wounded, he makes his way through Spain back to England. He returns to combat in time for the Allied invasion of France. On October 12, 1944, he shoots down five German fighters. On November 6, while piloting a prop plane, he shoots down one of the new German jets and damages two more. By the end of the war, he is credited with thirteen and a half kills.

Yeager's achievements are all based in his abilities. He has worked his way up, and he continues to prove himself constantly. Though he is commissioned as an officer, he does not have the college degree that most officers have, and that, in fact, disqualifies him from consideration when the Mercury astronauts are being selected. What he does have, aside from the skills of a great pilot, is the willingness to test himself every day, both in the air and on the ground. He takes up the most dangerous planes, and once off the flight line, he drinks hard and drives fast. Most importantly, as the drawl from the cockpit shows, he remains cool and efficient in the face of any problem. Other pilots imitate Yaeger's drawl to show they can reflect the same cool efficiency in the face of danger. Yeager's hands-on piloting is constantly contrasted with the sort of automatic, pre-experienced flying the astronauts do, even as they fight to prove that they have both the coolness and the flying skills Yeager embodies.

In personality, at least, the other central character in *The Right Stuff* seems a great contrast to Yeager. John Glenn, the most famous of the seven original astronauts, has not climbed his way up from the gas fields, and his voice has a choirboy's earnestness unlike Yeager's cool. He shares, however, Yeager's excellent flying record as a Marine Corps pilot. He has been in combat in both World War II and Korea and made the first coast-to-coast supersonic flight. On the ground, though, he is neither a fast driver nor a hard drinker. He drives an aging Peugeot, an underpowered car that is a great contrast to the Corvettes and Triumphs and other sports cars the rest of the astronauts drive. And while the other astronauts may blow off steam partying, John Glenn rises early to do miles of roadwork in full view of everyone.

Glenn's lifestyle seems not just Spartan but ostentatiously Spartan. In the same way, his idealistic and fluent speech at public appearances seems designed to attract attention to himself—and perhaps improve his chances of becoming prime pilot on the project. He is, of course, in competition with all the other pilots to be selected for the first Mercury flight. His lifestyle is utterly sincere, but it may also make him a more attractive candidate for the top slot, and ambition has never been something he has spurned—as shown by his record of finding the assignments in which he can most distinguish himself, in peace and war. Glenn is ready to excel in the space program, which strikes him as a new branch of the military, even if it is officially a civilian operation. It has the same urgency of war and the same joyous patriotic esprit—and on top of that, no one outranks him. Glenn's straight-arrow character and ambition seem early in the book to make him a military goody-two-shoes, especially in contrast with the other pilots. But in the end, his integrity makes him an attractive character. He is willing to tell off his comrades for their sexual indiscretions—but he is also willing to tell off the administrator of NASA when he thinks the space agency is trying to exploit Glenn's wife for political purposes, even though it may mean losing his chance to go into space. When he talks about family, as when he talks about country, he means it.

Glenn is in his element in public appearances, which turn out to be a large part of the astronauts' duties. The three naval aviators in the group,

222

Alan Shepard, Wally Schirra, and Scott Carpenter, may not be so enthusiastic about the appearances, but they have both the social skills and the charm to handle them. Scott Carpenter has the most in common with Glenn. Carpenter shares Glenn's sincere devotion to family, having even done something unimaginable to most pilots, choosing to fly multiengine patrol planes rather than fighters because of his wife's concerns for his safety. He also shares Glenn's interest in the scientific aspects of the space program, something that most of the astronauts think of as a distraction from the serious business of flying.

Alan Shepard is the most private of the group, a man with no intimates. He, in fact, perplexes his fellow pilots. There are two sides to his personality, which Wolfe names the Icy Commander and Smilin' Al. The first, a punctiliously correct naval officer who neither drinks nor smokes and attends a Christian Science church with his wife, is the one they see most often in their Virginia base. The second, who is smiling and friendly and enjoys fast cars and a good time, appears more often when they are away from home, training at Cape Canaveral. He is full of jokes and loves to repeat the Bill Dana "José Jimenez" routines about cowardly astronauts he has heard on the Ed Sullivan show. As the pressure mounts on Shepard, the only effect anyone notices is that the two personalities seem to alternate more frequently. Shepard is, however, as strong a personality as any in the group, and perfectly willing to stand up to anyone, including John Glenn at his most moralistic.

Like Shepard, Wally Schirra comes from a military family and has graduated from the naval academy. He has a fine war record from Korea and has tested both planes and the new sidewinder air-to-air missile. His personality, however, never takes on the "icy commander" edge. He is amiable most of the time and willing to display his emotions, including rage and frustration. He talks about "maintaining an even strain," and goes about doing so by indulging in pranks and practical jokes and fast cars. In contrast to Glenn with his roadwork, he argues that any exercise that is not fun is bad for the nerves. In the air, he is as cool as anyone, and people who underestimate him because of his joker personality are surprised to find what he can accomplish when he devotes himself to a project.

Among the things the astronauts from the air force share is a discomfort with public appearances. Their service has not had the "officers and gentlemen" tradition of the navy, and they feel awkward every time they are asked to "say a few words." Gus Grissom and Deke Slayton bond with each other almost immediately. They are both taciturn men, with little to say about anything but flying, and both are sometimes annoyed by the third air force pilot, Gordon Cooper. Cooper seems naïve, and also given to bragging about his exploits at Edwards—where he was in engineering while Slayton was in the more prestigious Fighter Ops. But Cooper is a natural pilot from a flying family, and he has done all he could to get into the program. Separated from his wife Trudy at the time of the psychological tests for the program and knowing that the military values family men, he first tells the psychologist that his home life is idyllic and then arranges a reconciliation to make it true.

The pilots' wives are important characters in *The Right Stuff*, though always secondary in the great, masculine enterprise. They are all presented to the world as brave and loyal women who give their husbands solid backing on the home front. In fact, their personalities are as varied as are those of the pilots themselves. Some, like Annie Glenn and Rene Carpenter, do to some extent fit the model of the perfect housewife awaiting her hero's return. But even these two show unexpected assertiveness at times. Annie Glenn refuses to have the vice president of the United States intrude into her house, and Renee Carpenter escapes the whole publicity machine NASA has created by going down to Cape Canaveral incognito when her husband's mission is at hand. Renee does possess the faith in her husband's safety that makes her an ideal pilot's wife: even when the word comes that his capsule may be lost, she is sure that he is safe—and consciously plans not to accept any report of his death until they find a body. Other wives, including Jane Conrad, do not bear up so well: she gets to the point of hallucinating about the visit of the bearer of bad news. With the exception of the publicity they must deal with, all the wives find the space program less taxing emotionally than were the years when their husbands were test pilots. Then they constantly worried about them. Bad news might come at any moment. Now they have only to watch the television to see that their husbands are still safe. In fact, they worry more about having to appear on television after the men have safely splashed down and, with Renee Carpenter in the lead, act out mock versions of the interviews, lampooning the inane questions they will face.

Several of the other wives have less idyllic marriages than the Glenns and the Carpenters, or, to put it another way, marriages based on a model that the press would be less likely to celebrate. Several see themselves as having made a deal with both their husbands and the service. In return for various sacrifices, they expect certain rewards, including both material rewards and a share in the adulation offered their husbands. Some, like Betty Grissom, are willing to put up with a great deal but also expect a great return and feel slighted if it does not come. They do not mind at all that their images have been airbrushed, both literally and figuratively, by NASA, *Life* magazine, and the press in general.

A number of the wives either fly themselves or come from flying families, and some other women also appear on the fringes of the flying fraternity, if only as nameless groupies. In Pancho Barnes, however, there is a woman who is almost a true member of the fliers' club. While Yeager and his comrades are breaking the sound barrier, she runs Pancho's Fly Inn, a low-rent resort near their base, which includes both stables for dude ranch ponies and an airstrip. She is foulmouthed, and her bar is full of flying mementos. But the woman who was born Florence Leontine Lowe has been a gunrunner for Mexican revolutionaries and a barnstormer. She has even broken one Amelia Earhart record as the woman who has flown the fastest. Pancho, however, seems like the relic of an earlier age—an age when women like Earhart could win fame as aviatrixes, and female pilots ferried warplanes to Europe. During Project Mercury men fly, and women worry and admire.

Among the many other characters in *The Right Stuff* are those who will later become famous as astronauts but do not make the cut for Project Mercury. We see much of the life of the test pilot through the eyes of Pete Conrad, but his impolitic defiance of authority keeps him out of the first set of astronauts. Neil Armstrong, who is described late in the book, represents a new generation of space explorers—still test pilots but more masters of engineering than pure "stick-and-rudder men."

MAJOR THEMES

Wolfe's great theme is the "the right stuff" itself. What is the quality that allows a man to be cool, efficient, and business-like when he is lying on his back atop what is essentially a skyscraper filled with explosives? Chuck Yeager himself questioned if there were such a thing. It seemed to Yeager that the term suggested that if you had it, it was because you were "born that way," while, in fact, if he was "better than average" at flying, "it was because I flew more than anyone else" (*Yeager* 319). But Yeager perhaps misunderstands what Wolfe means by "the right stuff," which involves not simply innate personal qualities but qualities proved and celebrated in a particular social context. The great pilots do not just have "it": they are constantly proving that they have it, and it is that competition and the ethos that goes with it that give a man "the right stuff," as much as revealing that he has it already.

The constant competition is another of Wolfe's themes. The image he uses is climbing a ziggurat, alluding to the ancient Mesopotamian pyramids that rose step by step with ever smaller terraces until one reached the temple at the top. The fliers Wolfe describes are constantly either moving up the ziggurat or being "left behind." The pilot lives in a world where there is a constant competition to prove that one has what it takes, which is something more than simple courage. "It" or "the right stuff"—the pilots themselves do not give the quality they so prize a name—includes coolness, intelligence, and the ability to apply one's skill in the most desperate situation. Those who do not have it are constantly being winnowed out. A third of them cannot make it through flight training. Still more cannot master carrier landings, and more fail at night carrier landings. Those who wash out of flying—or even those who end up flying transports rather than fighters—have failed some primal test of manhood. At every level of his career, the pilot has to prove he has it or be left behind. And one could be left behind not just for reasons of nerve or skill but because of something uncontrollable, such as a medical problem. Fighter pilots developed a culture in which they could prove to themselves that they had it. They would engage in aerial acrobatics and in the mock dogfights known as "hassling," which were officially forbidden but unofficially tolerated or even celebrated. The need to prove one had it would lead many never to admit they were in trouble, even as their planes were on the verge of a crash.

Even beyond the flight line, the pilots test themselves. What Wolfe calls "Flying & Drinking and Drinking & Driving and so forth"—and the "so forth" includes sexual adventures with the flying groupies—is more than just youthful indulgence. It is, in fact, another part of the constant competition, the constant testing. The pilot who can drink, drive, and then fly is passing a test his sober comrades are not. Eventually, what divides those who have it from those who do not is something larger than success or failure in training. It is life and death. Those who keep moving up in the world of pilots are those who stay alive. The pilots do not talk directly about the code that binds them; nevertheless, they pass along their doctrine. The first assumption is that "there are no *accidents* and no fatal flaws in machines," or as Pete Conrad puts it, "No single factor ever killed a pilot; there was always a chain of mistakes" (35). The implication is that any crash is the fault of the pilot and that a pilot who truly has "the right stuff" will be able to work his way out of even the most desperate situation. The greatest test is combat. Many who had left the service for the reserves volunteered for active duty during the Korean War. The American fighter pilots of that conflict racked up a glorious record—in contrast to the more inconclusive results on the ground. It remains clear that every man is being tested, either moving up or washing out in the most permanent way. After the war is over and one cannot display one's prowess in combat, the field for proving one's mettle becomes flight testing.

The airfields on which the pilots test themselves are often located in ugly patches of country, in "low-rent" areas, but the pilots feel themselves superior to the whole population of non-pilots. In fact, even when their social standing was declining, all military officers were coming to feel superior to civilians. Any indulgences of their own aside, they thought of themselves as having higher standards than those who lived the ordinary life, which they saw as characterized not by discipline and honor but by hedonism and acquisitiveness. The ziggurat the test pilot climbs is, in some ways, simply an elaboration of the usual path of an officer's career, where those passed over repeatedly for promotion must retire or resign. The hierarchies of the military, and especially of the officer corps, are thus not simply the relics of the aristocratic cultures that created the ethos of the profession of arms. They are a cultural system that produces what it is intended to produce: men willing to risk their lives coolly and efficiently.

The world of the officer, with its clear class structure, includes their wives, and the Military Wives Compact is another of Wolfe's themes. Especially when we are seeing the Space Program through the Betty Grissom's eyes, we hear about the unofficial agreement that Betty, at least, firmly believes in. The military wife gives up many things. She will have to move often, get by on low pay, go without her husband's company for long periods, and live in constant fear for his safety. In return, she receives several benefits. She is part of a real community that sees to all her basic needs, from housing to health care. What is more, she is part of the close-knit family of a unit—and few units are as tightly knit as fighter squadrons. She has a place in a status system. When an officer is promoted, his wife is, in effect, promoted as well. Since a charming wife can improve an officer's chances of promotion, the system is, to some extent, reciprocal. Where the wife does not receive as much as she expected in return for her sacrifices, there is real anger.

As in many of Wolfe's works, the religious impulse is a major theme in *The Right Stuff*. The pilot's feeling of being in a select group—as well as the ecstasy of flying—gives some pilots an almost religious feeling, the sort described by Antoine de Saint-Exupéry and a very few other pilots who tried to capture their experience in words. Indeed, everyone working on Project Mercury and caught up in the fervor of the project feels a "religious dimension that engineers, no less than pilots, would resist putting into words" but all feel (231). Here they are not so different from the religious groups Wolfe describes in *The Electric Kool-Aid Acid Test*, except that, unlike the Merry Pranksters, certainly, their efforts are directed to a common, public goal. Wolfe also discusses extensively how John Glenn's Presbyterianism—the faith Wolfe was raised in—shapes his career. Clearly again building on Max Weber, Wolfe shows how a devout Protestantism feeds, rather than restrains, worldly ambition.

Wolfe also explores the role publicity plays in the lives of all the fliers. They both long for and loathe it. One problem is that reporters get the facts wrong, as the film *Breaking the Sound Barrier* does in a most extreme form. A still more serious problem, however, is that they intrude on the flying fraternity's zone of privacy. They ask questions about things pilots would never discuss openly, such as bravery or fear. On the other hand, the pilots all have healthy egos and crave adulation even while wishing to keep both their personal and communal privacy. Wolfe's larger theme when discussing the press coverage of Project Mercury is its pre-scripted quality. It is as if the press as a whole has decided beforehand what the story will be, and then proceeds to write it, ignoring as much as possible anything that might detract from it. Since, in this case, the story is to be a positive and heroic one, the astronauts and their wives do not object. "The Genteel Beast," as Wolfe calls the press, both swarms the astronauts and ignores their flaws, and even protects them when, as is the case with Gus Grissom, they may have made a major error.

A final major theme is single combat. The press makes the seven original astronauts national heroes as soon as they are introduced. Wolfe speculates on why those selected for Project Mercury are greeted with such adulation, even before they have achieved anything—or even begun training. In 1959, the space program is filling the role in the collective psyche that single combat did in earlier cultures. History and legend are full of stories of individual warriors who go out before their armies to face a single foe. David facing Goliath is a prime example. The idea of single combat died out centuries ago, as warfare become total. But with nuclear weapons and "mutually assured destruction," total war itself has become obsolete. The conflict between the superpowers must be played out in other spheres. One of those is the space race, where America seems to be facing defeat, since, thanks to several televised tests, most people think that "our rockets always blow up." The situation appears especially dire because the national assumption is that the nation that first puts a man in space will win the Cold War, just as it seemed in ages gone by that the army whose champion was victorious in single combat would win the battle. The astronauts, even before they are placed atop the rocket that seems to the public to be fated to blow up, are given the adulation that a nation's champion, in the old sense, deserves.

A HISTORICAL READING: HEROES OF
THE COLD WAR

The Right Stuff chronicles events beginning in the 1940s and ending early in the 1960s. It was written and researched, however, during the 1970s. While the gap in time may not seem great, it includes the period that saw the greatest changes in American culture ever. While most of the men Wolfe wrote about were still alive when his book was published, the world that produced them was gone. There is always a tension between the values and assumptions of two eras in a historical narrative, whether it is fictional or nonfictional. Nathaniel Hawthorne's *The Scarlet Letter* and Francis Parkman's *France and England in North America* reveal as much about the values and outlooks of the nineteenth century, when they were written, as they do about the seventeenth and eighteenth centuries, which they describe. A historical narrative is always either a celebration of one's own age or a critique of it. One can either show the past as the bad old days that gave way to the current glory or depict it as a golden age from which society has fallen away. In nineteenth-century Britain, for example, Thomas Babington Macaulay (1800–1859) published a *History of England* (1849–1861) focusing on the Glorious Revolution of 1688 that toppled King James II and put William and Mary on the English throne. Macaulay's real point, however, was that the liberty and prosperity England now enjoyed was the result of the triumph of Protestantism and the Whig party in politics. He contrasted the glorious England he saw around him with the benighted period when Catholic King James and the Tory party were in power. During the same period, another English writer, the architect Augustus Pugin (1812–1852), published a book called *Contrasts* (1832). In that work Pugin uses both words and pictures to compare the artistic beauties and social solidarity of medieval Catholic England with what he saw as the artistic decadence and social squalor of modern Protestant England. His point is that England had lost its way because it had abandoned the Catholic faith and the gothic artistic styles that went along with it. Both Macaulay and Pugin use the past as a means of judging the present. In the same way, Wolfe seems to be using the story of Project Mercury as a yardstick against which to measure then present-day America—and to find it wanting—though he also acknowledges the follies and excesses of the era of Project Mercury.

The two eras could hardly be more different, and they were divided by the vast chasm of the 1960s—a period we might reasonably date from the assassination of President Kennedy in 1963 to the fall of Saigon in 1975. The 1950s were a period of unprecedented prosperity but also a time of genuine fear. The threat of nuclear war was real. Children learned to "duck and cover" in school, and there was a market for back-yard bomb shelters. Communism seemed a real threat. The time was also one of forthright patriotism. There was a real feeling of communal investment in public projects, ranging from the interstate highway system to the space program, and indeed a general trust in government. The echoes of the nation's triumph in World War II were still resounding. There was pride in the military, in which a good proportion of the male population still served, if only briefly, thanks to the draft. The nation was governed for most of the decade by General Eisenhower, who had brought about victory in Europe, and he was succeeded by John Kennedy, a navy hero from the Pacific campaign. With that energetic, charming, glamorous young president, who had not yet become the subject of scandal, a new age seemed at hand. He called his program the New Frontier, and breakthroughs seemed possible in every area, from science to social relations.

That era of self-confidence was destroyed by the events of the 1960s. The nation lost the war in Vietnam, and the deferment system saw to it that the rich and well-educated were much less likely to serve in the military than the poor and disadvantaged. Objections to the war were widely translated into contempt for the military and those serving in it. Trust in government, which the war weakened, became still more tenuous thanks to revelations about lawbreaking at the highest levels during the Nixon administration. Even as technology advanced, doubts about it began to appear, especially as pollution became a real problem. The Civil Rights movement, which had been predominately nonviolent, developed a radical wing. And the social roles that had seemed so fixed in 1960 suddenly became fluid with the women's movement and the "sexual revolution," which changed utterly not just the ways in which men and women related to each other, but also the way they studied, trained, and worked.

After those convulsions, the nation seemed to have lost its bearings. The economy was in trouble, suffering from both recession and inflation. Things were made worse by an "energy crisis," resulting in part from the Arab oil embargo. There was a general lack of trust in public institutions, including the military. President Jimmy Carter himself diagnosed the problem, though he seemed powerless to remedy it. In 1979 he told the nation that it suffered from "malaise." He had earlier noted that the nation lacked any great common purpose, something that would provide what William James called "the moral equivalent of War."

It was to this culture that Wolfe presented his own version of an old story, one that almost all Americans thought they knew. The account of the astronauts is by implication an attack on the culture of the 70s, a time when nothing would so engage everyone that traffic would stop all over the country, as it did when Alan Shepard was launched into space. *The Right Stuff* is a critique of the era in which it was written and a lament for an era that is irremediably past. For part of the nation's diminishment is that it has turned away from the great adventure on which it had embarked thirty years before: the last moon shot had taken place seven years before, and there would not be another one for the foreseeable future. Indeed, Wolfe's work on the space program began with the final Apollo launch.

Wolfe describes lost values, particularly those associated with the military's officer corps, without turning his heroes into plaster saints. He thus makes it all the more plausible that a return to those values might be possible. At the same time, he suggests it is possible that those heady days of shared national investment in the deeds of a few brave men may be gone forever. After all, even the memory of the original seven's exploits is fading, as the almost wistful ending, "Oh yes—which one was he?" (436) suggests.

The mood of America has changed considerably over the years since 1979—and mostly for the better. (While America seemed to have fallen behind its foreign competitors, especially Japan, in the 1970s, in 2001 it is clearly ahead economically, as well as having triumphed when the Cold War came so unexpectedly to an end.) The careful reader of *The Right Stuff*, however, will do well to recall that it was written for a time when America felt that it had fallen behind. It was, in a sense, in the great tradition of what is called the American Jeremiad—a rebuke to the nation for falling away from its ideals—though without that genre's fierce denunciation and with much more humor. It was a call to the nation to reclaim the values that had made it great.

7

The Bonfire of the Vanities
(1987)

No Justice, No Peace!
—Chant associated with protests led by Reverend Al Sharpton

The city of Florence in the 1490s was dominated by two figures, a friar and a financier. The financier, Lorenzo de Medici, was ruler of the city in everything but name. The friar was Girolamo Savonarola, a Dominican who preached spellbinding, prophetic sermons denouncing corruption and Medici control of the city's government. He also forcefully called upon the people to repent. Florentines had been especially enamored of festivals, gambling, and personal adornments. In 1497, during the heretofore licentious season of carnival, Savonarola conducted the "bonfire of the vanities," in which citizens burned jewelry, sensual pictures, playing cards, and other things that might distract them from a sober Christian life. That event is one of the iconic moments in the history of the Renaissance and was enshrined in the memories of readers of English literature by George Eliot, whose historical novel *Romola* (1863) is set in Florence during Savonarola's time.

New York City in the 1980s, like Renaissance Florence, was a city of great wealth and culture torn apart by politics and factional strife. While that strife did not rise to the level of civil war, as it did in Florence, it often seemed just as bitter, especially since it was so often linked to race. And financiers and preachers again dominated a great city's life. Corporate mergers, high-yield "junk bonds," and insider trading scandals made Wall Street a larger part of the news than it had been since the crash of 1929. And the leaders of ethnic communities, especially among African Americans, were often preachers like the Reverend Al Sharpton. While they could not, like Savonarola, take control of the city, they certainly could make its leaders think that they could bring them down.

Wolfe's novel is panoramic satire, and very few groups come off looking very good. It is also the portrait of a very specific period in American history. For example, much of its plot would be different if it were set in the age of the cell phone, or an era when voice-activated tape recorders could be hidden in a pen or a cigarette lighter.

PLOT

New York City is suffering from racial tension. The mayor and other white leaders are intimidated by Reverend Bacon, a black leader who can fill TV screens with demonstrators. But Sherman McCoy hardly notices such public matters. He devotes his attention to his role as chief bond trader for a Wall Street firm and to the affair he is carrying on with Maria Ruskin. He arouses his wife Judy's suspicions when he leaves his Park Avenue apartment to call Maria, dials his home instead, and asks for Maria when Judy answers. That close call does not deter him, and not long afterward he picks up Maria, who has been in Italy, at Kennedy airport. They become lost in the Bronx on their way back to Manhattan, and at an on-ramp that is partially blocked with trash cans, they encounter two young black men in what they are sure is an attempted carjacking. In the course of the incident, Maria takes the wheel of the car, and they escape to Manhattan, not sure if they have hit one of the young men as she drove off. Sherman suggests reporting the incident, but Maria, fearing publicity, refuses. Sherman is at first elated by the feeling of having fought off attackers, but by the next day he is so worried that he begins making uncharacteristic mistakes. Despite his million-dollar income, he is deeply in debt and worries that everything might collapse around him, especially if he is touched by some sort of scandal.

A young man named Henry Lamb has twice been brought to a Bronx hospital; he was first treated for a broken wrist and then diagnosed with a concussion. His mother says that he reported having been hit by a Mercedes, but she has disappeared. Assistant D.A. Larry Kramer is given the case, but he is more interested in the flirtation he is beginning with a juror in the case he has just won. Not much is done in the investigation until pressure is brought on the police and D.A. by the Reverend Bacon. Kramer goes with detectives Martin and Goldberg to meet Mrs. Lamb at Bacon's headquarters. (She has avoided the police out of fear of being arrested for outstanding parking tickets.) She gives them a description of the car and some possible numbers from the license plate. One of Bacon's allies, the attorney Albert Vogel, persuades journalist Peter Fallow to feature the case in the *City Light*, and stories start to appear in the newspaper just as McCoy is beginning to relax. The stories do not match the facts as McCoy knows them, but they so rattle him that he botches the major deal he has been working on for months, losing his firm $6 million. He sees his family lawyer, who tells him he is probably in little danger from the law but also suggests that he talk to a criminal lawyer, Tommy Killian.

The stories and the demonstration Bacon has organized get the attention of the D.A.'s office, and the investigation proceeds. The detectives check the possible matches for the Mercedes and license plate, including McCoy's. McCoy, who has not yet called Killian, is worried, and even though he thinks his car is undamaged, refuses to let them look at it. The refusal makes him their prime suspect. McCoy is now getting advice from Killian, who wonders if Maria will sign a statement corroborating McCoy's version of events. McCoy worries because Maria has disappeared, and Killian eventually suggests that McCoy secretly record her when they next speak, a step he rejects. Kramer is contacted by a legal aid attorney whose client, Roland Auburn, has been indicted on drug charges. In return for a reduced charge, Auburn will give his version of the Lamb case: a Mercedes, with a man driving and a woman in the passenger seat, hits Lamb on Bruckner Boulevard; the driver, after stopping to look, coldly drives away. When shown several photographs, Auburn picks out McCoy. D.A. Abe Weiss decides to have McCoy arrested, even though Bernie Fitzgibbon, the chief of his criminal division, counsels against it because several things in the case, such as a good boy like Lamb hanging out with a drug dealer, do not make sense. Fitzgibbon is only able to persuade Weiss to let Killian bring McCoy in, instead of having him arrested in his apartment.

McCoy receives the news from Killian while talking with the chairman of his firm about his recent errors. He then has to tell him, his father, and his wife about the arrest. He does not tell the whole truth. His wife offers him support but not love or affection. The arrest and booking, a humiliating ordeal for McCoy, includes threats from other prisoners. After he is arraigned and released on bail, he must make his way through a crowd of Bacon's demonstrators. He vows never to go through such an experience again, even if it means blowing his brains out. He is mobbed by reporters the next day when trying to walk his daughter to the bus. He begins to doubt Killian but changes his mind when Killian tells him about plans to get his version of events in the papers. He is soon alone in his apartment except for lawyers and bodyguards, since Bacon has surrounded it with protestors. The president of his co-op board suggests that he move out, and that, he tells Killian, makes him so angry that he gives up any idea of suicide and decides to fight it all.

Fallow has tried to talk to McCoy directly. He has also discovered the identity of the woman who was in the car with him. He decides to find Maria by working through her husband, an elderly Jew who made his money flying pilgrims to Mecca. Fallow meets him for lunch after claiming to be writing a story on him, and the old man dies of a heart attack at the table. Fallows turns that event, and the funeral, where he sees McCoy trying to talk to Maria, into newspaper stories. McCoy, convinced by Killian at last, wears a wire, but Maria says nothing helpful, although she agrees to see McCoy again soon. While all this is happening, McCoy is still living the life of a socialite. The strange thing is that he becomes a more attractive guest once the charges against him become public.

The D.A.'s, especially Kramer, are pushing the case, even though the police have discovered from some young men picked up in a crack sweep that Roland Auburn was showing Henry Lamb how to "take off a car," so the young man really was injured in an attempted carjacking. All the same, Kramer is sent to Maria Ruskin to give her the message that she will be granted immunity if she "comes clean" about McCoy. She reports the offer when McCoy sees her in the apartment she has sublet for her assignations, but she discovers McCoy is wearing a wire before he can get her to say again that she was driving the car. He flees from the apartment feeling thoroughly ashamed and recognizing that he may have lost his last chance to avoid jail.

Maria testifies at the grand jury, supporting Auburn's version of events, and McCoy is indicted. A story in the *City Light* quoting the landlord of Maria's "$331-a-Month Tryst Pad" has McCoy worrying about the remains of his marriage, but it gives Killian's private investigator an idea. He discovers a tape recorder the landlord has used in an attempt to catch illegal subletters. The tape he takes from it includes a conversation between Maria and McCoy in which she confirms she was driving. Since the tape was illegally made, it cannot be used as evidence, but McCoy, who has learned from Killian that one can legally tape one's own conversations, says he made it himself. The next day, McCoy is taken in for another bail hearing. Killian tells the presiding judge, Myron

Kovitsky, that the grand jury testimony was tainted and offers the tapes as proof. McCoy commits perjury, swearing that he made the earlier tape as well as the later one by wearing a wire. The second tape makes it appear that Kramer told Maria what to say and threatened her with jail if she did not comply; the first suggests that she was lying before the grand jury. Kovitsky dismisses the case. There is a near riot involving Bacon's people. Kovitsky tries explain to them that he has defended them by defending neutral justice, but he gives up and the judge, lawyers, and defendant all retreat.

The final chapter is presented as a newspaper article published a year later. Henry Lamb has died, and McCoy has been indicted for manslaughter. He had earlier faced trial for reckless endangerment after the D.A. obtained a new indictment from a second grand jury, but the trial ended with a hung jury—the white and Hispanic jurors favoring acquittal. On the strength of his forceful prosecution of McCoy, D.A. Weiss has been reelected to another term. Judge Kovitsky, on the other hand, lost the support of the Bronx Democratic Party and was defeated at the polls. Kramer has been removed as prosecutor in the McCoy case since it has been discovered that he has tried to secure Maria's "rent-controlled love nest" for the former juror with whom he is carrying on an affair.

McCoy now presents himself, both in statements and in his mode of dress, as a "professional defendant." When he appears for arraignment after six hours in the holding pens, he has been injured in a "dispute" with other prisoners, but he says it is a matter he will handle himself. A jury has awarded Lamb $12 million in Albert Vogel's civil action against McCoy, and all McCoy's assets are frozen pending an appeal. Since McCoy cannot pay him, Killian has withdrawn from the case, and McCoy, who now lives in a small apartment, is defending himself. His wife, who has moved to the Midwest with their daughter, appears in court during his arraignment. Maria is expected to testify in the new trial, although she did not in the previous one, and Peter Fallow has won a Pulitzer Prize for his articles on McCoy.

CHARACTERS

The central figure in the novel is Sherman McCoy, who at the beginning of the novel thinks of himself as a "Master of the Universe," taking the name from one of his daughter's toys. At thirty-eight, he feels he is on top of the world. He is tall, handsome, and successful, the top bond trader at his firm, earning almost a million dollars a year. He also comes from a fine background. His father is a semiretired lawyer who once headed a major Wall Street firm, and McCoy thinks of him as "the Lion of Dunning Sponget," though after his own troubles he realizes that he is just a little boy who has been pretending to be the powerful father all these years. McCoy has gone to all the right schools, including Yale. He has an attractive wife and a perfect little girl. His good fortune and success had given him an extreme sense of entitlement. He treats all his advantages as only his due, and he expects even more. One of the things that he expects is a gorgeous young mistress as well as a wife of forty.

Early on McCoy also sees himself as the keeper of values and upholder of standards. He is willing to tell off a fellow bond trader for reading a newspaper when he should be selling securities. He contrasts his true Knickerbocker values with the gaudiness of provincial nouveau riches who have recently come to New York. And he disapproves of homosexuals, whom he seems to see everywhere. He is utterly correct in his dress, and consciously assumes expressions of command, modeled on his father's. In the course of the novel, many of these attitudes are stripped away, and Wolfe, using a strangely postmodern rhetorical strategy for a writer usually thought of as conservative, suggests that no unitary self existed in McCoy. Rather, he was the construction of his environment, and when that environment changes radically, so does McCoy's very self. Once arrested and treated as a common criminal, McCoy thinks he has died. A new character is created by the new environment—a professional defendant. He gives up ideas of honor, taping his mistress without her knowledge. He gives up ideas of honesty, committing perjury when he needs to do so. He feels residual guilt for these actions, but since only they seem to offer him a chance of staying out of jail, he commits them anyway. Playing on the old saying about how experience can change one's outlook—"a conservative is a liberal who has been mugged"—Wolfe describes a parallel trajectory: "a liberal is a conservative who has been arrested" (504). McCoy, in his new incarnation, finds sympathy welling up in him for other persecuted groups, including homosexuals. Finally, there is some hint that this new McCoy is more like the one who existed before his sense of entitlement was stoked by Wall Street success. Facing his bail hearing, McCoy recalls with his wife the happy days when they lived in Greenwich Village, and he would give her a raised-fist Black Power salute as he went to work to show he was not being seduced by Wall Street, he was only using it to achieve their ends. At the arraignment described in the epilogue, he turns to her and gives that salute again.

Larry Kramer also feels he is owed more by life, but his feeling is fueled by a building resentment rather than a sense of entitlement. He has gone to a first-rate law school but is working for very little money for the Bronx D.A.'s office, while his classmates are making lots of money in private practice. (His feeling of the nobility of his calling wears thin.) His apartment is cramped. His wife seems less attractive and more provincial than she once did, and she does not seem to admire his work at all. He envies the people who seem to be living life to its fullest, and he decides to be one of them. He tries to seize his moment in part through his relationship with juror Shelley Thomas, but his pursuit of the McCoy case is also a way of rising out of the mire he feels he is in. Prosecuting a rich white defendant will make him look like a hero—both to Shelley and his wife—and it will help him take a higher place the power structure of the D.A.'s office. His longing for distinction in this case leads him to suppress all doubts about his witnesses and his evidence and to play demagogically to the mob. His decision to act on the idea that he is owed more by life has the same consequences McCoy's does: he loses everything he has when his relationship with a juror becomes public.

Kramer lives in a world dominated by the Irish and their values. Detective Martin and Bernie Fitzgibbon exemplify the values of the Donkeys, as they call themselves. They have a stubborn courage and a commitment to a certain form of loyalty, which Tommy Killian and Quigley, his private investigator, also hold to, even though they are now working for the defense. Killian calls it the "Favor Bank," and contracts made on the Favor Bank are inviolable. The Donkeys also show a macho toughness—and often a willingness to press people, especially minorities, a bit too far. Others in law enforcement conform to those values, even if they are not themselves Irish, like Martin's partner Goldberg. Kramer seems torn between acting like the Irish cops and prosecutors and taking the more political route exemplified by the Jewish politicians who hold onto their positions despite the rising power of blacks and Hispanics.

Abe Weiss and the mayor are two such characters. They are both attacked by Bacon's people—and both attacked at times in anti-Semitic language. They do not, however, respond by denouncing the demagoguery, much less the anti-Semitism. Rather, they follow Bacon's line on the McCoy case so as to encourage him to direct his ire—and his mobs—somewhere else. They stay in power, for the moment, by doing the will of the rising groups. A third Jewish elected official, Judge Kovitsky, shows a more impartial commitment to justice: he objects to allowing anything besides the legal facts to influence the course of justice. He is also unwilling to ignore, as the mayor and Weiss are, anti-Semitic slurs. Kramer sees him as a "Jewish warrior" (108)—if also as a foul-mouthed courtroom tyrant. But he is not the model Kramer finally chooses to follow.

Kramer's fellow D.A.'s and the detectives are Jewish, Irish, and Italian, and they prosecute mostly blacks and Hispanics. The mayor, the Bronx D.A., the head of Pierce & Pierce, and even the English editor of the *City Light* are Jewish. (About the only institutions in the novel without Jewish leadership are Reverend Bacon's organization and the Episcopal diocese—both headed by blacks.) There are surprisingly few WASPs (White Anglo-Saxon Protestants) in a novel dealing with the centers of power in both business and politics, and all seem to be ineffectual. Just as McCoy's father has been reduced from the level of Lion of Dunning Sponget to that of a senior partner with a small office and a shared secretary, McCoy's WASP associates are no longer the powers they once were. Rawlie Thorpe, the one old friend who keeps calling McCoy during his troubles, seems to have been cast in a shadow at Pierce & Pierce since his divorce—not because of any scandal, but because he seems to have developed a sense of irony, even about bonds. Pollard Browning, president of the co-op board, cannot even get McCoy to leave his co-op during the demonstrations. While there are still plenty of "young white men baying for money on the bond market" at Pierce & Pierce, the real power is elsewhere.

One of the new centers of power is in Reverend Bacon and his organizations. That he is headquartered in a turn-of-the-century Riverside mansion shows how the New York City power structures created by whites are being taken over by other groups. Bacon's authority derives in part from his clerical title—a title bestowed on him essentially by his mother, a famous gospel singer—and in part from his imperious presence. He can speak the language of the structures of power and turn it to his own ends. He knows that few white leaders, in either politics or the press, will be willing to attack a black leader directly, so he is free to ignore their concerns and threats—even threats of audits. His own threats of demonstrations and charges of racism are enough to get action—or donations—from those in power. He appears in public always as either the comforter or the righteous voice of the people. His associate, Buck Jones, can organize the events that create the pressure, complete with death threats and anti-Semitic slurs.

The journalists in the novel are outside any of the structures they report on. That point is emphasized by the fact that both the publisher, Sir Gerald Steiner, and the principal journalist on the case, Peter Fallow, are Englishmen who view all the people they report on, to a greater or lesser extent, as barbarians. (Many of the Americans in the novel seem to agree with them: several, including Ed Fiske and Gene Lopwitz, seem to wish they were English.) Steiner is enamored by the romance of the tabloid press to such an extent that he runs a money-losing paper just so he can enjoy it. For Fallow, who spends a good deal of the novel struggling with hangovers and trying to ward off memories of the night before, journalism seems not to be so much a profession as a way of avoiding impending ruin. In fact, he does little original reporting. He is fed stories by Albert Vogel and gets a lucky tip from one of his expatriate English cronies. He is, however, able to write them up in a sensational style, and he is not hindered in the process by any concerns about getting at the real truth.

There are very few women in *The Bonfire of the Vanities*, and they are not particularly well developed. McCoy's wife Judy appears quite rarely, in part because we see her from McCoy's point of view, and for most of the novel she is turning a cold shoulder to him. She is attractive and successful as a society interior designer, but, as his affair with Maria makes manifest, McCoy is not satisfied with her. What she seems not to give him—and what Larry Kramer's wife Rhoda does not give *him*—is an admiring audience for his descriptions of his triumphs. Both wives instead treat their husbands' professions with some irony, something the men cannot stand. In response, McCoy works up some resentment against Judy, who enjoys the position his wealth gives her but, unlike him, does not come from a wealthy background. When Judy gets Sherman's incriminating phone call—and still more when the rest of the story comes out—she withdraws affection from him while going on, insofar as she can, with the rest of the marriage. She clearly thinks the rift between them came, not with his affair, but when he allowed Wall Street, and his idea of himself as one of its Titans, to become the center of his life.

Maria Ruskin, McCoy's mistress, is a flat character, almost the traditional femme fatale. She is young and very attractive, and she has used those advantages to marry an aged financier for his money, which she spends freely. She also has a number of lovers, whom she seems to control skillfully. Certainly she gets McCoy to follow her lead after the incident in the Bronx, reminding him that she was in the driver's seat. Having come from the South, and clearly not from an upper-class background, she is another outsider in New York society and seems free to use all its structures to get what she wants or to protect herself. When she disappears to Italy, it seems that she is ready to leave McCoy in the lurch, but whether she is that disloyal is never clear, since he betrays her by taping her before she betrays him by offering false testimony at the grand jury. The other "other woman" in the novel, Shelley Thomas, is hardly developed at all. She seems simply Kramer's ideal audience for his war stories—at least until we hear what she thinks about men in New York beginning dates with "two or three hours of My Career" (514).

The rest of the women in the novel fall into a few set types, and it may be Wolfe's point that women in New York society choose to play a very limited number of social roles. There are the society hostesses, who all use a set repertoire of artificial signs of intimacy to manage their guests. There are the women, designers and realtors, who use society for their trade or hobby (the predatory real estate agent, Sally Rawthrote, is the best example of this group). And there are the older and younger women at the fashionable parties, the "social x-rays," middle-aged women who have starved themselves so it can never seem that the years have added a pound to their figures, and the "lemon tarts," the blond young girlfriends or second or third wives of successful men. What is excluded, Wolfe points out, is any woman whose figure suggests the image of "Mother" (334).

LITERARY MODELS

Wolfe's explicit literary models in *The Bonfire of the Vanities* are the great multiplots novels produced during the nineteenth century in both England and France. There is also, however, an important American model. Probably the greatest American novel about money and the ways in which it can warp human beings is F. Scott Fitzgerald's *The Great Gatsby*, and *The Bonfire of the Vanities* mirrors Fitzgerald's novels in one central part of its plot. Gatsby is destroyed because of an auto accident. While Gatsby is driving with his adulterous lover, his car strikes a woman, who is killed. Her husband tracks him down and shoots him. In *Bonfire*, McCoy is brought low because of another auto accident: his car strikes a young black man, who eventually dies. He is prosecuted for the death. The locations of the accidents are not too distant from each other, McCoy's in the Bronx, Gatsby's farther East on Long Island. But perhaps the most telling link between the two events is that in each case the man is not driving. It is the woman who is in the driver's seat when the people are hit. The man, who has done the same thing out of vanity or infatuation on a still larger scale, has let the woman take the driver's seat, and that leads to disaster.

The novel also includes several patterns of literary allusions. The most obvious is to Edgar Allan Poe. The young man who eventually dies lives in the Poe Homes, which are near where Poe once lived, and an English poet who speaks at one of the fashionable parties the McCoys attend compares the modern world to Poe's story, "The Masque of the Red Death." In that story a prince shuts himself off from his people during the plague, locking himself and his friends up in his palace where they revel at a costume ball. The prince is offended when he hears that someone has appeared dressed as Death and sets out to find him. When he does, he discovers his guest is Death himself. The analogy between the prince and the rich who try to insulate themselves from the poor of their city is clear. Wolfe uses Poe to underscore the inevitability of suffering anywhere affecting even those who seem most safe.

MAJOR THEMES

The Bonfire of the Vanities is essentially the work of a moralist. Few serious works of literature in recent decades have so relentlessly celebrated conventional morality. While Wolfe shows the allure of the unconventional, he also shows that breaking the boundaries of conventional morality is usually not liberating. Rather, it traps one in a still more desperate situation than one was in before. Wolfe makes his point through the most traditional of methods, poetic justice. All the figures who have been upholders of morality and then decide to cross the line are brought low by the end of the book. McCoy, the embodiment of Knickerbocker values, is broke and under indictment, and it all stems from his adultery. Kramer, the defender of justice, has lost his chance to distinguish himself—and may lose everything—because of his affair with Shelley Thomas. And Henry Lamb, the good boy, is dead because he fell in with a hard case who wanted to show him how to manage a carjacking. The roots of disaster are just as clear as they are in such great moralistic Victorian novels as George Eliot's *Adam Bede*, where the decision of a nice young man to dally with a maid leads to death, disgrace, and prison. It is interesting that Wolfe shows these consequences only for those who have been true to conventional morality and then choose to step out of line. The characters who are amoral from the beginning, such as Maria and Peter Fallow, flourish.

It is significant that the central act that leads, in one way or another, to all the other disasters is adultery. (If McCoy had not begun his dalliance with Maria, Henry Lamb would still be alive and Larry Kramer would not have destroyed his career by trying to get her apartment for

Shelley Thomas.) While free love, open marriage, and other such slogans are less often heard since the AIDS epidemic made multiple sex partners so clearly a prudential, as well as a moral, question, it is certainly true that American literature since World War II has, if anything, celebrated sexual exploration, adultery, and divorce. Wolfe, on the other hand, treats it as the primal betrayal. In part it is disastrous because it inevitably sets the person who commits it on a continued course of deception. Since McCoy must lie to his wife, he cannot go to the police or even cooperate with them when they come to him. What would have been just a frightening incident had he been alone in the car becomes his downfall because his mistress is with him.

A related theme is vanity itself. McCoy and especially Kramer are not lured into adultery purely through lust—though there is plenty of that present, and they both are fully alive to the sexual attractions of almost all the women they meet. Rather it is because they feel that they are owed an attractive woman who will gaze at them with admiration as they display their splendid selves. Other sorts of vanity appear throughout the book. McCoy is proud of his clothes—but so is Roland Auburn, who will only wear the brand new running shoes that are de rigueur on the street. Kramer is proud of his physique and preens by flexing his muscles. All the central characters, McCoy, Kramer, and Fallow, want to be recognized as more important than others—especially other men.

In *The Right Stuff*, Wolfe described a form of male competition that produced heroes. In this novel he describes less productive forms. The bond-trading floor at Pierce & Pierce includes no women, and McCoy thinks of it as being like an air force squadron, where "[y]ou were either capable of doing the job and willing to devote 100 percent to the job, or you got out" (61). But the competition here is directed to producing no public good, only money, and the sacrifices it implies for personal or family life seem out of all proportion. If the value of masculine competition is dubious on the bond floor, it is deadly on the street. Fitzgibbon describes Henry Lamb's decision to go along with Auburn in terms of a threat to his masculinity: Auburn was "taunting the kid, because he's such a mama's boy" (582). Still another form of masculine competition seems to shape the culture of the police and the D.A.'s office.

Another theme that Wolfe traced in earlier books that turns up in *The Bonfire of the Vanities* is the lure of the bohemian. In days past, when McCoy visited Maria's apartment with no worries about incriminating phone calls, much less criminal charges on his mind, he thought, "How bohemian! How . . . *real* this place was" (18), though that appeal is completely dead for him by the time he makes his final visit. In the same way, Larry Kramer is drawn to the carefree, youthful scene he sees around him. He wants to "seize the Life for himself" (47), using the same phrase that the bohemian surfers in "The Pump House Gang" use.

A large theme in the novel is the unfettered power of the press, which can hound citizens and publish half-truths at will. (Wolfe does not romanticize the profession he has worked in for so many years.) Indeed, publicity and celebrity are themes throughout the novel, where the TV cameras are present from the first scene to the last. Besides exploring the connections between publicity and politics, Wolfe also examines the odd notion of celebrity in America. Being a celebrity makes one attractive, whether the publicity is bad or good. McCoy becomes a social lion after the press has portrayed him as a heartless hit-and-run driver.

A POLITICAL READING: TWO NATIONS?

Except for sweeping historical novels, most works of fiction focus primarily on the experience of the individual. The form has proven ideal for the artistic exploration of private psychological experience—or of "sensibility," as an earlier age would have put it. Nevertheless, many novels are also explorations of public, and indeed, political issues. The great naturalist authors, such as Émile Zola (1840–1902) were not just involved in politics personally; they used their art to explore the political problems of their times. A political reading of any novel, whether the novel is openly political or not, will consider what political issues are raised by the novel and what stance, explicit or implicit, the author takes on those issues.

Benjamin Disraeli, the greatest leader of the Conservative or Tory party in nineteenth-century Britain, was also a novelist. While Tom Wolfe does not list him as one of his models, he has much in common with him. Like Disraeli, Wolfe presents a radical critique of the nation for conservative ends. In Disraeli's novel *Sybil: or, The Two Nations* (1845), the two nations are the rich and the poor, and they are hostile to one another. The rich feel little responsibility for the plight of the poor, and the poor are led by corrupt leaders toward useless violence. Disraeli imagines a reconciliation, like the "Tory democracy" he championed in real life, in which the aristocracy protects the people from oppressive trade and government and the people follow them rather than radical demagogues. In *The Bonfire of the Vanities*, there are at least two nations, for the divisions of class are complicated by race. Though Wolfe presents a clear analysis of the problems caused by the divisions between these nations, his satirical vision does not present any clear solutions, certainly not the romantic ones Disraeli envisioned.

Wolfe depicts a world in which different groups are thoroughly segregated from one another. Until he gets into trouble, McCoy needs to have little contact with any workingman beyond his doorman at home, the attendant at his garage, and the shoeshine man at the office. He goes to work in a taxi and returns home in a chauffeured car provided by his employer. Professional men of his father's generation took the subway to and from work, rubbing shoulders with the lower classes as they did so, but McCoy's generation has insulated itself from contact with people unlike themselves. One of the indignities Kramer has to suffer as a civil servant is that he must take the subway to work, but once at the Bronx County building, he is almost as insulated from the poor as McCoy is. Wolfe compares the building to the Rock of Gibraltar, and it does indeed seem to be a fortress in foreign territory. The judges and prosecutors always lunch in the building, since there is no longer any place to eat in the desolate area around it and, in any case, they fear for their lives when they leave its guarded walls.

The great division, of course, is racial. The McCoys live almost entirely among white people—even their servants are Hispanic rather than black. They may, rarely, meet a black person of their own class at a charity party but not at a "society" one. When McCoy and Maria get lost in the Bronx, they are terrified not just because the area is dangerous but because it is mostly black. McCoy assumes that the two young black men who confront him on the ramp are out to attack him even before they do anything. His assumption is correct about one of them, but it is based on nothing but the situation, including the race of the young men. The housing projects where Henry Lamb lives are almost entirely black. There are few places where the races meet, and in the novel they are usually places of confrontation, such as the courtroom or the demonstration.

Wolfe shows this division harming all members of society because it makes it almost impossible for people to deal with each other using the neutral principles that bind society together. In America, those neutral principles are embodied most definitively in law. As its usual allegorical representation shows, the law is supposed to be blind to everything but the facts of the case and the principles of justice. It is supposed to be beyond the influence of race, class, wealth, or personal connections. Everyone brought before the bar of justice is supposed to be equal. In both costume and language, American judges symbolically put aside their personalities in order to take on the role of neutral arbiters: they wear robes instead of personally distinctive clothes and refer to their decisions, not as their own, but as those of "this court." The ideal that the system seeks to embody is that no one should be judged by an interested party, whether that is a capricious tyrant or an impassioned mob.

What has gone wrong is that much of the society Wolfe describes has lost faith in that ideal, and instead of trying to make it a reality, has abandoned the very ideal of impartial justice and neutral principles. American history, of course, gives many groups, and especially black Americans, ample reason to think the ideal of equal justice was never a reality. The centuries of slavery, segregation, and lynching show that until recently in many places in this country it has been an ideal that applied, if at all, only to a part of the population. Groups like Reverend Bacon's do not trust that the system has been reformed and will, if left to proceed on its own, produce neutral justice. Bacon mocks the very idea of justice as a "blind woman" (655). Instead, he and his followers resort to political pressure and demonstrations that verge on mob violence to force the criminal justice system to produce the ends they want.

Almost everyone is, in fact, powerless in the face of the mob, or more precisely, in the face of charges of racism. Accusations of racism trump any other consideration: even the almost equally poisonous charge of anti-Semitism. The powers of the state—the mayor and the district attorney—bow before Bacon's protests. There is, in fact, no way to counter the charges that "Weiss Justice is White Justice," so demands that the case really be treated like every other case, such as those pressed by Bernie Fitzgibbon, are ignored. Once what we have called "the race card" since the O.J. Simpson trial has been played, there is a great danger that the justice system will be guided not by facts and neutral principles but by political expediency. The degeneration of the legal system from a means of insuring justice into an arena in which biased actors perform political theater is perhaps the most troubling of the themes Wolfe explores.

With only a few exceptions, everyone is swept up in the same tide and driven to seek a result that is unjust. (McCoy is certainly not guilty of manslaughter, at least, since he was not driving the car when it struck Henry Lamb.) Only a few figures resist the demands of the mob. The most important of these is Judge Kovitsky. Kovitsky is the exemplar of a devotion to color-blind justice. Although he is a minor character in the novel, he is in some ways its moral center. His first appearance in the novel shows him worried about ethnic divisions: the insults from the prisoners that bother him are the anti-Semitic ones. (He notes, in salty language, how ironic those taunts are, considering the importance of Jews in the Civil Rights movement.) In his last appearance, he alone stands against prosecutions based on the demands of the mob. He realizes that if the ideal of neutral justice is abandoned, it will, it the end, hurt the powerless much more than the privileged. For that reason he calls himself "their only friend" when referring to the demonstrators outside his courtroom. But his idea of trying to explain that to them seems Quixotic, and even he abandons it before he can leave the building. Defending the ideal of neutral justice in a racially polarized society seems hopeless, and his election defeat only underscores that point. Kovitsky's defeat is a sort of "poetic injustice" that matches the literal injustice he fights in his court.

Instead of neutral principles, the system seems to be based on power. But power is a divided and complex thing in Wolfe's world, and rarely appears in a pure form. Indeed, almost none of those who are motivated by considerations of power will admit that—even to themselves. Kramer and Weiss want to further their careers, but they also want to think they are really furthering the cause of social justice. Convicting "the Great White Defendant" will burnish their own self-images as tribunes of the people—as well as encouraging those people to keep them in power, instead of replacing them with members of their own ethnic groups. Even Sir Gerald Steiner, who uses the McCoy story to sell newspapers and buy off racial protesters, thinks of himself as a crusading journalist. What is more, all these characters—and the mayor—are Jews and feel a traditional commitment to black causes, even in an era when black groups are often anti-Semitic, as well as a certain antipathy toward the WASP power structure. (The ethnic divisions Wolfe describes go well beyond black and white: white ethnics, such as the Irish and Italians who fill the police department and the D.A.'s office, have almost as little in common with WASP's as with blacks.)

Raw power is, nevertheless, one of the great motivators in the novel. Kramer feels it most intensely when he confronts Maria Ruskin and her lawyers. He feels "the inexpressible pleasure of possessing" the power of the state—"the power of the government over the freedom of its subjects" (591). Abe Weiss is, in Kramer's mind, at least, "totally given over" to that power. And they do, indeed, wield it. They can put almost anyone in jail, for a time, and strip him of the most basic personal dignities. The irony is that that power, which seems absolute to the person being handcuffed or fingerprinted or locked in a cell with dangerous men, is so precarious. It cannot be used as its possessor would choose. Weiss—and the mayor—find themselves forced into courses of actions (essentially, alliances with Reverend Bacon) that they would never freely choose. But to keep their power, they must use it so as preserve their positions. The real power is with those who can force the current possessors of political power into action—and in this case, that action is to ignore principles of neutral justice and to side with the mob.

A further irony in the way power works in the novel is that privilege is no protection and that the "marginalized" are the most powerful. No part of the power structure closes ranks behind McCoy in order to protect one of its own. The police and prosecutors seem to have no deference for wealth or position, and McCoy is, in any case, not one of their own, since they are Jews and Irishmen. His wealth only makes him a better target. The power structure, on the other hand, does cower before the mob. The assumed moral superiority of any black leader, even one with dubious financial dealings, makes it impossible for most white politicians to confront Reverend Bacon directly, much as they might like to. With a mob and the press behind him, he can make the holders of power do what he pleases. He does not need to take the titles of power any more than Lorzeno de Medici or Savonarola needed to call himself "duke" in order to rule Florence. (With his bond business, Bacon is a financier as well as a preacher.) As he explains to Ed Fiske, institutions, the government as much as the mainline churches, deal with him not to achieve their announced ends, but for "steam control" (150). They cooperate with him, directly or by following his lead, for fear of an uprising, either in the streets or at the polling booths.

Florence in the Middle Ages and the Renaissance produced great wealth, great art, and great literature. Its factionalized politics also produced almost uninterrupted civil strife and bloodshed—and sent many of its greatest artists into exile. In showing modern New York as a battleground of factions where the Enlightenment ideals of "equal justice under law" are abandoned in favor of identity politics, Wolfe warns that any state that allows power to be controlled by the desires of faction unrestrained by neutral principles may find itself facing the sort of humiliations, public and private, that Florence did.

A Man in Full
(1998)

"A man's a man for a' that."

—Robert Burns

African American poet Sterling Brown described a "man in full" in his 1938 ballad, "Break of Day." Big Jess is a coal-heaver on a steam loco-motive, and he faces lynching because he refuses to give up his job when times turn hard and white men want to take his place. Big Jess might seem to have little in common with Charlie Croker, the hero of Tom Wolfe's latest novel. One is a black man working a backbreaking job on the railroads in the days of segregation, the other a white real estate developer in the capital of the New South. Yet they are linked in several ways. Both are trying to hold on to what they have achieved in the face of what looks like certain ruin, and both find their lives and choices determined, in part, by race and the history of the South. Still more important, both are shaped by an ideal of manhood. It includes physical strength: Charlie recalls a folk song about his namesake that declares, "Charlie Croker was a man in full / Back as broad as a jersey bull." But it includes a vision of integrity, honor, or self-respect as well. The ques-tion they each face is, finally, what must one do—and what must one be willing to lose—in order to be a man in full.

The novel explores many serious social, political, and moral issues, but like most of Wolfe's work, its surface is more often than not comic. Wolfe even indulges in a number of in-jokes—for example, naming Atlanta's police chief Elihu Yale, after the benefactor of the university where Wolfe did his graduate work, or giving one of the minor figures tastes in clothing very like his own and explaining that the man is "determined to be a Character" (527). Yet the serious issues remain. Some of Wolfe's characters struggle with the issue of where to find value when material goods have failed them, and the traditional sources of meaning, such as religion, are not a living part of their experience. Others deal with questions of racial identity in a world where power and even wealth are crossing the old color line. In painting his panorama of Atlanta in the 1990s, Wolfe attempts to capture both the creative vibrancy of American material culture and the spiritual or moral malaise coexisting with it.

PLOT

Charlie Croker seems to be enjoying all the trappings of success as an Atlanta real estate developer, including weekends quail hunting at his beloved south Georgia estate, Turpmtine, where he entertains old friends like Inman Armholster. Even so, Charlie's world is collapsing around him. His business is nearing bankruptcy, and he is suffering from an arthritic knee and from growing doubts about the wisdom of having left Martha, his wife of many years, for Serena, his young trophy wife, and about his own potency. He has to face humiliations such as a "workout session" at PlannersBanc, his main creditor, where bank officers Harry Zale and Raymond Peepgass, men who were deferential to him when they wanted his business, insult him and demand that he sell off part of his empire to pay his debts. He holds on to the things that symbolize his success, the plantation and a corporate jet, and decides to lay off 15 percent of the workers at the food distribution company he owns, Croker Global Foods.

Meanwhile, there is trouble brewing in Atlanta. The football coach at Georgia Tech has called Roger White, an African American partner in an establishment law firm, to help him with a potentially explosive situation. A black star on his team, Fareek Fanon has been accused of raping a young white woman during Freaknick, the gathering of mostly black college students for spring break in Atlanta—and that young woman is Armholster's daughter Elizabeth. If the charges are made public, they could have awful consequences not just for the team, but also for city, which might split along racial lines. White is brought in because of his contacts with the mayor, Wesley Dobbs Jordan. The mayor agrees to do what he can, assuming it is in the best interests of the city. He also recruits White to gather information on André Fleet, his likely rival in the upcoming election. Fleet is running on the idea that members of the black elite like Jordan are not in close enough touch with the "real" black majority of the city, but his chief financial backer, the mayor reveals, is Inman Armholster.

Charlie's problems tell on him. He begins sliding into depression and insomnia as the demands for money become more insistent. But his problems also ramify across the country. Conrad Hensley works in the freezer at the Croker Global Foods warehouse near Oakland. It is hard work, but it gives him a chance to save his money, buy a condo for his wife and children, and climb into the middle class. One night he saves the life of his friend Kenny during an accident in the freezer, but before the shift is over receives a notice telling him that he has been laid off. Unemployment brings him the contempt of his mother-in-law—and also of his wife Jill—and he tries to get a new job. He goes to Oakland to take a typing test but finds that the warehouse work has left his hands and fingers too huge for the keyboard. While he is taking the test, his car is unjustly marked for towing by a meter maid, and he spends a Kafka-esque day trying to get it back. When he is finally at the impound lot, he is told he cannot have the car without paying more than he expected—or has. Feeling he has been treated unjustly and seeing his car being damaged, he tries to take it away. In the ensuing altercation a man suffers a heart attack, and Conrad is arrested. He winds up in the jail at Santa Rita, convicted of a felony since he has refused a plea bargain. Jill visits him once but seems unlikely to support him. He fears the prison gangs, and the threat of homosexual rape hangs over the whole institution.

Raymond Peepgass is separated from his family because of an affair with a woman who has filed a paternity suit against him. He and Harry Zale continue their pressure on Charlie, and Peepgass develops an idea that would allow him to profit personally from Croker's collapse. If Croker could be persuaded to simply hand over his deeds instead of going through bankruptcy, the property could be quickly sold without adverse publicity for the bank. Peepgass thinks he could put together his own syndicate to buy the property and take millions in commissions. As part of his plan, he seeks out Martha Croker. She feels like the "superfluous woman," and her efforts to change that seem futile. She tries to reenter society by buying a table at the opening of a daring show of homoerotic art at the High Museum but finds that no one pays attention to her. Her guests are more interested in Charlie, who has allowed Serena to book a table so that they will not seem to be in financial trouble. Peepgass is the only person who seems to want to talk to her. Peepgass later learns from her that Croker drove down the prices of the land he needed for his latest development by staging a confrontation between the Ku Klux Klan and André Fleet's group in the area.

The mayor has developed a plan to settle the Fanon problem, which is becoming public through an Internet site. He wants a prominent white businessman—Charlie Croker—to appear with him in public and call for fair play for Fanon. In return, PlannersBanc, which holds many of the city's deposits and would not want to lose them, will end all pressure on Croker and restructure the loans. Roger White is to make the proposal. He has already spoken up for Fanon at a televised press conference and has enjoyed the support from blacks of all classes that it brought him. Croker's own attempts to get more cash into his business have failed. He has tried to interest liberal Jewish businessman, Herb Richman, in making Croker Concourse his corporate headquarters by making him part of a weekend at Turpmtine, but he has only succeeded in offending him, and when Croker's private plane touches down back in Atlanta, it is seized by Zale, Peepgass, and some sheriff's deputies. Croker manages to sabotage the plane before they can fly it away, but he has still been humiliated.

Conrad Hensley is seeing horrible things happen in the Santa Rita jail. His only solace is a book that was sent to him by mistake. He wanted a thriller called *The Stoic's Game*, but got instead *The Stoics*, the works of the ancient philosophers. He finds that Epictetus, especially, speaks to him. Here is the rule for his life, an explanation of all that has happened to him. He comes to feel full of the "spark of Zeus" and unknowingly prays for the first time. He is now able first to stand up, in a small way, for a pathetic homosexual inmate who has been raped by a prison gang, and then to use the strength in his hands to best the leader of the gang when he confronts him. He is faced with retribution from the gang but escapes it, thanks to an earthquake that destroys the jail. He drags his cellmate to safety and then flees, getting both clothes and a jeep at the army reserve center across the fence. He drives off to find Kenny, who uses his connections with Vietnamese traffickers of immigrants to get Conrad a trip to Atlanta. Once there, another part of the Vietnamese network gives him papers creating a new identity for him. He finds a new home, and in it, miraculously it seems, he discovers a copy of the book he lost in the earthquake. When working as a home health aid, he draws on his prison experience to defend an elderly couple from an extortionist. They praise him so highly that he is assigned to the service's most important new client: Charlie Croker.

White has presented the plan to Croker, who is dealing with more pressure from the bank and other creditors every day. Croker cannot see how he can honorably do what is asked: he has more than once promised Armholster to do anything he can for him. But he does agree to meet Fanon, who is not at all deferential to the old white football player. Croker does not know what to do: he cannot imagine what he will say to Inman and his other friends if he speaks up for Fanon, but he knows he will not see much of them in any case if he loses his money and position. He decides what to do after he receives a videotape from Zale. It tells the story of his inciting racial conflict to get the land he needed. Knowing that if that story comes out he will be finished, he calls White and agrees to the plan. He also soon decides to have the knee-replacement surgery he has been putting off. The hospital will be a refuge for him.

It turns out not to be a refuge, however; Roger White finds him there, and demands clearer commitments from Croker about when he will make his statement. He later appears at Croker's home while Charlie is doing his physical therapy with Conrad, and Conrad sees the older man humiliated into agreeing on a date to appear at a press conference with the mayor. By this point Peepgass's syndicate is in place. Herb Rickman has invested in it, although he knows how shady the plan is, and Martha Croker and Peepgass have become lovers, though each finds the other more comfortable than passionate. But the plan is not going anywhere now that the bank's executives have decided to take the pressure off Croker. Roger White is enjoying being a political player and elated that he can intimidate someone of Croker's stature. Charlie Croker, however, is still in a quandary. He becomes more and more interested in Conrad and the book he is always reading, and even borrows it. To escape from White and all the pressure, he takes his family and Conrad on an out-of-season trip to Turpmtine. There he tells Serena about his problems. She is all for his making the statement. She says that she has gathered from Elizabeth Armholster, who is a friend of hers, that what happened was not the rape her father describes but simply two young people "hooking up." That view of things, which would protect the fortune Serena has married, does not help Charlie. What does help is a serious talk with Conrad. Conrad feels that he has been brought by Zeus to turn the man who fired him into a means of spreading the Stoic message. Charlie asks what Epictetus would say about his predicament, and the two men share their stories. In the end, Charlie decides not to lie or flatter, and to go to the press conference to talk about the Divine spark.

At the press conference, he tells about the deal that was offered him, says that he is walking away from all his property, and then goes on to speak about Stoicism. The mayor responds by saying that he is acting treacherously. Martha and Peepgass are watching on television. She is saddened by what she sees as the breakdown of someone who was once great. Peepgass is delighted: if Croker goes ahead and turns over his deeds, his plans for his syndicate can go forward. Roger White is angry at Croker, but before he can confront him, he is hearing delightful messages of support from black politicians. Charlie has achieved just what the Stoics promised. For the first time in ages, he feels serene.

In the epilogue Roger White visits the mayor the day after his reelection. It turns out that the Croker incident was the turning point in the campaign, even if it did not go as planned. The mayor got stronger support from the black community because he stood up for Fanon. Fleet could not support Fanon more strongly than the mayor did, but neither could he reject him, which is what Armholster wanted him to do, so he lost the money he needed for his campaign. Charlie Croker did turn over his deeds and leave everything, and he is now preaching Stoicism in South Georgia and Florida. A TV show, *The Stoic's Hour*, is in the works. Conrad went back to California and turned himself in, citing his Stoic beliefs, and the judge released him. He is preaching with Charlie. Croker's property sold for more than expected, and Peepgass's scheme was discovered by the bank. He lost his job but has married Martha Croker. The mayor is pleased with how things have turned out, thinking he has done his best for both Fanon and the city of Atlanta, and Roger White is seriously thinking about a career in politics.

CHARACTER DEVELOPMENT

The central figure in *A Man in Full* is, of course, Charlie Croker. All the other male characters are, to greater or lesser extents, simply his foils, characters who set off his virtues and flaws by their contrast with him. He enacts several traditional American roles, though none of them perfectly. All are roles that American intellectuals tend to sneer at. He has had the sort of rags to riches career often associated with the novels of Horatio Alger. He has been a football star in college and still enjoys his reputation as "the Sixty-Minute Man," one of the last players to excel at both offense and defense. He has made his money through dealing in real estate, a line of work most famously treated by an American novelist in Sinclair Lewis's *Babbitt*, a book whose hero's name entered the language as a synonym for the narrow-minded and self-interested provincial booster. Finally, he is very much a man of the South. While he sometimes plays the role of the master of the Old Plantation and delights in being called "Cap'n Charlie" by his staff at Turpmtine, he does not really fit the role of the "Southern Gentleman" in a linen suit. Rather, he plays that other Southern male role, the "good old boy," the lower-class rural white Southerner who retains his country manners no matter how far he rises in the world.

Croker turns out to be more complicated than intellectual stereotypes would suggest. He is indeed a man who values other qualities more than intelligence. Even at sixty, he is proud of his physical strength and of his displays of prowess, both on football field and during his tour of duty in Vietnam. He has, nevertheless, had the intelligence to create an empire starting with little beyond his football fame and a socially adept wife. And the impulse behind his empire building seems to be more than simple acquisitiveness; he has expressed a real creative urge in bringing his developments into being. His skills as a salesman have shown some insight into human nature. Even his self-presentation as a good old boy is, in part, an act he puts on deliberately, either when very comfortable or as a mask against possible embarrassment.

Croker also has a sense of honor—one he has violated several times. His Southern ideal is not the romantic, aristocratic one of *Gone With the Wind* but one that keeps more of its rural heritage and connection with nature. It involves not just strength and self-reliance but also integrity and a loyalty to one's retainers. Charlie believes in those values, but as he has moved up in the world, he has been caught up in the glamour of wealth and the comfort of position. He has betrayed his first wife, who made possible his successes. He has overreached economically and faces the shame of bankruptcy. He has amassed land through machinations that would bring ignominy down on him if they became public. And though he talks about the hands at Turpmtine who depend on him, he shows no loyalty to the staff that works for him in the Croker Global plants. He has climbed to the top of the economic and social pyramid and now faces the prospect of giving it all up if he is to keep what is left of the honor he has already tarnished. His dilemma results in part because he has always proved his self-worth through competition—in sports, war, and business. In that way he is utterly unlike men such as his Chief Financial Officer Wismer Strook and Conrad Hensley, who want lives of safety, not risk. He is facing, perhaps for the first time, the question of what to do when one loses the great competition.

For Conrad Hensley, the goal in life is not to win big. He does not even dream of becoming rich. He wants instead to work his way into the bourgeoisie. He is a child of Bay Area hippies, who quote Ken Kesey's maxim "go with the flow" and use the term "the whole bourgeois trip" to reject anything that involves order, planning, or hard work. Conrad hates the squalor he has been raised in and aspires to the life his parents scorn. Even when his favorite professor at a community college speaks slightingly of it, Conrad loves the idea of the bourgeois life, with its insistence on order and morality and financial stability (171). He genuinely wants a safe, middle-class life, which in his mind means nothing grander than a condo in the suburb of Danville, but he struggles under the burden of a wife and two children. He has tried to live up to his bourgeois ideals, even at great cost to himself: he chose to marry Jill when she became pregnant, rather than abandon his child. With only the beginnings of an education, he relies on clichés to express his deepest values, but he shows genuine courage in trying to achieve the bourgeois life others take for granted. Many other men of his class, such as Kenny and his friends who take "crash'n'burn" as their slogan, seem to have given up on it.

While Charlie has risen to wealth from the rural lower classes, and Conrad is a child of bohemia, several other men are the children of the bourgeoisie. Raymond Peepgass, who always chose the safer path until his sexual indiscretion landed him in trouble, is one example. When he tries to be a swashbuckler like Charlie, Peepgass seems to be acting out of character, and it is not surprising that in the end he gives up passion for comfort.

Two other characters are still more firmly bourgeois, even though they find their membership in that class problematic for other reasons. Roger White and Wesley Dobbs Jordan are from exactly the class described in E. Franklin Frazier's *Black Bourgeoisie* (1957). They are from the old black elite, which tended to be light in skin color, and they are both graduates of the black elite's flagship college, Morehouse. They have succeeded by the standards of the white bourgeoisie: they are highly educated, live in attractive neighborhoods, and are successful in their careers. The question they face is how far they can be part of white society and how far they can have real solidarity with blacks from social backgrounds of which they have no real experience. Wesley Jordan handles this question, as he handles most, through the use of irony. He will play the role of an Afro-centric collector of Yoruba artifacts or of a high-fiving street brother, but always with the suggestion that he *is* playing a role and expects others to know he is. Roger White II, on the other hand, is almost perfectly comfortable in the elite white world. Since his college days he has been saddled with the nickname "Roger Too White," which fits him all too well. He loves European high culture, and, if anything, looks down on white businessmen because they do not dress as well as he. But as the novel progresses, he comes to enjoy feeling that he is accepted, even celebrated, as a member of the black community. His political awakening is in part the result of his realization that race does matter and that he likes feeling part of his community.

Fareek Fanon has never had the opportunity to become bourgeois. As it was for Charlie Croker years before, college football has been his path to success. For him, however, financial success has been almost immediate, and he has not had to learn to follow, as best he can, the rules of society in order to get ahead. He has not had much opportunity to learn those rules, since the black bourgeoisie, including White and Jordan's parents, abandoned his part of Atlanta years before, leaving behind an underclass with its own values, as well as its own fashions and language. We see enough of Fareek to know he is arrogant, impertinent, and selfish. Whether or not he is guilty of rape is an open question. He denies it, and the versions of events recounted on the basis of Elizabeth Armholster's confidences by her father and Serena Croker conflict. It is clear, however, that Fareek has thought of her only as a sexual object.

The other women prominent in the novel have played the same role in Charlie Croker's life, at least initially. His attraction to Serena seems to have been almost purely sexual. He certainly was not drawn to the investments in the art market she was trying to interest him in through the auspices of PlannersBanc. She, on the other hand, plays the manipulative femme fatale. She seems to have been mercenary in every part of her relationship with Charlie—the mayor suggests that women like her hurry to have children only to seal their tie to the rich old men they have married—and Charlie comes to wonder why he married her. He feels he cannot look to her for support in times of trouble. When he does tell her what is weighing on him, she advises him to take the course of action that will protect their joint fortune, without much regard for any concerns involving morality or honor he may feel.

Charlie's interest in Martha was also largely sexual to begin with. He is even proud, when he thinks of it, that while he married well, he did not marry Martha for her position but for her beauty and charm. Her skills have aided him over the years, but years and pounds have made her a less obvious object of a sexual fantasy. Having thrown it away, he misses his life with her. She is still more devastated. She has been betrayed and shamed. She finds herself trying to meet a physical ideal appropriate for few women and for almost none her age. She has lost her social network, becoming almost invisible without Charlie. In response, she settles for Peepgass, a man without the strength and drive she found so exciting in Charlie and one who will need a lot of maintenance, but one who at least—having thrown his own bourgeois life away—appreciates the comfortable life she can provide.

STRUCTURE AND POINT OF VIEW

The structure of *A Man in Full* has a great deal in common with that of *The Bonfire of the Vanities*. Several plots intertwine. The central one involves the fall of a man from a position of power and wealth; the others show men of less grandiose positions whose successes or failures are entwined with the central figure's fate. All the plots build up to a climactic event that brings all the figures together, and the novel ends with an epilogue in which many loose strands are tied up in the form of reports from not entirely reliable sources.

One of the major differences between the two novels is that in *A Man in Full*, the characters do not just confront each other at the end. One *transforms* another. Sherman McCoy stands in the same courtroom with Larry Kramer and Peter Fallow, but they view him only from the outside and use him for their own ends. In their different ways, Raymond Peepgass and Roger White play similar roles in the story of Charlie Croker. Conrad Hensley, on the other hand, listens to Croker's story and brings him the essentially religious message that changes his life. Since Conrad has been brought to Atlanta from California by a series of improbable events—including an earthquake, something the insurance companies still call an "act of God"—*A Man in Full* seems to have something in common not only with those novels that use coincidence to underscore irony, but also with those works, so common in Victorian times, in which coincidence is the sign of the action of Providence.

The other great difference between *A Man in Full* and Wolfe's earlier novel is that parts of it are told from the points of view of a woman and of a black man. Women's perspectives are very rare in the earlier novel, and blacks are observed only from the outside. In Roger White and Martha Croker, Wolfe tries to describe from the inside what it is like to look in on, from very specific vantage points, the white male world of the

South. Whatever the sections recounted from their points of view tell us about upwardly mobile African Americans or wealthy divorcées of a certain age, they tell us a great deal about Charlie Croker, a man who has only the vaguest idea of what blacks and women think about him.

Like many long works of fiction, *A Man in Full* has the flaw of being too short: that is, its ending seems rushed, and issues that have been raised are not explored. The most notable such issue is depression. Charlie Croker is described as depressed, in the clinical sense, but that explanation of his torpor and malaise is abandoned when Conrad Hensley and Epictetus appear with their philosophical solution to his predicament. Conrad works in Charlie's life like a deus ex machina, the literary term for an improbable character or event that solves a problem in the plot. The name comes from the practice of some ancient dramatists of having a god descend from a machine above the stage to set all things right. Wolfe uses the device several times in *A Man in Full*, notably when the earthquake releases Conrad from prison just when he is in the greatest danger.

MAJOR THEMES

In *A Man in Full*, as in *The Bonfire of the Vanities*, Wolfe explores the way American cities are developing at the turn of the twenty-first century. The Atlanta of the second novel is, however, very different from the New York of the first. New York as Wolfe presents it, is an established center of world culture and business. A WASP elite to some extent controls the business world, and society still is shaped by family and school connections, even as new ethnic groups are taking political control of the city. As in traditional European cities, wealth remains in the city center, in places like Park Avenue. Atlanta, on the other hand, is more like a new model of the American city, described by Joel Garreau in his book *Edge City* (1991), one of the few books Charlie Croker has devoured. In the newer model of the American city, downtown may remain a business and financial center. As in Atlanta, it may even come to be a center of international business. But the residential, shopping, social, restaurant, and even business centers will be elsewhere, in satellite city centers— some, like Buckhead, within the political limits of the city, some far beyond it. Atlanta, which is a new creation among the cities of the South, not one with centuries of tradition, like Richmond or Savannah, is a perfect example of this trend. New cities are built by developers like Charlie Croker, who has simply taken the inevitable expansion one step too far out into the country, for now. The growth, even the creativity, is on the edge.

The political power in the center city, however, is completely out of the hands of whatever white elites once held it. In the urban core, political power is already controlled by a black power structure, and whites must learn to do business with them. That political power has passed from one racial group to another is only one of the many changes that characterize Atlanta, and by extension other groups of edge cities and the rest of American culture. There is really no old elite; only a series of groups who ascend to power. The institutions that seem most like bastions of an aristocratic tradition are really the home of a series of parvenus: Charlie Croker belongs to the Piedmont Driving Club, but he is by birth a poor boy from below the "gnat line." He owns a plantation, but it is not the ancestral estate; it is a property that has been held in succession by a series of newly rich men. Other elites find their hold on position just as tenuous. The older black elite exemplified by the mayor and Roger White faces competition from those who present themselves as more authentically black. Everything, in other words, is dynamic, and there is great excitement for those willing to make things happen.

Continuing racial separation is another of Wolfe's themes. In the Atlanta he presents, segregation is long gone, but what has replaced it is not exactly integration. Blacks are in positions of power, part of the city's black-controlled political system and full members of traditional white institutions, such as Roger White's law firm. Socially, however, they still move in a world separate from that of white Atlantans in similar positions. They do not do so because they are excluded from white society: it is significant that both Jordan and White have been approached about joining the Piedmont Driving Club and passed up the opportunity. Instead, they choose to make racial identity primary and let it trump affiliations based on such things as social class, education, and professional position. Roger White is especially uncomfortable with having to make this choice, but comes to enjoy the feeling of being part of a community that prizes him. That separatism, rather than integration, has come to be valued in some parts of African American society is certainly true: Jordan and White themselves discuss, with some irony, the Afrocentric movement, and American culture has seen a rise in "identity politics" and the loss of faith in integration, much less "assimilation." Through Jordan and White, Wolfe suggests that in the great debate among black intellectuals embodied by Booker T. Washington and W.E.B. Du Bois, Washington has been proved just as right as Du Bois. Washington is often stigmatized as an accommodationist, one willing to tolerate discrimination while seeking the economic improvement that would gain the respect of whites. In the new Atlanta, powerful whites show the greatest possible respect for blacks: they come to them for help because they have taken control of important institutions in government and business, even if they do not move in the same social circles. (Interestingly, one of Wolfe's sources, Garreau's *Edge City*, paints a much less bleak picture of racial division in the new Atlanta. He describes many of the new edge cities to which middle-class blacks have moved as thoroughly integrated and reports that a third of the Atlanta area's black citizens live in predominantly white neighborhoods [145]).

Another theme Wolfe explores is the consequences of the "sexual revolution," including the consequences of divorce. Conrad cannot hear the expression without disgust. To him it means the sordid world of his parents, who never bothered to get married. He cannot forget the shameful discovery of his parents sprawled naked on the floor with another couple after a night of group sex. His own decision to marry Jill after he gets her pregnant is a response to the loose affiliations of his parents. For most of the other characters, the sexual revolution has had three great consequences. The first is the disappearance of customs of sexual modesty, especially among the age group that would once have been tended by chaperones and subject to parietal rules. The disappearance of "dating" in favor of "hooking up" makes possible the ambiguities surrounding the incident involving Fareek Fanon and Elizabeth Armholster.

The second consequence is a culture in which divorce is no longer stigmatized, and that fact shapes the lives of many of the figures in the novel. Charlie, among others, is able to shed the woman who has built up his career for a trophy wife and still hold his head up in society, something that would not have been true in an earlier era. (In the same way, Raymond Peepgass's wife does not hesitate to throw him out after discovering his infidelity.) Wolfe shows the dilemma of the abandoned middle-aged wife through several characters. The most notable of the group is Martha Croker, but it also includes her friend Joyce and Jill's mother, a woman who is passing her bitterness toward men on to her daughter, even though Conrad is not at all likely to follow his father-in-law's example. He also makes it clear that another consequence of divorce is that fathers play a much diminished role in their children's lives: Charlie seems to hardly know his son—he is unlikely to do better with his infant daughter—and Peepgass has little to do with any of his children. (Fareek Fanon exemplifies a part of the culture where fathers have abandoned their roles still more completely: his father is merely a man who was pointed out to him once.)

The last great consequence of the sexual revolution is the rise of un-realistic sexual ideals. Women suffer from them more directly, having to try to meet the physical ideal of a "boy with breasts" even when that does not suit their age or body type. But men who succumb to the idea that sexual ecstasy is all around them and that they are almost entitled to a share of it fare almost as badly: both Croker and Peepgass spoil their lives seeking it. If Martha is correct, even Charlie's business failure was wrapped up with his sexual transgression: his attempt to prove himself the greatest of developers was a way of proving his continued potency to his trophy wife.

Wolfe shows that many different facets of American society are related to each other in unexpected ways. Some of the connections are economic: Charlie's overreaching in Atlanta real estate means unemployment north of Oakland. Others are cultural. For example, Wolfe shows the culture and fashions—and even the values—of prison rippling through society. That point is made explicitly by the mayor, who shows Roger White ghetto boys who dress in deliberate imitation of convicts, wearing their pants low and "do-rags" on their heads because belts and hats are not allowed in prison. But it is also clear in contexts where no one is likely to have even met a convict. White is appalled, in an early scene, that the rich black college students in town for Freaknic are dancing to rap songs that are essentially paeans to rape. The women at DefinitionAmerica, including Martha Croker, exercise to the same music, moving to the words, "Ram yo' booty." Kenny and the crash'n'burners at the Croker Global freezer listen to country metal music that shares prison slang with rap, and they are proud to know the inmates' lingo. In the Santa Rita pod, the raps are performed extemporaneously but with the same theme of rape: the refrain is always, "Give it up, bitch," whatever topical verses are added to terrorize inmates like Conrad. It appears that the culture is not imposing it bourgeois values on the underclass: it is making the underclass's values its own.

Wolfe's most important theme in *A Man in Full* is manhood itself. The novel includes several different conceptions of manliness, and its climax comes as Charlie Croker adopts a new idea of what a man should be. From the beginning of the novel, Charlie is associated with masculine symbols: bulls, snakes, stallions. (He even takes his guests at Turpmtine into the breeding barn to see a stallion mount a mare.) He has had what Herb Richman calls this *"thing* about Southern manhood" (523), and he played out the role perfectly, showing his physical prowess in many ways. He has been a football star and a war hero. He is, if you ignore Martha's contribution, a self-made man in business. He has remained close to nature, hunting and raising horses. His gun house at Turpmtine is decorated, not just with phallic weapons, but also with trophies of animals he has killed himself. He does not accept the modern tolerance for homosexuality, since he sees, as he tells his guests in the breeding barn, "the male and the female" at the root of everything.

Charlie associates all his success with his sexual prowess. He believes that "his performance as a developer [. . .], as a creative person, was bound up with his sexual vitality." He fears losing everything if that goes, and even rationalizes his abandonment of Martha as "*necessary*, in order to maintain his vitality" (227). (It seems his sexual vitality actually disappears as his business reverses plunge him into depression.) Other characters certainly see Charlie's masculinity as part of his business success. Peepgass is annoyed that men like Charlie think they can use "their stronger wills, greater guile, and higher levels of testosterone" to manipulate "banking types" like Peepgass himself. Of course, there is so much truth in that assumption that the bank has to bring in Harry Zale for the "Male Battle" (38) of the workout session. In fact, the whole confrontation between Charlie Croker and PlannersBanc is described in terms of male rituals of dominance and competition, including combat and boot camp.

Male competition and dominance are still more obvious in the Santa Rita jail, a world "gorged with anger and testosterone" (418). There the gang leaders are men who have seized their position of power through the most brutal sort of male competition, and they keep it through their ability to dominate others. Domination is often sexual, conveyed with the threat, implicit or explicit, of rape. Society is little more than a dominance hierarchy like those among many social animals, with an alpha male lording it over all the others. The exciting brutality the larger culture celebrates, through rap music or High Museum's show of homoerotic prison painting, is a terrifying reality to Conrad in Santa Rita.

It is in that setting that Conrad refines his own idea of manhood. For him, manliness has to do with such purely human concepts as honor and integrity. He looks with scorn on the inmates who have a chance to be the alpha male in the pod: "What kind of manhood," he asks himself, "was it to look the other way and not snitch when a brute decides to have his way with the hide of another human being" (453). He "reject[s] the pod's code of false manliness," the same view that is being spread, with perhaps some mitigating irony, through the culture. Instead, Conrad's view of manliness includes qualities that have been little spoken of since the women's movement stigmatized them as imposing a permanent position of weakness and dependency on women. His view of manhood includes chivalry: manliness requires that the strong protect the weak. And his views could be labeled with the feminist term of abuse "patri-archal," since he is the one man in the novel who takes his responsibil-ities *as a father* seriously. In fact, as Conrad awaits the retribution that must come because he has dared to help the brutalized homosexual in-mate and to stand up to the Nordic Bund's alpha male, he thinks about that responsibility, thinking that someone will have to tell his son what a man really is.

Other characters in *A Man in Full* need to be told the same thing. Wolfe's point, indeed, seems to be that as the idea of "manliness" has been drained of its moral dimensions, all that has been left is a bestial quest for dominance and position in a status hierarchy. Charlie Croker is ready to give up his integrity to keep his position and finds the strength to change his mind only after Conrad shares his view of man-liness with him. At the end of that conversation, Conrad recounts the story of Agrippinus, one of the philosophers Epictetus describes. Rather than take part in one of the Emperor Nero's degrading spectacles, he risks death or exile. While the Senate is trying his case, he carries on with his usual routine. When told that he has been sentenced to exile and the confiscation of all his property—precisely the loss of the wealth and social position that Charlie fears—his only response is that it is time for dinner. Conrad's comment on the story is "Charlie—*there* was a man" (710). For Conrad, manhood is characterized not by position in the dom-inance hierarchy but by utter indifference to that hierarchy. That true manhood is a matter of the soul, not the body, is the essence of the faith he finds in the course of what is, perhaps surprisingly, a religious novel.

A RELIGIOUS OR ETHICAL READING

Some novels are happily amoral and invite the reader to enjoy the pleasures of language and narrative without making ethical judgments. Others are primarily psychological, and call on the reader to experience the inner mental states of various characters before seeing their actions through any moral lens. Still others have so clear an ethical framework that the reader hardly need think about it: the good are rewarded, the wicked punished, and poetic justice rules the world. Novels of these kinds can be read from a religious or ethical perspective. It is interesting to consider how moral questions are foregrounded or pushed to the side. But it is still more interesting to use the lens of religion or ethics to study works in which characters are themselves struggling with religious and ethical issues. It is interesting to consider, for example, what theology Huck Finn develops when he decides to "go to Hell" rather than betray a friend, to ponder what drives Graham Greene's narrators to seek—or reject—holiness, to explore the grotesque and violent responses of Flannery O'Connor's characters to grace, and to think about the ethical struggles of characters in a world without God in novels such as Nick Hornsby's *How to Be Good* (2001). Since its central characters are confronted with religious and ethical questions and long for some link to a transcendent source of meaning, *A Man in Full* invites a religious or ethical reading.

In *The Electric Kool-Aid Acid Test* Wolfe portrays Ken Kesey as an exemplary prophet, one who draws others to himself through his own experience of ecstasy. In *A Man in Full*, Wolfe presents the other kind of religious leader that Max Weber describes, the ethical prophet who attracts followers by teaching them how to live. Indeed, the prophet in question cannot communicate his vision through his personal charisma, as Kesey does, because he exists only in the pages of a book. To emphasize that Conrad's conversion to Stoicism is, to begin with, purely intellectual, Wolfe has him learn of the new faith through the driest possible medium: a scholarly book containing "the complete extant writings of Epictetus, Marcus Aurelius, C. Musonius Rufus, and Zeno"(397). Conrad is not likely to find spiritual meaning in drug-induced visions: having grown up in a house that always smelled of marijuana with parents who were "Beautiful People," if not seekers on the level of the Merry Pranksters, he sees intoxication as only the path to squalor. But a teacher who can show him how to live a good life, despite all the obstacles, speaks to his needs.

Conrad is, indeed, attracted to Epictetus the teacher, as well as to his doctrine. He feels that Epictetus really knows his condition in life, since he also was imprisoned and lived as a slave. The little philosophy that Conrad has encountered in community college seems to speak to people who are free and whose problem is choosing among almost endless possibilities—people like the middle-class bohemians who gathered around Ken Kesey. Epictetus assumes that the individual has very few choices. You cannot control the actions of others, and you will often be subject to their choices physically or materially. But with the few choices you have, you can either keep your integrity or throw it away. In reading the long-dead philosopher, Conrad feels he has not simply been taught;

he has been understood: Epictetus would know why Conrad could not take a plea bargain if it meant saying he was guilty when he was not. Epictetus, alone among philosophers as far as Conrad knows, looked his tormentors in the eye and said, "You do what you have to do, and I will do what I have to do, which is live and die like a man" (411).

In drawing his portrait of a man saved by Stoicism, Wolfe builds on a real figure he encountered during his research for *The Right Stuff*, an American pilot shot down over Vietnam and imprisoned and tortured in the infamous prison known as "The Hanoi Hilton," and who reported that he could not have survived the ordeal if he had not read Epictetus and been able to recall his teachings (Cash). That flier was undoubtedly Admiral James Stockdale, who since the war has written several books on his experiences and the strength Stoic philosophy gave him. Stockdale, like Conrad Hensley, was an actual prisoner and faced the literal choices that Epictetus imagined: torture or dishonor. Wolfe is perhaps even more daring when he suggests that Stoicism might speak to those who have everything to lose, instead of next to nothing. The chapter entitled "Epictetus in Buckhead" is, in fact, still more unlikely than the one called "Epictetus Comes to Da House." Yet by the time he reaches Charlie Croker, Conrad has been almost an exemplary prophet himself; he is so full of the joy that Epictetus has given him that he attracts others to his creed.

Conrad's reaction to Epictetus makes it clear that Stoicism for him is not just a philosophy; it is a religion. He does not merely accept an intellectual proposition; he opens himself to the divine, the holy. He takes seriously the idea that Zeus has given him a "portion of divinity," and it, not the "corpse and quart of blood" that are his body, is what he must protect. He wants to be a "vessel of the divine" and sometimes truly feels that he is—never more so than when he is defending the weak against the brutal idea of manhood that rules in prison and spreads beyond its walls.

That Conrad feels he must defend the weak is, as Wolfe acknowledges, a departure from Classical Stoicism. Like other ancient religions, the Stoics held what Robert Graves called the "religious principle that ill-luck is catching" (xii). As Conrad tries to decide what to do about the inmate the prison gang is brutalizing, he wrestles with Epictetus's dicta, which seem to suggest that while we are responsible for our own choices, we are responsible for ourselves alone. Conrad tries to make them apply to the situation before him and keeps wondering, "What *was* the obligation of the Stoic, the man of noble spirit, to the people around him?" (446). He even grows angry at Epictetus for a moment. He then decides that aiding the weak is, in fact, the very trial that Zeus has sent him. Conrad thus adds a Christian conception of compassion to the Stoic message, while retaining its essential point that a man is the choices he makes.

Conrad becomes eager to spread the message of his newfound faith, which has been strengthened not just by his feelings of transcendence but also by the providential pattern he sees at work in his own life. By the time Charlie Croker asks to borrow the book, everything seems to fit part of a larger plan. He has been brought through everything to recruit Croker into the "service of Zeus" (689). He feels that the book is not just a set of interesting intellectual propositions. Rather, it is alive. It is, in other words, not simply philosophy. It is, for him, Holy Scripture. And Charlie, like a born-again Christian, is also eager to study that scripture and apply it to his life. After his conversion—and his public professions of faith—he feels a tranquility new to him, for he also has come to feel that he is filled with a divine spark and impervious to all the troubles that have tormented him.

Conrad finds a fertile field for his "Zeusian" missionary work because traditional religious systems seem to have lost their power in the world Wolfe describes. The society he portrays is thoroughly post-Christian. (Conrad, for example, has had no religious training at all.) Black characters go to church, but what they find there seems more political than spiritual. The only white characters who talk about church are Conrad's elderly landlords, and they only complain that the Episcopalians have better hymns than do Methodists like them. If religion has played any roles in the Crokers' lives, we do not hear about it, and they certainly do not call on it in times of trouble. What vestiges of Christianity remain in their society are toothless. Charlie notices that even the Baptist deacon at the exhibition at the High Museum is unwilling to appear offended, lest a principled objection to sodomy appear as homophobia, one of the most stigmatized forms of the one remaining sin, intolerance. Since the institutions that presented a common source of values no longer play that role, it is not surprising that Charlie should grasp at a philosophy that emphasizes the spark of the divine within each individual.

A Man in Full reveals a significant departure from Wolfe's earlier analysis of human motivation, or at least a development of it. In many of his earlier works, particularly *The Right Stuff*, Wolfe celebrates a culture of competition. It is that culture, not the inherent qualities of the individual, that produces achievement. Charlie Croker has lived in the same world, as a football player, as a soldier, and as a real estate developer. But when he is no longer "climbing the ziggurat" but rather tumbling down it at a great rate, he has to find another source of value, one based entirely on his own internal qualities and choices, not on his socially validated successes. In *The Bonfire of the Vanities*, Wolfe suggests that the self is socially constructed: Sherman McCoy is a different person when he loses his place in society. Charlie Croker is afraid of suffering a similar fate. He will not be "Cap'n Charlie" without his wealth and plantation. The message Conrad brings to him is that he has a self—a character—independent of his society, and that message allows Charlie to make his choice. Conrad has made the same choice himself: before his confrontation with the gang leader, he realizes he has cut "his last tie to the earthly beings from whom men are used to deriving their courage and support" (455). He has, from that point on, only his "spark of the Divine" to rely on.

The central issue in *A Man in Full*, finally, is whether it is possible to have a value system that is not socially validated. Conrad, building on the Stoics, finds that it is. A man—and all our Stoics seem to be men—can protect his character, his spark of the divine, and he does that by making sure that the few choices he can make are honorable ones. He must be uninfluenced in any moral choice by the actions of others—even when the results of the action will be pain, or shame, or bankruptcy. A man can, in other words, keep his integrity, which means completeness. The title of the novel comes to refer to the man of integrity, who is complete in himself and independent of the society to which he might once have looked to for validation, not the man whose back is strong as a Jersey bull.

Bibliography

BOOKS BY TOM WOLFE

Nonfiction and Miscellanies

The Electric Kool-Aid Acid Test. 1968. New York: Bantam, 1969.

From Bauhaus to Our House. New York: Farrar Straus Giroux, 1981.

Hooking Up. New York: Farrar Straus Giroux, 2000.

In Our Time. New York: Farrar Straus Giroux, 1980.

The Kandy-Kolored Tangerine-Flake Streamline Baby. New York: Farrar Straus Giroux, 1965.

Mauve Gloves & Madmen, Clutter & Vine. New York: Farrar Straus Giroux, 1976.

The New Journalism. Ed. with E.W. Johnson. New York: Harper & Row, 1973.

The Painted Word. New York: Farrar Straus Giroux, 1975.

The Pump House Gang. New York: Farrar Straus Giroux, 1968.

The Purple Decades: A Reader. New York: Farrar Straus Giroux, 1982.

Radical Chic & Mau-Mauing the Flak-Catchers. New York: Farrar Straus Giroux, 1970.

The Right Stuff. New York: Farrar Straus Giroux, 1979.

Novels

The Bonfire of the Vanities. New York: Farrar Straus Giroux, 1987.

A Man in Full. New York: Farrar Straus Giroux, 1998.

OTHER WORKS BY TOM WOLFE

"Commentary" in *Frederick Hart, Sculptor*. Introduction by J. Carter Brown; essays
    by Homan Potterton et al.; designed and produced by Marshall Lee. New
    York: Hudson Hills Press, 1994.
*The League of American Writers: Communist Organizational Activity Among American
    Writers, 1929–1942*. Dissertation. Yale University, 1956.
"Literary Technique in the Last Quarter of the Twentieth Century." *Michigan
    Quarterly Review* 17 (1978): 463–472.
"Lost in the Whichy Thicket." *New York* [*New York Herald-Tribune* supplement]
    (18 April 1965): 16.
"Stalking the Billion-Footed Beast." *Harper's*. November 1989, 279:1674, 45–56.
"Tiny Mummies! The True Story of the Ruler of 43rd Street's Land of the Walking
    Dead!" *New York* [*New York Herald-Tribune* supplement] (11 April 1965):
    22.
"Why They Aren't Writing the Great American Novel Anymore." *Esquire*, De-
    cember 1972: 152.

INTERVIEWS WITH TOM WOLFE

Collection

Scura, Dorothy, ed. *Conversations with Tom Wolfe*. Jackson: University Press of
    Mississippi, 1990.

Arranged in Chronological Order

Dundy, Elaine. "Tom Wolfe . . . but Exactly, Yes!" *Vogue* 147. 15 April 1966, 124,
    152–155. In Scura. 6–17.
Buckley, William F. "Tom Wolfe and the Painted Word." *Firing Line* (PBS TV) 9
    July 1975. In Scura. 73–94.
Gorner, Peter. "Tom Wolfe: In Big League as a Writer." *Chicago Tribune*, 7 De-
    cember 1976. In Scura. 99–102.
Blue, Adrianne. "The Earthling and the Astronaut." *Washington Post Book World*,
    9 September 1979. In Scura. 103–105.
Gross, Martin L. "Conversation with an Author: Tom Wolfe." *Book Digest Mag-
    azine*, March 1980, 19–29. In Scura. 121–128.
Flippo, Chet. "The *Rolling Stone* Interview: Tom Wolfe." *Rolling Stone*, 21 August
    1980, 30–37. In Scura. 129–157.
Gilder, Joshua. "Tom Wolfe." *Saturday Review*, 8 April 1981, 40–44. In Scura. 158–
    166.
Levine, Martin. "An Interview with Tom Wolfe." *Book Digest*, November 1981,
    60–61. In Scura. 167–171.
McLeod, Mary V. "*CA* Interview." *Contemporary Authors, New Revision Series* 9,

ed. Ann Evory and Linda Metzger, 536–539. Detroit: Gale, 1983. In Scura. 178–185.

Thompson, Toby. "The Evolution of Dandy Tom." *Vanity Fair*, October 1987, 118–127, 160–164. In Scura. 199–220.

Taylor, John. "The Book on Tom Wolfe." *New York Times Magazine*. 21 March 1988, 46–58. In Scura. 255–266.

Plimpton, George. "The Art of Fiction CXXIII: Tom Wolfe: Interview." *The Paris Review* 33 (1991): 92–121.

Reilly, Charlie. "Interview: Tom Wolfe." *Onthebus* 7: (1993 Winter–1994 Spring): (13), 226–229.

Gray, Paul. "A Man in Full." *Time* (2 November 1998): 88–96.

Applebome, Peter. "A Man in Tune with His Heritage; In His New Novel, Tom Wolfe Unearths His Southern Roots." *New York Times*, 11 November 1998.

Cash, William. "Southern Man." *San Francisco Examiner*, 29 November 1998.

Rehm, Diane. "The Diane Rehm Show: Tom Wolfe: *A Man in Full*," December 1998.

Scott, Janny. "How to Persuade with a Feather (or a Quill); An Editor with an Instinct for the Jugular and the Diplomatic." *New York Times*, 20 January 1999.

Greig, Geordie. "Ahead of His Time." *Sunday Times* (London), 30 May 1999.

REVIEWS

Collection

Shomette, Doug, ed. *The Critical Response to Tom Wolfe*. Westport, CT: Greenwood, 1992.

The Kandy-Kolored Tangerine-Flake Streamline Baby

Commonweal 82 (17 September, 1965): 670–672.
New York Times Book Review (27 June 1965): 8.
Newsweek (28 June 1965): 90.
Saturday Review 48 (31 July 1965): 23.

The Electric Kool-Aid Acid Test and The Pump House Gang

America 119 (31 August 1968): 136.
Atlantic Monthly 222 (September 1968): 134.
Commonweal 134 (20 December 1968): 413.
New Statesman 77 (9 May 1969): 660.
New York Times Book Review (18 August 1968): 1.
Saturday Review 22 (27 December 1969): 32.

Radical Chic & Mau-Mauing the Flak-Catchers

Harper's 242 (February 1971): 104.
New Statesman 82 (17 September 1971): 404.
Partisan Review 38 (3 November 1971): 335.
Time (21 December 1970): 72.
Washington Post Book World (6 December 1970): 5.

The Right Stuff

Atlantic 244 (October 1979): 107.
Library Journal 104 (15 October 1979): 2228.
New Republic 181 (20 October 1979): 38.
New York Times Book Review (23 September 1979): 1.
Saturday Review (15 September 1979): 35.
Time (24 September 1979): 81.

The Bonfire of the Vanities

America 158 (2 April 1988): 363–363.
Commonweal 115 (26 February 1988): 120.
New Criterion 6 (February 1988): 5.
New Statesman (12 February 1988): 31.
New York Times (22 October 1987): c25.
Punch 294 (12 February 1988): 44.
Wall Street Journal (29 October 1987): 30.

A Man in Full

Economist (7 November 1998): 89.
Newsweek (2 November 1998): 83.
New York Review of Books (17 December 1998): 18.
New York Times (28 October 1998): e1.
San Francisco Chronicle Sunday Review (15 November 1998): 1.
Wall Street Journal (30 October 1998): w1.
Washington Times (15 November 1998): b8.
Times (London) (29 October 1998): 44.

Articles and Books About Tom Wolfe

Anderson, Chris. "Tom Wolfe: Pushing the Outside of the Envelope." In *Style as Argument*, 8–47. Carbondale: Southern Illinois University Press, 1987.
Bellamy, Joe David. "Tom Wolfe as Visiting Martian." In *Literary Luxuries*. Columbia: University of Missouri Press, 1995. 126–136.

Bloom, Harold, ed. *Tom Wolfe: Modern Critical Views*. Broomall, PA: Chelsea House, 2000.

Bonca, Cornel. "Very, Very Ridiculous: Tom Wolfe, Chronicler of the Comfort Class," *Orange County (CA) Weekly*, 1 December, 2000.

Card, James. "Tom Wolfe and the 'Experimental' Novel." *Journal of American Culture* 14 (1991): 31–34.

Cohen, Ed. "Tom Wolfe and the Truth Monitors: A Historical Fable." *CLIO* 16 (1986): 1–11.

Cooper, Rand Richards. "Tom Wolfe, Material Boy: Embellishing a Doctrine." *Commonweal* (7 May 1999): 11–15.

Corliss, Richard. "By the Book: Some novels that are now also films." *Film Comment* (27 March/April 1991): 37–8+.

Crawford, Sheri F. "Rebel-Doodle Dandy." *Journal of American Culture* 14 (1991): 13–18.

———. "Tom Wolfe: Outlaw Gentleman." *Journal of American Culture* 13 (1990): 39–50.

Edwards, Thomas R. "No Country for Old Men." *Over Here*. New Brunswick, NJ: Rutgers University Press, 1991.

Epstein, Joseph. "Tom Wolfe's Vanities." *The New Criterion* (6 February 1988): 5–16.

Fishwick, Marshall W. Introduction. *Journal of American Culture* 14 (1991): 1–10.

Hartshorne, Thomas L. "Tom Wolfe on the 1960's." *Midwest Quarterly* 23 (1982): 144–163.

Harvey, Chris. "Tom Wolfe's Revenge." *American Journalism Review* 16 (1994): 40–46.

Hersey, John. "The Legend and the License." *Yale Review* 70 (1980): 1–25.

Konas, Gary. "Traveling 'Further' with Tom Wolfe's Heroes." *Journal of Popular Culture* 28 (1994): 177–192.

Lewin, Leonard C. "Is Fact Necessary? A Sequel to the *Herald-Tribune-New Yorker* Dispute, *Columbia Journalism Review* 4, no. 4 (Winter 1966): 29–34.

Lounsberry, Barbara. "Tom Wolfe's American Jeremiad," In *The Art of Fact*, 37–64. Westport, CT: Greenwood, 1990.

MacDonald, Dwight. "Parajournalism: Tom Wolfe and His Magic Writing Machine. *New York Review of Books* (26 August 1965): 3–5

———. "Parajournalism II: Wolfe and *The New Yorker*. *New York Review of Books*. (3 February 1966): 18–24.

Masters, Joshua J. "Race and the Infernal City in Tom Wolfe's *Bonfire of the Vanities*." *JNT: Journal of Narrative Theory* 29 (1999): 208–227.

McKeen, William. *Tom Wolfe*. New York: Twayne, 1995.

Molesworth, Charles. "Culture, Power, and Society." In *Columbia History of American Literature*, ed. Emory Elliot, 1023–1044. New York: Columbia University Press, 1988.

Porsdam, Helle. "In the Age of Lawspeak: Tom Wolfe's *The Bonfire of the Vanities* and American Litigiousness." *Journal of American Studies* 25 (1991): 39–57.

"Reports." *Columbia Journalism Review* 4, no. 2 (Winter 1966): 29–34.

Ross, Charles S. "The Rhetoric of 'The Right Stuff.' " *Journal of General Education* 33 (1981): 113–122.

Rouse, Parke. "Tom Wolfe Unchanged by Fame." *Journal of American Culture* 14 (1991): 11–13.

Smith, James F. "Tom Wolfe's *Bonfire of the Vanities*: A Dreiser Novel for the 1980s." *Journal of American Culture* 14 (1991): 43–50.

Sojka, Gregory S. "The Astronaut: An American Hero with 'the Right Stuff.' " *Journal of American Culture* 7 (1984): 118–121.

Stull, James N. "The Cultural Gamesmanship of Tom Wolfe." *Journal of American Culture* 14 (1991): 25–30.

Teachout, Terry. "Reconsiderations: You Don't Say: *The Bonfire of the Vanities* (Review Article)." *The New Criterion* 11 (January 1993): 57–59.

Varsava, Jerry A. "Tom Wolfe's Defense of the New (Old) Social Novel; or, the Perils of the Great White-Suited Hunter." *Journal of American Culture* 14 (1991): 35–41.

Other Works Consulted

Adler, Renata. *Gone: The Last Days of the New Yorker*. New York: Simon & Schuster, 1999.

Capote, Truman. *Music for Chameleons*. 1980. Reprint, New York: Vintage, 1990.

Chicago Crime Commission. *Gangs: Public Enemy Number One*. Chicago: Chicago Crime Commission, 1995.

Frazier, E. Franklin. *Black Bourgeoisie: The Rise of a New Middle Class in America*. New York: Free Press, 1957.

Garreau, Joel. *Edge City: Life on the New Frontier*. New York: Doubleday, 1991.

Glenn, John, with Nick Taylor. *John Glenn: A Memoir*. New York: Bantam, 1999.

Kerouac, Jack. *On the Road*. New York: Viking, 1957.

Kesey, Ken. *The Further Inquiry*. New York: Viking, 1990.

———. *One Flew Over the Cuckoo's Nest*. New York: Viking, 1962.

———. *Sometimes a Great Notion*. New York: Viking, 1964.

Lee, Martin A., and Bruce Shlain. *Acid Dreams: The Complete History of LSD: The CIA, the Sixties, and Beyond*. New York: Grove Press, 1985.

Pearson, Hugh. *The Shadow of the Panther: Huey Newton and the Price of Black Power in America*. Reading, MA: Perseus, 1994.

Perry, Paul. *On the Bus: The Complete Guide to the Legendary Trip of Ken Kesey and the Merry Pranksters and the Birth of the Counterculture*. New York: Thunder's Mouth Press, 1990.

Salamon, Julie. *The Devil's Candy*: The Bonfire of the Vanities *Goes to Hollywood*. Boston: Houghton, 1991.

Thompson, Hunter. *Fear and Loathing in Las Vegas: A Savage Journey to the Heart of the American Dream*. New York: Popular Library, 1971.

———. *Hell's Angels: A Strange and Terrible Saga*. New York: Ballantine, 1967.

Trollope, Anthony. *Thackeray*. 1879. London: Trollope Society, 1997.

White, E.B. *Letters of E.B. White*. New York: Harper & Row, 1976.

Yagoda, Ben. *About Town: The New Yorker and the World It Made*. New York: Scribner, 2000.

Yeager, Chuck, and Leo Janos. *Yeager: An Autobiography*. New York: Bantam, 1985.

Index

About the Author

BRIAN ABEL RAGEN is Professor of English at Southern Illinois University at Edwardsville. He is the author of *A Wreck on the Road to Damascus: Innocence, Guilt, and Conversion in Flannery O'Connor* (1989). He has contributed numerous articles on American literature to journals and reference works. He is the editor of the journal *Papers on Language and Literature*.

Critical Companions to Popular Contemporary Writers
Second Series

Julia Alvarez by *Silvio Sirias*

Rudolfo A. Anaya by *Margarite Fernandez Olmos*

Maya Angelou by *Mary Jane Lupton*

Ray Bradbury by *Robin Anne Reid*

Louise Erdrich by *Lorena L. Stookey*

Ernest J. Gaines by *Karen Carmean*

Gabriel García Márquez by *Rubén Pelayo*

John Irving by *Josie P. Campbell*

Garrison Keillor by *Marcia Songer*

Jamaica Kincaid by *Lizabeth Paravisini-Gebert*

Barbara Kingsolver by *Mary Jean DeMarr*

Maxine Hong Kingston by *E.D. Huntley*

Terry McMillan by *Paulette Richards*

Larry McMurtry by *John M. Reilly*

Toni Morrison by *Missy Dehn Kubitschek*

Chaim Potok by *Sanford Sternlicht*

Amy Tan by *E.D. Huntley*

Anne Tyler by *Paul Bail*

Leon Uris by *Kathleen Shine Cain*

Gloria Naylor by *Charles E. Wilson, Jr.*

Critical Companions to Popular Contemporary Writers
First Series—*also available on CD-ROM*

V.C. Andrews
  by *E.D. Huntley*

Tom Clancy
  by *Helen S. Garson*

Mary Higgins Clark
  by *Linda C. Pelzer*

Arthur C. Clarke
  by *Robin Anne Reid*

James Clavell
  by *Gina Macdonald*

Pat Conroy
  by *Landon C. Burns*

Robin Cook
  by *Lorena Laura Stookey*

Michael Crichton
  by *Elizabeth A. Trembley*

Howard Fast
  by *Andrew Macdonald*

Ken Follett
  by *Richard C. Turner*

John Grisham
  by *Mary Beth Pringle*

James Herriot
  by *Michael J. Rossi*

Tony Hillerman
  by *John M. Reilly*

John Jakes
  by *Mary Ellen Jones*

Stephen King
  by *Sharon A. Russell*

Dean Koontz
  by *Joan G. Kotker*

Robert Ludlum
  by *Gina Macdonald*

Anne McCaffrey
  by *Robin Roberts*

Colleen McCullough
  by *Mary Jean DeMarr*

James A. Michener
  by *Marilyn S. Severson*

Anne Rice
  by *Jennifer Smith*

Tom Robbins
  by *Catherine E. Hoyser and Lorena Laura Stookey*

John Saul
  by *Paul Bail*

Erich Segal
  by *Linda C. Pelzer*

Gore Vidal
  by *Susan Baker and Curtis S. Gibson*